Self-Employed Tax Solutions

Help Us Keep This Guide Up to Date

Every effort has been made by the author and editors to make this guide as accurate and useful as possible. However, many things can change after a guide is published—regulations are revised, phone numbers change, etc.

We would appreciate hearing from you about your experience with this guide and how you think it could be made better and kept up to date. While we may not be able to respond to all comments and suggestions, we'll bring them to the attention of the author. Please send your comments to the following address:

The Globe Pequot Press
Self-employed Tax Solutions/Reader Response
Editorial Department
246 Goose Lane
P.O. Box 480
Guilford, CT 06437

Thanks for your input!

Self-Employed
Tax Solutions

QUICK, SIMPLE, MONEY-SAVING, AUDIT-PROOF
TAX AND RECORDKEEPING BASICS
FOR THE INDEPENDENT PROFESSIONAL

Second Edition

June Walker

Guilford, Connecticut

Text design by Nancy Freeborn

The Library of Congress has cataloged the first edition as follows:
Walker, June.
   Self-employed tax solutions : quick, simple, money-saving, audit-proof tax and recordkeeping basics for the independent professional / June Walker.
     p. cm
   Includes index.
   ISBN 0-7627-3071-4
    1. Small business—United States—Finance. 2. Self-employed—Finance, Personal.
  3. Self-employed—Taxation—United States. 4. Small business—Taxation—United States. I. Title.

HG4027.7.W3514 2004
343.7306'2—dc22

3 1984 00275 1806

2004051137

ISBN 978-0-7627-4890-7

Printed in the United States of America
10 9 8 7 6 5 4 3 2 1

To my guy, Warren Sloat

Contents

Preface

"She is passionate about providing reliable and understandable information [to the self-employed] about taxes and the IRS." (*Southwest BookViews*)

"All the tax myths I had heard about being an individual in business were suddenly cleared up by June Walker using lots of easy to understand, real life examples." (Paul D. Gregg)

"An indispensible book for the sole proprietor, freelancers and others." (*The New Mexican*)

That's what reviewers said about the first edition of **Self-employed Tax Solutions.**

I was surprised by some who said that it "reads like a novel" and is "funny." I think of it instead as a group of short stories; the humor, when it comes up, springs from my well-founded skepticism about and irreverence toward the supposed wisdom of the mahogany-office accountants.

Let me welcome you to the second edition of **Self-employed Tax Solutions** and assure you that it has everything contained in the earlier edition.

Only some fine-tuning and a bit of cleanup were required because the tax basics of self-employment have not changed. For example, items like the per-mile auto deduction change every year, but the method of recordkeeping for business mileage does not vary.

The major change in these pages is organizational. In this edition, the chapters are grouped into parts, to make the book easier for you to use and faster for you to reference. The parts are: Self-employed—What Does That Mean?; Business Expenses; Income; Recordkeeping; and Taxes.

Although I hadn't intended to write an inspirational work, many readers have gone out of their way to tell me that **Self-employed Tax Solutions** has instilled in them an unexpected confidence. They can approach self-employment issues with poise, ready with the knowledge to ask the right questions and able to judge the accuracy of the answers they get.

Armed with the clear, useful, easy-to-understand tax and recordkeeping basics in this book, I know that you, too, will develop the confidence to move forward with assurance in your independent endeavor.

I wish you much success in that indie venture, whatever it is.

June Walker
Santa Fe, New Mexico

Acknowledgments

To my clients go my greatest thanks. They make me think, laugh, and utter profanities. Some are wealthy enough to be Republicans. Others are barely making it. All of them, however, are talented, resourceful, accommodating, intelligent, and fun. Pat Cerasiello—musician, composer, music professor, and bandleader—is one of my star-quality clients. He best summed up the financial situation of many artists with: What's the difference between a large pizza and a musician? Answer: A large pizza can feed a family of four.

Some clients have brightened what could be a dull tax time with notes like the following (sometimes addressed to the Tax Goddess or the Tax Ayatollah). From a *New York Times* reporter: "Here is my tax material, late, naturally. I am poised between Pakistan (nuclear bombs) and Kosovo (impending genocide), business as usual. . . . Hope all is well with you." From an artist in New York: "Once again and forever, I offer my deepest thanks to you. In a world where, as Dylan has it—even the swap meets are pretty corrupt—you assist those in need. In need of yer bitchin' advice, that is! Let's rock even harder next year." Responding to a seminar I was about to give, a New Jersey psychologist suggested the following ad: "Bring me your tired, your disorganized, your jumbled indies yearning to live free. The wretched refuse of the IRS. Send them, the self-employed, to June." From an award-winning writer after tax prep turned his brains to mush

and his prose to doggerel: "June, June—It's tax time soon. So what do I owe? I don't want to be slow. Try to limit the blow. I just need to know."

Other clients helped in specific ways. Daran Moon, Cloudsifter, and Diane Oberlin read various chapters and suggested changes. Dr. Natalie Brown, psychologist, advised when I used psychologically inappropriate examples. Dr. Ruth Gage, after reading an early draft of the chapter "How Long to Keep Records," supplied my favorite editorial comment: "You told me more about penguins than I really wanted to know." Farn Dupre, editor of *Family* magazine, walked me through several editorial quandaries. Literary agents Stuart Bernstein and Susan Bergholz and writers Samuel G. Freedman, John Katzenbach, Elizabeth and Michael Norman, Gail Buckland, and Paul Colford—all were generous with their time and sage advice. Roger Styczynski has been my computer guru and technological savior since computers used keypunch cards to store data. Frances White, designer, equally nimble with color, line, and phrase, was there for me whenever I got stuck. Christine Davies, writer and entrepreneur, encouraged me from the beginning and put me on course for turning my talks and workshops into a book.

I have been lucky to have the support of friends like Sally Hindes, who trekked through bookstores with me checking out the competition; Terri Lonier, founder of Working Solo, Inc., willing to share a bottomless bag of ideas; and that indispensable friend of writers, the Authors Guild.

Thanks to my children Lisa Sloat, Sarah Sloat, Thatcher Keats, and Shane Keats, and their spouses and children for their support and sometimes just for their love and joy. A special thanks to Shane, whose encouragement was unflagging and whose ideas were abundant, and to Thatcher and my daughter-in-law Karen Crumley for their comments and suggestions on the manuscript.

And a flourish of trumpets and drumroll for my husband, Warren Sloat, who taught me how to write.

Introduction

Artists,

astrologers,

psychologists,

personal trainers,

pet sitters,

writers,

real estate appraisers,

coaches,

creators of intellectual property,

graphic designers,

investment counselors,

carpenters,

information technology consultants,

Web site designers,

solo performers on the stage and in the business world . . .

each of you is unique.

Yet despite your uniqueness you all have one thing in common—

you are all self-employed!

You may call yourself by another name— sole proprietor, freelancer, indie, subcontractor, free agent, independent professional—but to the taxing authorities, all these descriptions mean the same thing. And the taxing authorities require all of you, no matter what you call yourselves, to follow the same rules.

According to the Internal Revenue Service, there are thirty-three million self-employed Americans! That's more than 23 percent of the workforce. And the biggest factor in the vast increase in self-employment is the one-person show, the independent professional—the indie.

Despite your growing numbers, the tax laws are written without you in mind. And as for your needs, the mahogany-office accountants don't have a clue. After meeting with most accountants, self-employed people stagger out glassy eyed, their minds a jumble of irrelevant and often incorrect advice.

You deserve better. You are (with a few exceptions) talented and spirited people, motivated and deeply interested in your work— bright, intuitive people whose talents probably outweigh your practical sense. But where do you find that practical know-how about business deductions, easy recordkeeping, estimated taxes. **Where do you go for the basics?**

You cannot succeed as a solo in business if you don't understand tax fundamentals. That's why I never cease to be puzzled by the mountains of books, DVDs, and audiotapes on self-employment that fill the bookstores. They are crammed with advice on marketing, home office zoning, office furniture arrangement, Internet use, dressing for success, and etiquette tips for business lunches. They coach you in confidence, motivation, and self-discipline and advise you to overcome uncertainty, fears, and self-doubt. But when it comes to taxes, they tell you to "keep good business records" and they provide a list of tax payment due dates. Instead of telling you how to keep your tax bill low or even whether you can deduct your trip to Grandma's as a business expense, they make hostile remarks about the IRS and then go on to the next subject—like the importance of feng shui in the arrangement of your office.

Let's face the facts. You can choose the wrong office furniture and survive. An uncultivated phone manner may lose a customer, but it's not the difference between life and death for a freelancer. An episode of fear and loss of confidence may do some harm, but you'll get another chance. Taxes are different. If you don't understand them and you gum up the works, you will find that getting the gum out is expensive, time consuming, and worrisome. The consequences include paying interest and penalties to Uncle Sam, spending a bundle to hire a tax professional to clean up the mess, going through the anxiety of an audit—and time away from your business. Such complications could prove fatal to your enterprise. It's a lot more serious than wearing the wrong tie at a product presentation.

I'm not saying that the books and videos about self-employment are trivial, but so many of them concentrate on the frills and ignore the essentials. I've never found one that adequately dealt with tax know-how. They are either too highly technical or written in a Taxes-Lite style that never gets beyond surface information.

This book is written for smart indies who don't know much about the tax and recordkeeping part of their enterprises but want to learn because they know that understanding taxes and keeping adequate records is indispensable to making it in the unforgiving world of self-employment. In more than twenty-five years of advising self-employed people, I have found that *you've got to know the basics.*

With *Self-employed Tax Solutions,* you will learn the basics.

I Am Self-employed, Too

For more than two decades, I've been an accountant and tax advisor with an unusual clientele made up almost entirely of self-employed people. Many have singular occupations and many are in the arts.

In the past I had offices in New York and New Jersey. Now I live in glorious Santa Fe, New Mexico, while my clients are scattered all over North America as well as Europe and the Middle East. Most have been with me for many years. And although it is rare, there are a few I've never actually met face-to-face (a *New York Times* reporter always on assignment) or those I seldom see (a South African opera singer who now performs in Europe). We communicate electronically. And if I'm in Santa Fe long enough, we may communicate telepathically!

My style suits the kinds of people I advise. I have written for many publications about finances and taxes with an emphasis on self-employment and on the tax problems of people in the arts. In my writing and seminars, I focus on fostering in the self-employed the same mastery in business matters that they possess in their creative or professional pursuits.

I maintain a deep respect for the talent and intelligence of those who have struck out on their own. My responsibility to my clients has always been to be clear and coherent in steering them past the obstacles that lie on the financial path of their chosen professions. Dealing with an atypical and spirited clientele has forced me to innovate with approaches centered on their particular needs.

In that way my perspective differs from that of other accountants—I don't expect the creative mind to think linearly even in its approach to business and taxes! I can't play the banjo, build furniture, fix a computer, or sell real estate. I don't expect a poet to do accounting, and I hope she doesn't expect me to write a sonnet.

Each time I meet with a client, I want him to understand more about his finances than he did the meeting before. Whether plotting tax strategy, gathering information for tax return preparation, or budgeting for irregular income, I guide my client so that he can do as much of the preliminary work as possible himself. The client who does the preliminary work on his own not only saves accountant fees but also enhances his own financial awareness.

By adjusting a financial procedure to fit my client's preferred method of recordkeeping, I get orthodox results via an unorthodox route. My role is part accountant, part guide, and part teacher.

By a method that I call the Most Simple System, I make complicated things simple and understandable. On one level it is a record-keeping method—a quick, easy, accurate, and foolproof method—of my own devising, and it's the only one you'll ever need throughout your indie career. If you use this method, you will never miss a tax deduction and you will be armed with solid backup in case you are ever audited. But the Most Simple System is more than recordkeeping; it's a mind-set, a deeply ingrained way of thinking about your business life as an indie.

Is the Most Simple System for You?

Yes, if you are:

- Self-employed.
- Not sure whether you're self-employed.
- Just starting out.
- Juggling both a regular job and a self-employed venture.
- Planning to freelance in the future.
- Already the sole proprietor of an established business.

Or if you:

- Are not satisfied with your recordkeeping method.
- Are confused about business expenses.
- Already have an accountant.
- Have never met with an accountant.
- Have never met with an accountant you understood.
- Have never met with an accountant who understood you.

Or simply if:

- Putting your tax material in order is a grueling chore.
- You want to overcome your tax-time terror.

Yes, if you earn:

- $5,000 a year.
- $50,000 a year.
- $500,000 a year.

Amount of income, even absence of income, does not limit use of the Most Simple System.

Yes, if you're full-time self-employed, just starting out, been at it for a decade, moonlighting, making a big profit, or losing money by the basketful.

Yes, if you're single, married, with kids, or supporting your parents.

Yes, if your time is limited. When you're in your own business and holding down another job or beset with family responsibilities, time is at a premium. You want to put all your energies into getting customers, making your product, or marketing your service. You want neither to struggle with bookkeeping nor to lose productive time doing it.

If you're reading this book, there's a good chance that you aren't keeping records, or you're keeping the wrong ones, or you don't know what to do with the records you do keep. You're either paying too much in taxes or hiding your income to avoid taxes. You need to get your records in order and learn how to keep your tax bill as low as legitimately possible. You've come to the right place.

What Can the Most Simple System Do for You?

- The Most Simple System will simplify your business life.
- The blurry boundary between what is personal and what is business will become clearer.
- You will begin to understand the tax consequences of your business decisions.
- You will know what is (and what is not) a business deduction and what to do with an expense receipt after you've got it.
- This recordkeeping method will take you a matter of hours per year—not per week nor per month, but per year. You'll understand it quickly.
- No matter what your level of recordkeeping sophistication, the Most Simple System will benefit you. It will provide the **foundation** for **all** your tax transactions.

My clients save thousands of tax dollars and countless hours of bookkeeping time and frustration because they know how to keep records. **Self-employed Tax Solutions** will show you how to do that, too. *Easily*!

My method calls for very little logging, no writing down of every expense in a daily journal, and no ledger system where you must write each transaction into a tiny green box. It guarantees no missed deductions. It is a perfectly acceptable method for gathering and arranging material for your tax return preparation. And it is complete backup for an IRS or state audit. I've handled many audits, and some of my clients have even handled their own: When the Most Simple System was used, the audit was a success.

This Is a How-to Book

In these pages I will show you, in the most simple way, how to miss not one single business deduction, how to keep records, and, therefore, how to pay the least tax legitimately possible.

In Part V, Taxes, you will get a full explanation of taxes. You will learn how your estimated tax payments can be calculated, when to pay which taxes, and what happens if you don't or can't pay a tax when it is due.

This is **not** a handbook on starting a business. This is **not** a tax preparation manual. This is **not** everything you need to know about indie finances. It is a book of basics—understanding self-employed status, income, expenses, recordkeeping, and timely tax payments. Just as you shouldn't attempt the high dive before you know how to swim, neither should you attempt to hire employees, establish a pension, or computerize your bookkeeping until you understand the basics.

Although you may have a tax professional who prepares your return, you still need the advice and how-to instruction of **Self-employed Tax Solutions.** The recordkeeping and worksheets that are part of the Most Simple System will prepare you to stride into your accountant's or tax practitioner's office, or to utilize one of the tax preparation services, fully prepared and confident that you have an accurate record of your income and a complete record of every business expense.

I have presented my Most Simple System to many people. When the presentation is one-on-one to a client, I'm invariably told that no one has ever before made taxes so easy to understand. And when I've presented the system to groups at seminars, I've often drawn applause at the end of the workshop—no small feat when you're talking taxes. The applause conveyed to me that the indie attendees—for the first time—realized that they could keep records and make the tax laws work for them without devoting a big chunk of their waking hours to the effort. One writer in attendance said, "I knew there had to be some way to save taxes, but nobody before had ever told me how to do it without a whole lot of time, sweat, and accountant fees." He said he didn't know anything about money, but he understood every word I said. So will you.

You too will find the explanations simple and easy to understand. The suggested method of recordkeeping is painless, mostly frustration free, and always adaptable to *your* style. This is the easiest system that you will have ever read about, ever tried, or, I'm sure, ever stuck with.

More than twenty-five years of tax and financial consulting have convinced me that the Most Simple System is the linchpin of indie business success. It will bring order out of chaos and give you firm footing as you find your way through the tax maze. It is truly the self-employed tax solution.

How to Use This Book

If you're like most of my clients, you will not start at page one and read straight through to the end of this book but will skip around looking for what interests you. I'm sure if you're really curious or baffled by, let's say, OFFICE IN THE HOME deductions, then you'll jump to that section of the book. So here are some hints to help you get the most out of your hopping, skipping, and jumping:

To know what it takes to be regarded as a self-employed in the eyes of the IRS (and to have the confidence of regarding yourself as one), read straight through to the end of Part I. Then, if you like, start skipping.

Subjects may be covered more than once at different places, for different reasons. This is a reference book. Refer to it often! There is a complete index.

Let me take a moment to explain this book's special features. For starters, there are lots of examples, some fictional—such as Caitlin Caterer and Lily Legal—and some actual IRS cases. Both types provide concrete examples of abstract theories and principles. Some of these

 examples are called Reality Checks, as indicated by the Reality Check icon at left.

About the fictional names: Yes, I know they are often corny. But many of them are based on actual situations of my clients, and I don't have to explain why I can't use their real names. So I use names that indicate professions. The names—like Syd System (the computer consultant software developer) and Billy Bride-snapper (the wedding photographer)—are mnemonic devices to help you understand and remember a complex tax situation. Some are alliterative and some more referential, like P. R. Bernays (the public relations guy) and Miles Mingus (the musician). Sammy Segar is my depiction of the clueless certified public accountant (CPA) who doesn't understand the first thing about the indie business world.

From time to time throughout the book, it will be necessary to explain some tax concept to you so that the material that follows makes sense. Each explanation will be noted by the WHATTACONCEPT! heading.

Other features in this book include:

- "IRS says" boxes that present the exact IRS wording on the topic under discussion.
- Any word set in SMALL CAPITAL LETTERS is a specific business expense deduction category. The BRILLIANT DEDUCTION! icon flags the first mention of an expense in a chapter.
- A worksheet icon in the margin indicates that there is a reference to a specific worksheet in the corresponding paragraph. You'll find the worksheets in Chapter Twenty-three, The Worksheets: Put It Together with the Most Simple System.
- Many terms in this **boldface** font can also be found in the glossary at the end of the book, where a slightly different definition may aid your understanding.
- The warning indicated by **ALERT!**

announces that there's something out of the ordinary that you need to store in your memory bank.

- As a handy reference, I included a "To Sum Up" at the end of some wide-ranging sections so that you could review the main concepts of that section more easily.

If an idea initially seems weird to you, please be patient, read on. Many of you will have read or been told other ways to keep your records or been given other procedures for determining the business merits of a deduction. Those ways haven't worked or you wouldn't be reading this book. This is not the method that the mahogany-office accountants will tell you about. It is not the way any book that I've read or lecture I've attended has ever suggested keeping records. *But it works!*

And of course the caveat: Things change. Tax law modifications were in the works as I wrote these pages and are ongoing as you read this. Before you make a major decision, ask questions, check with your tax advisor, be aware.

Good luck in your indie venture.

I welcome comments, questions, and suggestions. Please send them by mail to The Globe Pequot Press, P.O. Box 480, Guilford, CT 06437. Or contact me through my Web site at www.junewalkeronline.com or by e-mail to june@junewalkeronline.com.

Self-employed—What Does That Mean?

You say you're self-employed. But will the IRS? The journey through the maze of tax rules governing the self-employed must be sure-footed; you've got to have the confident stride of someone who not only considers himself self-employed but can prove his self-employed status to the IRS. In the Introduction I noted that the self-employed go by various names—freelancers, sole proprietors, free agents, indies, solos, subs. The IRS, however, classifies all of us by one official title: **independent contractor.**

To determine independent contractor status, the IRS looks at two conditions:

1. Are you really self-employed or are you an employee?
and
2. Are you running a business or is it a hobby?

You need to establish that you are **both** self-employed **and** engaged in a business in order to qualify as an independent contractor for tax purposes.

Before looking at the requirements for being a self-employed in business, let's look at the difference between pay received by an employee and pay received by a self-employed, and the tax consequences of each kind of remuneration.

CHAPTER ONE

W-2 or 1099: Pay Received by an Employee or by a Self-employed

A new client of mine said upon our first meeting that she hadn't yet decided how she would treat the income she had earned for the year so far—as self-employed income or not. I had to tell her, "Sorry, but if the income has already been earned, then it's too late—most likely that decision has already been made for you!"

Often those who work part-time or fill in for staff shortages aren't sure under which basis they are working—as employees or independent contractors. There are times when a person gets called to a job, gets paid, and never thinks about whether she's self-employed or not. Income is income, right? Not so when tax time rolls around. The amount you have to hand over

A view of income

You sold your car, won the lottery, the boss gave you a raise, the stock Dad gave you just hit the roof and you sold it. There are all kinds of income, some of it taxable, some not. In tax jargon there's a classification for every kind of income. Problem is, the classification may change depending upon the circumstances. For instance, grants and scholarships are sometimes considered *earned* income, but sometimes not. Tax-free interest and dividends, although not taxable, may be included as income for certain calculations.

to Uncle Sam will depend upon whether you were paid as an employee or as a self-employed.

For our purposes let's use the following income definition: **Earned income** is payment for services performed. It is money or goods that you receive in the form of salary, wages, professional fees, tips, etc., for work that you do. Earned income is not money or things you receive for reasons other than work. For instance, earned income is not a gift from Grandma, nor unemployment compensation, nor dividend income, nor insurance proceeds.

There are only two types of earned income:

- W-2 earnings
  and
- Self-employed income

Let's see how to tell the difference between the two.

 Reality Rick Reporter writes a feature story on sailing that was not assigned by his editor, but the editor likes it and the piece is published in the newspaper's Sunday supplement, *Jaunty Journal*. Rick is paid $1,000 for this feature. In his next paycheck the $1,000 payment is added to his regular weekly salary. Taxes were withheld. ***That $1,000 is W-2 earnings.***

Rick then decides to send the same piece to *Mariner's Monthly*. The magazine accepts it virtually unchanged and will also pay him $1,000. Two months after publication Rick receives a $1,000 check from the magazine. No taxes were withheld. ***That $1,000 is self-employed income.***

Simply stated: ***If taxes are withheld, it's W-2 income; and if no taxes are withheld, it's self-employed income.***

From the two publications, Rick earned the same amount of money for the same piece of work; however, he generated two different types of earned income.

It is important to understand the distinction and to keep them separate in your records. Why? Because they are treated differently on your tax return, and the tax you pay on each is not the same.

W-2 income is referred to as salary, wages, paycheck, take-home pay, or regular income. Those who earn W-2 income are called employees. I call them W-2 people. At the end of the year, W-2 people receive a Form W-2 from their employers stating income and withholdings for the year. The government also receives a copy of the W-2.

Self-employed income can be called commissions, fees, royalties, stipends, or freelance income. Self-employed people are dubbed freelancers, consultants, sole proprietors, indies, subcontractors, or just gutsy. Self-employed income is *not* under-the-table, off-the-books, or paid-in-the-parking-lot income. (More on that later.)

If a self-employed is paid $600 or more in one year by an individual or corporation, then that individual or corporation should send the self-employed a federal Form 1099 at the end of the year stating "nonemployee compensation" paid. The government is also sent a copy of the form. Even if the self-employed receives no 1099—because his earnings were less than $600 or the payer neglected to send it—*the income is still taxable and must be claimed on his tax return.*

How Do W-2 Earnings Compare to Self-employed Income?

Astrid Astrologer's *gross income is $20,000* a year as a self-employed. She has a neighbor whose *total wages are $20,000* a year as a supermarket employee.

Let's look at how the same income amounts compare from the perspective of *take-home pay* for the employee and *net income* for the self-employed. They are not alike!

Take-Home Pay

W-2 people often refer to the money they receive on payday as take-home pay. Take-home pay is important because it's what the W-2 person lives on until the next paycheck.

The amount she takes home is considerably less than her gross wages or actual salary.

From gross wages some of the following payroll deductions must and others may be withheld by the employer:

Federal income tax
State income tax
City or local income tax
FICA (Social Security tax)
Medicare tax
Unemployment insurance
Disability insurance
United Way contributions
Pension contributions
Savings plan deductions
Medical insurance
Pretax child-care costs

For W-2 people: *gross wages* minus *deductions* equals *take-home pay.*

Rick Reporter, who made $1,000 extra for the piece in his paper's Sunday supplement, did not *take home* an additional $1,000. Deductions probably reduced it to about $600 in *take-home pay.*

Keep in mind:

- A W-2 person's income tax is calculated on gross wages.
- With her take-home pay she buys food, pays the rent, plays the slots at the casinos. But she doesn't make the tax payments on it: Her employer has already withheld the tax and sent it on its way to Uncle Sam and the state tax folks.

- When a bank loan officer asks a W-2 person to state her income, the banker is asking about **gross wages.**

Net Income

Net income is the amount a self-employed has left after subtracting his business expenses from his gross self-employed income.

Rick Reporter did receive a check for the full amount of $1,000 from *Mariner's Monthly* magazine. His only expense was a $20 express mail fee.

The	$1,000	is his *gross* self-employed income.
Less	20	expenses.
The balance of	$ 980	is his *net* self-employed income.

For self-employed people: *gross self-employed income* minus *self-employed expenses* equals *net self-employed income.*

Keep in mind:

- A self-employed's income tax is calculated on his net income.
- With his net income he buys food, pays the rent, goes to the movies—**and** pays taxes.
- When a bank loan officer asks a self-employed to state his income, the banker is asking about **net income.**

You'll learn more about income in Part III.

Now that you understand what distinguishes W-2 income from self-employed income, you may think that you have it all figured out. Have someone pay you and withhold no taxes and kazam!—you're an independent contractor. Oh, if it were only that easy! For as I'll show you in the next section, **it is not the method by which one is paid but the nature of the business relationship that determines whether or not one is self-employed.**

CHAPTER TWO

What Determines Employee or Self-employed Status? It's All about Relationships

Many business relationships are straightforward and clear-cut. A fifth-grade teacher in the city school system is unquestionably an employee. If that same teacher tutors children on weekends and during the summer, in his home, with his materials, in the subjects he chooses—not out of the goodness of his heart but to earn enough to build an addition to his home—then tutoring is a self-employed endeavor.

However, in some work situations the lines get blurry. What if the school supplied the teacher with all the materials? What if the school scheduled the students' tutoring sessions? What if the students paid the school and then the school paid the teacher?

Or suppose Syd System, a software developer, leaves his job at the Callous Company and then completes a project for the company for a flat fee? Is he truly self-employed or actually still an employee? And what if five years after leaving the company, he is operating his own business but has always had and still has only one client—the Callous Company?

Employee? Self-employed? With both the teacher and the software developer, the blurriness is real. However, in other cases the issue is deliberately obscured in order to save the business owner time and money.

Reality ✓ Manny Mailorder, although still working out of his home, just can no longer handle all the business himself. But Manny is reluctant to take on the added hassle of payroll, withholding taxes, insurance and pension requirements, and the periodic reports required when a business has employees. So when he hires Stevie Stamplicker to come in five days a week, he has Stevie sign a contract saying that he is an independent contractor. Believing that the contract is all that he needs to establish their relationship, he pays Stevie as a **consultant.** But anyone who examines the nature of their relationship would conclude that Manny is an employer and Stevie is an employee.

This contrivance of phony self-employment doesn't come up only in the nation's mom-and-pop shops. Back in the 1990s the IRS ruled that many of the people working at Microsoft had been wrongly classified as independent contractors. They worked the same hours as other workers who were designated as employees, performed the same functions, and reported to the same supervisors. As far as the IRS was concerned, they were employees—despite words written in a contract—because Microsoft controlled the "manner and means" of their work. Microsoft and the workers had an employer-employee relationship, and it's the relationship that counts.

As the IRS goes looking for tax money that has been slipping between the cracks (whether through legitimate cracks or man-made fissures), it has been reclassifying many independents as employees. The consequences of misclassification can be severe. If the IRS reclassifies independent contractors as employees, back payroll taxes and penalties can hit the employer hard.

The former independent, now classified as an employee, must file his tax return as an employee and may lose many of his business deductions—or, if the deductions remain applicable to his new employee status, they must be moved from the self-employed section of his tax return to the employee section where their tax-reduction value dwindles. The reclassification could also eliminate his health insurance deduction and force him to give up his self-employed pension.

If Stevie Stamplicker, like the workers at Microsoft, is an employee, then he and his employer need to face up to it and not stretch and squeeze the criteria to make his status look like that of a self-employed.

Beware of some old husbands' tales out there that say you're considered self-employed if:

- You have a contract.
- You're paid on commission.
- You have a business bank account.
- You work sporadically or part-time.
- You work for more than one person.

Not one of these is surefire proof of self-employment. Take heed: *If you claim to be self-employed, you must be able to prove it.*

To cover both the contrived and the honestly complicated situations, the IRS has put together a guide to help determine whether someone is an independent contractor or an employee. Until recently the IRS used twenty factors in making that determination. Now it has focused the criteria upon a single issue: *control versus independence.*

Does the worker perform independently? To what degree is her work controlled? It is a question of relationship, it is a matter of degree, and it is measured in three categories:

1. **Behavioral control:** Who directs and controls what will be done and how it will be done?
2. **Financial control:** Who directs or controls the business aspects of the work?
3. **Type of relationship:** What facts show the type of relationship?

The table on the next page provides detailed comparison of the differences in business relationships between an independent contractor and an employee.

Let's explore the differences in business relationships with the following Reality Checks.

 The question of independence and control gives us more perspective on the case of Syd System, the software developer who left the Callous Company but for the following five years has had only the company as a client. As the IRS sees it, having a single client suggests that Syd is really an employee. However, there are other factors that lend credence to his claim that he is an independent contractor with a home-based business:

He is paid an agreed-upon price for a job project and does not submit hourly bills; he works at home, using his own computer and other equipment; the Callous Company does not provide him with supplies; he is not required to or invited to attend staff meetings; when called to meet with company officials, the date is set at his convenience; he works no specific hours and determines his own work schedule except that he is required to deliver various phases of the work on dates set by the contract.

All these suggest that although he works for a single client, he is a bona fide independent contractor.

 Ted Tilesetter shows up for work, bringing along his own tools, whenever the Confounded Construction Company calls him to a job. Sometimes he will work for five or six weeks at a time. He sets tiles in various houses in the order that the company specifies. The company supplies the materials and pays him on a per diem basis. Ted does not have a place of business and does not offer, advertise, or promote himself to work for other construction companies. Although he cites the sporadic nature of his work as evidence of being an independent contractor, he is actually a part-time employee.

 Lily Legal does corporate legal work for three companies and bills them by the hour, sending invoices that itemize her work. The bills also include expenses for long-

WHAT'S YOUR BUSINESS RELATIONSHIP?

CATEGORY	SELF-EMPLOYED	EMPLOYEE
BEHAVIORAL CONTROL Who controls what is done and how it's done?	• Works how, when, and where she chooses. • Uses own tools and equipment. • Purchases own tools and equipment. • Uses own methods. • Chooses own assistants. • Decides who does which part of the work. • Sets own work schedule.	• Told how, when, or where to work. • Told what tools and equipment to use. • Given or told where to purchase supplies. • Given extensive training and/or instruction. • Told what workers are to assist with the work. • Told what work must be performed by a specific individual. • Told what order or sequence to follow.
FINANCIAL CONTROL Who directs and controls the money?	• Pays own business expenses except for specific costs set by contract, e.g., mileage. • Has fixed ongoing costs regardless of whether the work is ongoing. • Has a significant financial investment in the facilities. • Advertises to her relevant market. • Available to her relevant market. • Maintains a visible business location. • Paid by a flat fee for the project or service. • May be paid an hourly rate (e.g., attorneys). • Can make a profit or loss.	• Is reimbursed for expenses, although may have some unreimbursed expenses. • Has no fixed business costs if she has no work. • Has no financial investment in her work facilities. • Does not advertise her services. • Works for one employer. • Has no business location. • Earns a regular wage. • Wage or salary may be supplemented by commissions.
TYPE OF RELATIONSHIP How is the relationship between the parties perceived?	• Contract describes the relationship. • Receives no benefits. • Engaged for the length of contract or project.	• Job description is provided. • Worker benefits are provided. • Engaged permanently or indefinitely.

distance calls, faxes, photocopies, postage, and travel. Does she have three jobs as a part-time employee? She claims to be an independent contractor, noting that she employs a part-time receptionist and files a W-2 for that employee every year. She rents office space, owns her own office equipment, and pays for her membership in professional organizations as well as an online legal research service. Although she has only three clients for which she works extensively, her relationship with them appears to be that of an independent contractor.

You can see that no single factor determines self-employed status. The IRS considers *all* evidence of control.

- Whether the worker is a self-employed or an employee depends primarily on the *extent* to which the individual or company receiving the service or product has the right to direct and control what the worker does and how she does it.
- The amount of instruction needed varies among different professions. Even if no instructions are given, sufficient behavioral control may exist if the person or company for which the work is done has the right to control how the work results are achieved.
- In highly specialized professions, a business may lack the expertise to control the worker. That alone does not negate an employer-employee relationship.
- The greater the degree of control, the more likely the worker is an employee.
- Independent contractors determine for themselves how the work is to be performed.

As far as the IRS is concerned, *if you claim to be self-employed, you must be able to prove it.*

Yet even if you prove that you're self-employed, you're only halfway through the IRS independent-contractor maze. To treat your income as that of a self-employed on your tax return, you still must show the IRS that you're running a business, not a hobby.

CHAPTER THREE

For Fun or Profit: Is Your Endeavor a Hobby or a Business?

Want to be classified as an independent contractor? You must meet two conditions. As explained in the previous section, the first is establishing yourself as a self-employed rather than an employee. The second is that you must be engaged in a *business.* It cannot be a hobby supported by Grandma's inheritance; it must be a real, honest-to-goodness business.

As pointed out at the beginning of this chapter, there are different tax consequences for pay received by an employee and for that received by a self-employed. If the self-employed can show the IRS that he's running a business, not just puttering away at a hobby, the financial

Taxes as a plus-minus formula

1. You receive various types of income—or "pluses." Examples: wages, fees, commissions, pensions, savings account interest, stock sale gains, unemployment compensation, Social Security benefits, lottery winnings.
2. Various kinds of deductions—or "minuses"—reduce your income. Examples: IRA contributions, business expenses, union dues, charitable contributions, mortgage interest, gambling expenses.
3. You subtract the minuses from the pluses. What you are left with is "taxable income."
4. You pay tax on your income. That's why it's called income tax.
5. Therefore, the more minuses, the less tax you pay.

impact can be more pronounced and he may end up with more money in his pocket.

If your self-employed expenses are greater than your self-employed income, you will have a **net loss.** That loss is subtracted from your other income (that is, from the part of your income that does not come from your self-employment). There are many reasons for self-employment, making money usually near the top of the list, but even losing money can be of some help if it gets those **overall** pluses down so that you pay less tax!

If you receive $50,000 in income from Grandma's trust fund in the same year that you have a $10,000 loss in your self-employed business, you get to subtract the $10,000 business loss from the $50,000 trust income. You are now looking at income of $40,000 instead of $50,000.

However, if you lose money as a self-employed, you may deduct the loss from Grandma's trust income or from any other taxable income only if the IRS considers your self-employed activity a **business.**

Because of the two-part proof, even if you are very clearly not an employee, you must still be able to show that you are a self-employed *in* **business.** And the way to show that you're in business is that you must be in it to make money.

THE IRS SAYS ABOUT

Being in Business . . .

In order for you to be engaged in a business rather than a hobby, *the goal must be to make a profit!*

The IRS doesn't insist that you actually make a profit, but there must be a reasonable expectation of one. It could be:

- A big chance of making a small profit
  or
- A small chance of making a big profit

If the purpose of your endeavor is not profit, any loss you incur from it may not be a minus against other income. Said another way: Your deductions are limited.

Here are two situations that clarify the difference between a hobby and a business.

Reality

Aunt Ada lives nicely off the income generated from her investments. She enjoys quilting very much, and every once in a while an acquaintance or relative buys something she's made. Ada keeps a hit-or-miss record of her expenses and does not advertise. She gives many of her quilts to her nieces.

Based on these facts, Aunt Ada has a hobby. If Ada sells $1,000 worth of quilted pillows in a year, she is allowed to deduct up to only $1,000 in quilting expenses, even if her costs were more than $1,000. Why? Because hers is a hobby, not a business.

	$1,000	gross quilting income
minus	$1,000	allowed expenses
equals	$ 0	net income

Reality

Trixy Trinkets, unlike Aunt Ada, has no investments. To earn a living she must work as a W-2 person. She has a regular job as a buyer's assistant at a clothing store where she earns $40,000 a year. Evenings and weekends she designs and makes silver jewelry. She can't keep up with the requests of those who want to buy her unique pieces. So she cuts back on the hours at her job in the clothing store to devote more time to designing, creating, and selling her jewelry. She's not sure how long it will take, but she's determined to leave the clothing store eventually and make a living as a jewelry designer. She was an excellent apprentice to a highly respected silversmith in her town and even helped him redesign his studio. She keeps careful records of how long it takes her to complete each piece and sets her prices by her records and the going market rate.

Based on these facts, Trixy is a self-employed jeweler. She is in business even before she quits her regular W-2 job. If Trixy sells $1,000 worth of jewelry, she may deduct as many business expenses as she incurs even if they amount to many thousands of dollars. If Trixy's net income is a loss, that loss can be deducted from her other income and could reduce her taxes.

	$1,000	gross jewelry income
minus	$3,000	expenses
equals	– $2,000	net income

Said another way: Trixy has a $2,000 loss. From her W-2 income of $40,000, she may subtract her $2,000 loss to arrive at an earned income of $38,000.

WHATTA**CONCEPT**!

What is negative income?

In accounting, subtraction and negative numbers are indicated by parentheses. For example, ($2,000) means negative $2,000 or subtract $2,000 or a $2,000 loss.

Therefore, the above example may be written as follows:

	$ 1,000	gross income
	(3,000)	expenses
equals	$ (2,000)	net profit (loss)

As said earlier, **an activity is a business if its goal is to make a profit.** If your activity **always** makes a profit, no problem—it's a business. Or if your activity makes a profit in **three years out of five,** no problem—it's a business. That's because the IRS presumes it to be a business if there is a profit in three out of five **consecutive** years (two out of seven for horse breeding, training, showing, or racing). The profitable years do not have to be consecutive, but the five years during which they fall must be consecutive.

Let's look at two situations. In the seven years since each started business, Cheech had a profit in only three years and Chong had a profit in four years. However, in any five consecutive years, Chong did not have a three-year profit. By the three-out-of-five-years IRS criteria, Cheech's endeavor would be considered a business. Chong would have to prove that his endeavor is a business.

Cheech A Business:	Chong Not a Business:
2001 loss	**2001 profit**
2002 loss	**2002 profit**
2003 profit	2003 loss
2004 profit	2004 loss
2005 profit	2005 loss
2006 loss	**2006 profit**
2007 loss	**2007 profit**

Dear IRS:

I'm self-employed and not making any money, but this is a business I'm running. Really!

What if you've **never** made a profit? If you can't prove you're in it for the money, then the IRS says you're not a business! And if yours is not a business, then you don't get to deduct your business loss from other income. So how do you prove you're doing something to make a profit if you're not making a profit?

A number of books advise entrepreneurs that the best way is to just "show a profit." That's like telling Miles Mingus to make the charts with a hit song three years out of five … or, if that doesn't happen, the mahogany-office accountant, Sammy Segar, CPA, suggests that Miles forget about a lot of his expenses, pretend he made a profit, and pay Uncle Sam more than is his due. **Pretty bad advice!**

If you know that your self-employed business is going to make you rich someday (even though you've had a loss every year since you started your new venture), how do you prove to the IRS that your goal is to make a profit?

THE IRS SAYS ABOUT
Proving a Profit Motive . . .

A profit motive is indicated if you **treat your activity like a business.**

Just as the IRS provides guidelines for determining self-employed or employee status, it also provides guidelines for determining if you're treating your activity like a business and thereby in it for the money.

If It Walks Like a Business and Talks Like a Business, It Must Be a Business

The following list will help you determine if you're doing whatever you're doing to make a buck. No single item on the list settles or resolves the issue, nor is this a complete list used by the IRS in making a decision, but these are the items normally taken into account. The IRS considers *all* the facts surrounding an activity in determining if the activity is engaged in for profit.

1. **Carrying on the activity in a businesslike manner.**
   - Are your books and records kept completely and accurately?
   - Is your activity carried on like similar businesses that operate at a profit?
   - If methods you used proved unprofitable, did you change your methods or adopt new techniques in an attempt to improve profitability?

2. **Expertise of the taxpayer or his advisors.**
   - Have you prepared to enter this business by studying the accepted managerial and technological practices of those already in the field?
   - Are your business practices similar to others in your profession? If not, are you attempting to develop new or superior techniques that may result in future profits?

3. **Time and effort expended.**
   - Do you put more time into marketing your business than you put into fly fishing?

   - Do you employ someone with the expertise you may not have or who puts in the time you are not able to?
   - Did you leave another job to devote more time to this activity?

4. **Expectation that assets used in the activity may appreciate in value.**
   - The term "profit" encompasses appreciation of assets. Will the land, equipment, or instruments used in your endeavor increase in value so that your future profit may be realized from the appreciation of your assets as well as from income?

5. **Success in carrying on similar or dissimilar activities.**
   - Have you taken a similar activity and converted it from an unprofitable to a profitable enterprise?
   - Have you had general success in running other kinds of businesses?

6. **History of income or losses with respect to the activity.**
   - Losses early in the history of a business are common. Are your losses due to heavy early expenses or have they extended beyond the normal time for this kind of activity to begin making a profit?

7. **Amount of occasional profits.**
   - There may be a disparity in the amount of profits that you make in relation to the losses you incur or in the amount of money spent on assets used in your activity. The purchase of a $3,000 camera, but not one photo sale, may tell the IRS it's a hobby. Do you have an opportu-

nity to make a substantial ultimate profit in a highly speculative activity?

- A software developer may work on a project for years before it is viable. Is your business the type that will have an occasional large profit but small operating losses over many years?

Note: Be careful of the next two.

8. Financial status of the taxpayer.

- If this is your only source of income, then you must be in it to make a profit.
- If, on the other hand, you've got large income from other sources and this activity generates substantial tax benefits, this could indicate to the IRS that the activity is not carried on for profit but as a homemade tax shelter.

9. Elements of personal pleasure or recreation.

- The IRS says "elements of personal pleasure or recreation" may indicate the lack of a profit motive.

Let's look at how these points were applied by the IRS. The following Reality Checks are summaries of cases from IRS files. Real names are used.

 The artist's road is a hard one. Stella Waltzkin, an artist, supported herself for some years by selling her art, teaching art, and designing fixtures for a lighting company. After receiving an inheritance, she no longer had to work, but she persevered at producing and selling her art. Over the next ten years, Ms. Waltzkin continued to lose

money on the sale of art. One year she claimed a $40,000 loss on $6,000 of gross income.

The IRS ruled her activity a hobby. But the federal courts overruled the IRS decision. "It is well recognized," the court noted, "that profits may not be immediately forthcoming in the creative field, and many artists have to struggle throughout their careers. This does not mean that serious artists do not intend to profit from their activities. It only means that their lot is a difficult one."

 The fisherman who was at sea. After six years out of the tuna-fishing business, Fisherman Lamb decided to get back into it. He bought a boat and obtained a license. But by the third year of his business, he still hadn't made a profit. That year he caught only one fish and his loss was a whopping $21,000! After taking losses on his tax return for five years, he quit the fishy business.

Claiming that he did not have a profit motive, the IRS disallowed his losses in two of those years. The IRS noted that he didn't fish that much, but Lamb contended that there are only fifteen to twenty good fishing days per year off the Maine coast. Lamb attributed his lack of success to diabetes, which had caused his eyesight to deteriorate.

The tax court ruled in Lamb's favor. It noted that he had substantial previous experience in the business and had shown evidence that he had gone back into it with a profit motive in mind. He kept records of weather and tide conditions and the locations of fish, obviously running the enterprise in a businesslike manner. The court attributed the cause of Lamb's poor catches to his poor eyesight, not to a lack of profit motive.

 The doctor who farms. The doctor spent his childhood on a farm. When he grew up, he thought farming would be a profitable second business. For seventeen out of eighteen years, he operated his farm at a loss. Not so surprising considering he worked there only on weekends. Guess the cows got pretty uncomfortable or the hay got pretty high. He intended to buy more land, increase the size of his herd, and devote more time to farming in the hope that these changes would bring in more income. But he never bought the land and instead put more time into his medical practice. The IRS ruled that he was operating the farm for pleasure rather than for profit.

 The lady farmers. The IRS was reversed when it disallowed nine years of deductions for a horse farm operated by a woman and her daughters. For nine years they bred, trained, raced, and sold horses at a loss. The IRS disallowed the losses. The tax court overruled the IRS, determining that the farm was operated with a profit motive because accurate records were kept, time and expertise were put into the work, and the women changed their procedures at the advice of experts.

 Yachting for fun or losses. Concerned that a taxpayer might be having too much fun in his self-employment (as in the earlier Reality Check about the farming doctor), the IRS has used personal pleasure as a factor to disallow business deductions. This case involved a yachtsman who leased his vessel to others then deducted his losses in the yacht-chartering business. The IRS noted that the yachtsman enjoyed sailing and contended that he was just engaged in a hobby. The tax court found for the yachtsman. "A 'business' will not be turned into a 'hobby' merely because the owner finds it pleasurable," the court ruled. "Suffering has never been made a prerequisite to deductibility."

The IRS has won some and lost some. They look at self-employment very closely if there's no financial need for the endeavor (Stella the artist or the farming doctor) or if it's a fun business (yachting).

Whether you're a self-employed artist or one of the other thirty-three million self-employeds now boppin' around the USA, you can make your lot less difficult by doing your best to meet IRS criteria. The real-life examples above should give you a sense of whether your manner of pursuing your activity is that of a self-employed in business or not.

Self-employment as Tax Shelter

A number of books, articles, and Web sites advocate going into a self-employed business as a terrific way to get a lot of write-offs on your tax return. The epitome of this style is a well-known author and money guru who glibly promises that "you can magically turn personal expenses into tax deductions." His online bag of tricks invariably shows that outsmarting the IRS is a piece of cake and that any taxpayer with his wits about him can't lose.

Writers of these articles and books are more interested in the tax consequences than in the business. This is a wrong and disallowed reason to set up a business. At worst it may lead some people to set up a sham business to cut taxes—a move that could bring them up against the IRS with costly consequences. At best, it's putting the cart before the horse.

The backward approach prevails in a number of books that promote the idea that having a business will set you up to pay no tax. The authors' contrivances usually feature a W-2 person who creates a self-employed sideline that allows him to convert personal expenses into business write-offs. The alternative scenario features one spouse with a W-2 job while the other spouse fabricates the self-employed job. All self-employed jobs are created exclusively to generate deductions. "Which spouse should create the deductions?" is a question one book poses.

In real life, decisions about self-employment are not made that way. One spouse may have a W-2 job for the sake of regular and steady income or health insurance coverage, while the other tries a hand at the riskier and more irregular income of self-employment. Don't get me wrong—I'm for taking every deduction legally possible, but going into business for that purpose is not what made America great or made any business succeed. Do you think Bill Gates or Oprah Winfrey got started in business to deduct personal expenses? Or do you think they were motivated by great opportunities?

It's the glib and muddled counsel of the tax-shelter promoters that gets the IRS breathing down our necks and gives us legitimate self-employeds a bad name. Remember, for the IRS to consider your activity a business, you must have a profit motive, not a tax-reduction motive!

To Sum Up Hobby versus Business

- Just because you are paid as a self-employed does not mean that you are self-employed.
- Specific factors determine whether you're an employee or self-employed. They have to do with the degree of control and independence in a business relationship.
- For the IRS to treat you as an independent contractor, being self-employed is only part of the picture; you must also be able to prove that you're in it for the money—that you're running a business.
- The more you treat your activity as a business, the more likely the IRS will see it as one. Portray a strong commitment to your business and, most important, keep complete and accurate records. The easiest place to start your recordkeeping is right here, with *Self-employed Tax Solutions.*

CHAPTER FOUR

Employee or Self-employed: Which Is Better?

Is self-employment for you? If you're still pondering that question, ignore the bad advice of the tax-evasion gurus who urge you to do it for the tax breaks. Although taxes matter vitally once you're in business, taxes are not, and should not be, the defining factor in your decision to go solo.

Let's begin the analysis of the pros and cons by dropping the gushy prose about the joys of self-realization that abound in working for yourself and about how "the real you" will bubble up from the depths when you "control your own destiny." Instead, I want to show you some of the considerations you need to face if you are thinking about going into business for yourself and weighing whether it is the right step for you.

Is it better to be self-employed or an employee? Here are several people who are asking themselves this question.

- A reporter for the *New York Times* earning $160,000 per year with oodles of employee benefits, including a pension plan and stock options, can no longer deal with incessant travel. She wants to adopt the life of a freelance writer with no editor dispatching her to Wichita on two hours' notice—but also no set income and no benefits.
- A guy who works in the local bakery getting paid a little above minimum wage has kept his mom's Hungarian pastry recipes and is sure there'd be more satisfaction and more money in his own busi-

ness. He could name it Marika's Marzipan after his sweet mother.

- A public relations executive making $300,000 per year, with mucho investments and even more client connections, has tired of the rat race—yet thoughts about going out on her own give her an awful stomachache.
- A woman with degrees in Russian, Spanish, and Italian and lots of volunteer experience, and whose youngest child is in school half a day, wants to be home when her kids are home. She is thinking of starting a home business as a publication translator and language teacher.

For some the choice is not so hard between self-employment and W-2 work; for others it is excruciating. There are a host of factors, personal and professional, in a decision about whether to go solo. Some of them are:

Situational: Do you have many family responsibilities? Do you have support from friends and family?

Talent: Do you have the skills to make it on your own?

Psychological: Do you have the temperament and the discipline necessary?

Financial: Do you have the money you need to get started? Or have enough saved to keep you afloat until your venture runs smoothly?

Benefits: Are employee benefits available through your spouse's employment? Can you afford the high bills of health coverage or can you take the risk of being without it?

Legal: Do you understand and can you handle your increased liability as an independent professional?

Ownership: Do you understand the differences as to who owns your work—the copyright or patent or recipe—if you create your creation as an employee? As a self-employed? As a work-for-hire?

The unknown: How prepared are you for an emergency such as getting hurt while working? A long bout with the flu? A shortage of clients? Computer crashes? Car breakdowns? A no-show babysitter?

Whether to be self-employed or work for someone else: There is no right or wrong decision. It's a choice only you can make.

Disadvantages of Self-employment

All the important disadvantages of self-employment can be summed as one big piece of bad news: Nobody is taking care of you. There's no big daddy to turn to. You alone are responsible for yourself—and often for a lot of others, too.

You are not paid for sick days; you must come up with the money to pay for your own health insurance; if you have a question about pensions, you can't run to the personnel office on the sixth floor to get an answer; there's no child-care subsidy. I am not saying that every employee has this kind of coverage and benefits, but I am saying that *no self-employed has them.*

When you work for yourself, you have no boss. You are both employer and employee, and in your dual role you must pay both the employee's share and the employer's share of Social Security and Medicare tax, called **self-employment tax (SE tax).** (You'll learn more about taxes paid by a self-employed in Part V.)

As for your pension, every penny comes from you, whereas in many companies employers contribute to the pensions of their employees. If you can't work or there is no work, you don't get paid, and you can't apply for unemployment benefits. Nor can you get worker's compensation for a work-related injury. *You are truly on your own.* It sounds daunting, but most independent professionals have faced all these considerations and have decided, as I also did, that (unless you believe in reincarnation) since you only live once, being your own boss is more fulfilling and more fun!

Advantages of Self-employment

The same thing that makes self-employment scary is what makes it attractive and adventurous. Nobody will take care of you, but instead of dwelling on that as bad news, embrace it as good news: It means you will be in charge. You will be responsible for yourself—and often for others, too. No big daddy will tell you what to do, how to do it, and when to do it. Nor can he fire you. You'll have more control of your time and your life. I'm talking practicality here, not psychobabble about women running with the coyotes or adolescent rebelliousness and your contempt for "the suits." (You may pick up a few "suits" as clients.)

Here's what I'm talking about. Do you want to work until three in the morning all week so that you can take four days off to go skiing? You can. Do you want to start the day late so you can have breakfast with your honey? You can. If you're not feeling great and want to work from your home in your pj's, you can. You can fit your schedule into the schedule of the rest of your family, maybe eliminating the need for expensive or inadequate child care. If you have a great idea, you can try it. If it doesn't work, you are responsible for that, too, but you can make changes and improve your idea without the need to play company politics with the sales department down the hall.

And with self-employment comes financial advantages. One of the less obvious advantages is the possibility of more money for the same work. Many companies have downsized (don't you love that word?), and former employees have been fired and then engaged as independent contractors. Why do you think that has happened? Money! It saves the company a big bundle in payroll taxes and benefits to hire someone as a freelancer rather than as an employee. So should you work for the same fee that you would be paid as an employee? No, you shouldn't. You should ask for more. You are costing the company a lot less than would employee Dennis Dubya-two, so how about splitting the difference? And if you're engaged by someone who has never run a business or never hired anyone to work for her, maybe you'll need to point out the financial savings to her and why she should use your services instead of those of the temp agency she's considering.

Self-employment comes with tax advantages as well. You are in control, so in many instances …

- You have more influence over business expense deductions.
- More business expenses are actually deductible.
- You get more flexibility in how much tax you'll pay and when you'll pay it.
- You get to decide when to spend money to help your business grow.
- You can influence when you receive income.
- You can distribute income to family members by hiring them as employees.
- You have a wide range of pension choices.

Some of these topics will be covered throughout **Self-employed Tax Solutions,** others are beyond the information included in this book. Nonetheless, you're on your way to being able to take full advantage of them in the future. For now let's look at two of the basic advantages: your own influence over business expense deductions and the greater deductibility of business expenses.

The IRS determines a business deduction as one that is "ordinary and necessary" to your profession. And who decides what is ordinary and necessary? The decision is based on (a) industry standards and (b) your employer. But as a self-employed, you are **your own** employer, and so you have a great deal of influence in determining which of your expenses are ordinary and necessary to your work. Therefore, as a self-employed, your deduction vista is expanded. You may get to write off many more business expenses than if you were an employee.

The other tax advantage to the self-employed that we'll look at here is the greater *actual* deductibility of business expenses. You'll remember that earlier in Part I, Rick Reporter sold a feature story on sailing to both his newspaper and to a sailing magazine. If he had spent $100 on reference books and magazines on boating to research the piece, then those **PUBLICATIONS** expenses would be a business deduction. For this example let's say that the publications were his only business expense on his entire tax return. Without question it is a legitimate $100 business expense. He would have to split the expense: $50 against his W-2 wage and $50 against his freelance income.

However, the $50 expense allocated against his $1,000 W-2 income is deducted on a part of his tax return that must exceed a certain minimum. He would not have met that minimum. As an employee, therefore, the $50 **PUBLICATIONS** expense would not actually be deductible from his income. The deduction would be lost, and the entire $1,000 W-2 income would be subject to income tax.

On the other hand, the $50 expense against his $1,000 self-employed income is deducted on a different part of his tax return where no minimum need be met. It would be fully deductible, and so only $950 of the $1,000 self-employed income would be subject to income tax.

More control in determining **ordinary and necessary** expenses and the straightforward deductibility of **all** business expenses provide powerful advantages to being self-employed. When these factors apply to a large portion of your income, they are especially advantageous. Note that Rick Reporter's other expenses—such as the canoe trip with his buddy, the visit to the maritime museum, the 4:00 A.M. phone calls to his fishing partner about problems in renting the sailboat—are all totally or partially deductible against his $1,000 freelance income. Such legitimate increases in deductions lower the overall tax of a self-employed.

Self-employed Tax Solutions will help you clearly understand and intelligently weigh the advantages and disadvantages of the freelance life. I hope that you'll choose it over the W-2 life.

If you're still undecided, you may want next to read Chapter Six, Thinking Like an Indie Business, which introduces you to business expenses; Chapter Sixteen, Camels or Cash, which introduces you to income; and the introduction to taxes in Chapter Twenty-five, Taxes: Your Fair Share. The information in those three chapters will help you make this life-changing choice. Then you can return here to read the next section, which explains sole proprietorship.

CHAPTER FIVE

The Most Simple Business Structure: Sole Proprietorship and Beyond

If you've decided that an indie business is for you, congratulations! But now what do you do? Well, according to the majority of books on entrepreneurship, the first step is to talk with a lawyer about incorporating. The lawyers—no surprise—say the same.

Incorporating is not the thing to do!

Every business conducts its affairs as a particular kind of **business entity** (or **business structure**). The organizational form you choose determines which tax and legal regulations will apply. For tax purposes the IRS gives a choice of the following kinds of business structures:

- Sole proprietorship
- Partnership (several types)
- Corporation (two types)

If you're a self-employed in business and you have done nothing about a business entity, your business is already structured. It is a **sole proprietorship.**

Self-employed Tax Solutions is a book of basics. There is no need to complicate when simplicity will suffice. For all but a few newly hatched solo ventures, a sole proprietorship is the way to go. And although most of the information and guidance in this book applies to all business structures, I'll focus on sole proprietorships.

What Is Sole Proprietorship?

A **sole proprietorship** is the most simple business entity. Did you have a lemonade stand when you were a kid? Or as a teen, did you babysit or do yard work? If you were doing it to make money, then you were a self-employed in business and your business structure was a sole proprietorship—and you probably weren't even aware of it.

How to Become a Sole Proprietor

It's simple. Just say, "I am a business." You need do nothing by way of notification. There are no papers to complete, no agency to contact. You simply engage in your business activity.

As soon as you sell or attempt to sell your service or product in hope of making a profit, you have "formed" a sole proprietorship.

Rick Reporter did that earlier in Part I. When he decided to try to freelance his sailing story, he became a self-employed in business. His business structure was a sole proprietorship. Even were Rick unable to sell the piece, and ended up with enough rejection letters to paper his walls, as long as he intended to make a profit as a freelancer he'd be a sole proprietor. He doesn't need a business name. He is as legit with a business card that simply states his name and contact information as he'd be were he to call his business Rick's Real Good Writin' and rent office space and open a business checking account.

Don't pay much heed to the pros and the how-to-be-a-business books that insist you have need of an accountant, a lawyer, a banker, an insurance agent, and a marketing consultant to become a business. Depending upon the kind of project you are embarking on—if you're a solo trucker shipping hazardous materials across state lines, for instance—or as your business grows or tax laws change, some or all of these professionals may be useful to your business, but they are not necessary for the early and instant formation of your business as a sole proprietorship.

You may never need to incorporate. The Feds say that nearly four out of five businesses in the United States are sole proprietorships. Yet just about every lawyer advises a budding indie to incorporate. In twenty-plus years of experience, I have found only one attorney who didn't answer "yes" when asked: "Should I incorporate?" And every new client who has come to me already set up as a corporation said he or she did it because "my attorney (or my accountant) told me to do it." None of them had a clear idea of why incorporation was supposed to be an advantage.

Forget the old husbands' tales and look at the facts. All business structures:

- Allow you to deduct business expenses.
- Allow some or all deduction of medical insurance.
- Allow for contributions to pension plans.
- Allow you to hire employees or subcontractors.
- Allow the other guy to sue you.
- Do not allow you to hide income.
- Do not allow you to write off personal nonbusiness expenses.

Once in a while there may be a good reason why a self-employed should incorporate, but if advised that you must do it, find out why. Be sure the professional explains to your satisfaction—and also to the satisfaction of a savvy friend, colleague, or relative—what makes incorporation necessary.

The Characteristics and Advantages of a Sole Proprietorship

- You and your business are one and the same.
- A sole proprietor and his business use the same tax year.
- Its income or loss is your income or loss. (This is referred to as pass-through, which we'll look at in a moment.)
- Its debts and assets are your debts and assets.
- Assets, originally for personal use, can immediately be used in your business without paperwork and without negative tax consequences. And there can be positive tax consequences without any cash outlay.
- It's the easiest, quickest, and cheapest business structure to set up and maintain with regard to recordkeeping, accounting, legal procedures, and fees.
- The most flexible business structure is a sole proprietorship.
- It is the only business structure that does not require a separate tax return. A federal Schedule C: Profit or Loss from Business and a few other pages are added to your personal tax return. These pages show the income and expenses of your independent endeavor.
- Only a sole proprietorship allows for a

simple, direct deduction of home office expense.

- A business loss can immediately reduce your other taxable income.
- Taxes are not paid twice on the same income, as can happen with a corporation.
- Recent tax law changes have made sole proprietorship the most tax-advantageous pass-through tax structure for a one-person business.
- A sole proprietorship allows for the most advantageous tax remedy when husband and wife work in the same business.
- It is easy to change from a sole proprietorship to another business structure —such as a partnership or corporation— when your situation warrants it.

Three Disadvantages of Being a Sole Proprietor—and Three Antidotes

1. You are personally liable. Yes, they can take your house if your massage oil gave someone a skin rash that ruined her performance at the piano competition and so destroyed her future earning potential. ***Antidote:*** Get adequate liability insurance appropriate to your business activities and assets. Insurance can be much less expensive than incorporating.

2. And the reverse: Business assets can be confiscated to pay personal debts. Yes, they could take your computer if you owe money on your credit card or to your dentist. ***Antidote:*** Watch your spending.

3. Audit rates are higher than for other business entities. ***Antidote:*** Don't flinch. Good

records will get you through an audit. That's one of the big reasons you're reading ***Self-employed Tax Solutions.***

A General View of Taxes and Income in a Sole Proprietorship

Any profit made by a sole proprietorship is income directly added to the tax return of the self-employed. Any loss is subtracted from other income on the tax return. If the loss is greater than the other income on the tax return, it can be used against previous or future earnings. Because of this kind of treatment of income, a sole proprietorship is called a **pass-through** entity. Pass-through means the income passes through the business directly, dollar for dollar, to the individual taxpayer. The sole proprietor—that's you—gets no wages or salary. Whatever profit or loss the business makes is the sole proprietor's, or owner's, ***net income.*** You can think of ***profit*** and ***net income*** as the same thing. Net income gets taxed.

The owner may end up with more or less money at her disposal than the amount shown as a profit or loss.

For instance, let's say that Caitlin Caterer charged a $3,000 oven to her credit card and made a single payment of $500. She would have a $3,000 business expense deducted on her tax return even though she shelled out only $500.

Think of Caitlin's money this way...

Gross sales	$10,000
Cost of oven	(3,000)
Net income on tax return	$ 7,000

or this way:

Money in	$10,000
Payment on oven	(500)
Money in the bank	$ 9,500

A sole proprietor is responsible for paying all his own taxes on his net income.

However, unlike a corporation where the tax liability is calculated solely on the activities of the business, the tax liability of a sole proprietorship, because it is calculated as part of your entire tax return, is determined by circumstances such as other income, personal expenses, whether there's a working spouse, and the number of dependents. Part V will present a complete explanation of taxes.

Regulatory Chores That May Be on a Sole Proprietor's To-Do List

A sole proprietor may need to look into permits, licenses, or other regulations.

 P. R. Bernays saw the storm approaching. The public relations firm where he worked had new management and was slowly sinking. P. R. had worked there for five years, long enough to learn the hype and hoopla of the business. He quietly took on a few clients of his own, working for them on weekends and evenings and using a few of his personal and sick days, too. Although he was still an employee of the troubled company, P. R. was also a self-employed in business.

By the time the firm went under, his own business was growing. P. R., already a sole pro-

prietor, had to do nothing about his business structure, but his decision to call his business "The Write Stuff" rather than to simply use his name meant he had to register the business name with the county clerk. The purpose of registration is to make sure that no two people in the same county use the same business name. P. R. also decided to convert his three-bay garage into an office, and so he had to deal with the friendly and courteous bureaucrats of several local agencies about zoning and construction permits.

All independent professionals, depending upon:

- The product they sell
- The service they provide
- The location of their businesses
- Whether they use a name other than their own as their business name
- Whether they have employees or hire subcontractors

May have to:

- Obtain various permits from state and local governments to comply with zoning or health code regulations.
- Obtain various licenses, perhaps registering the business with the state.
- Show proof of insurance.
- Register to collect and/or pay state sales or gross receipts tax.
- File for the use of a trade name. Often referred to as a DBA—"doing business as."
- Contact a federal agency about federal regulations for various kinds of businesses; for instance, a weaver who raises

his own sheep must comply with textile regulations, and the maker of Bobbie's Beef Pot Pies must observe regulations on the preparation of meat products.

- Obtain a federal identification number, also called an employer identification number (EIN).

We'll look at why you may need to obtain a federal identification number in a moment. Most of the other governmental rules that apply to aspects of your solo business are required and administered by local and state agencies, not by the Feds. You will have to make calls, check on the Internet, visit your library, and consult your county tax office to find out the full scope of your responsibilities. Bear in mind that these rules apply to partnerships and corporations as well as to the sole proprietor.

ALERT! Every jurisdiction overflows with rules and regulations. Some you must follow closely, while others you can let slide because nobody pays any attention to them. Don't slap down $500 for a certain permit and later discover that you are the first to apply for it in fifty years. On the other hand, don't skip a $200 license the lack of which could shut you down. Get in touch with business associations for such information—many of them allow you to attend one meeting as a visitor without being required to join and pay dues.

Federal Employer Identification Number (EIN)

Use your Social Security number as your sole proprietorship's identifying number, unless:

- You must withhold taxes from a subcontractor you've hired.
- You hire one or more employees.
- You set up a self-employed retirement plan.
- You deal in products that require you to file a federal excise or alcohol, tobacco, and firearms return.

If one or more of the above applies to your business, you will require a nine-digit EIN. Since all these situations are beyond the basics covered in this book, be sure to consult your tax pro should any of them arise.

If you obtain an EIN, use it for all your business correspondence with the federal government. Don't use your Social Security number for this purpose unless specifically asked for both numbers. Never use someone else's EIN. If you buy a business, you cannot use a previous owner's EIN.

Other Business Structures

If four out of five businesses in the USA are sole proprietorships, that leaves one out of five that's structured differently. The other choices are **partnerships** (a sole proprietorship is a one-owner business; a partnership is for more than one owner and is a pass-through entity) and two kinds of corporations (a regular, called a **C corporation,** is not a pass-through entity; an **S corporation** is a hybrid—part partnership and part corporation). I do not want to confuse you by going into detail about these other business entities since they will not apply to you at this time. If you are considering a business structure other than a sole proprietorship, be sure to get sufficient and clear advice before traveling down that road.

I want to say a few words about a **limited liability company** (LLC). It's the new kid on the block. The important thing to know is that an LLC is not a federal tax entity but a *legal business structure* set up under the laws of *each* state. Because LLCs are formed under fifty different sets of state law, the tax and legal treatment of an LLC may vary from state to state. If you ever consider setting up an LLC, be sure that your tax professional understands the legal aspects as well as the tax ramifications. If not, consult an attorney familiar with the LLC structure.

If your business is an LLC, it has liability protection similar to that enjoyed by a corporation. You are not personally liable for the debts or liabilities of the LLC. That means a disgruntled supplier could go after your office equipment (a business asset) as payment for a delinquent invoice but could not confiscate your kitchen appliances (personal assets).

Regulations governing an LLC depend upon the state of organization. To my knowledge, every state now allows a one-person LLC to be structured as a sole proprietorship for federal tax purposes. If, as a sole proprietor, you foresee potential liability problems because of the kind of business you are in, then speak to an attorney about forming an LLC.

If more than one person formed an LLC, they could choose a partnership or an S corp structure or, in some states, a C corp structure for federal tax purposes.

Some states recognize another legal entity called a **limited liability partnership** (LLP). This is available in certain states to certain professions, such as doctors or attorneys or accountants. An LLP bears many similarities to an LLC.

Remember: LLCs and LLPs are legal designations, not tax structures. Setting up an LLC requires professional help, a setup expense, and in many states an annual fee.

As your indie business grows and changes, you may want to review your business structure. But for almost all independents, sole proprietorship is the right first choice.

Part I has laid out the basic principles and the initial steps of self-employment. As you continue through *Self-employed Tax Solutions,* you'll learn about the day-to-day operation of an indie enterprise. The rest of the book, therefore, is material you will certainly consult over and over as your business develops.

Business Expenses

How-to books and IRS manuals on recordkeeping generally start with instructions about recording income. Yet anyone who has ever been in business knows that expenses come first. A landscaper doesn't get paid before he buys the equipment; he's paid after he cuts the grass. *Self-employed Tax Solutions* starts where it makes the most sense, with expenses coming before income. Let's start with the pleasures of taking deductions. Income will be covered in Part III.

CHAPTER SIX

Thinking Like an Indie Business: An Introduction to Business Expenses

So what makes an item or event a business expense? Common sense (you know, that's the commodity your mother wished you had) would tell you that business expenses are the costs you incur to run your business—the money you must spend in order to make money.

THE IRS SAYS ABOUT
Business Expenses . . .

To be deductible, a business expense must be both *ordinary and necessary.* An **ordinary expense** is one that is common and accepted in your field of business. A **necessary expense** is one that is appropriate and helpful for your business. An expense does not have to be indispensable to be considered necessary.

Okay, but what is ordinary to an astrologer? What is necessary to a computer games inventor? The answer: Anything you do that relates to your work, that stimulates or enhances your business, nurtures your professional creativity, improves your skills, wins you recognition, or increases your chances of making a sale may be a business expense and therefore deductible.

 When Astrid Astrologer goes to another astrologer for a reading, that isn't a personal expense; that's a business expense, and deductible. It's just as legitimate a deduction as the one a management executive takes for attending a seminar on product presentation.

Reality Ivan Inventor—of computer games, that is—shouldn't assume that buying someone else's computer game can't be a business expense. Even if he stayed up half the night fighting invaders from another galaxy, he was researching the competition. The purchase of the game is a business deduction.

Astrid and Ivan are independent professionals. When Ivan fills out a form that calls for his signature and "title," he writes "owner" next to his name. Both Ivan and Astrid are in business. Ivan's business is inventing computer games. Astrid's business is reading horoscopes for clients. Very simply, Ivan's business is Ivan. Astrid's business is Astrid. There must be in the life of every self-employed a moment of illumination, a shift in understanding, a reconfiguration of brain circuits, a vision of herself or himself as a business—a solo act, but a business nonetheless. It's a new mind-set that is essential for an independent professional. We might call this new way of thinking the indie business way.

With this section begins the presentation of a lot of information about business deductions, but what underlies this material is more fundamental than information. It invites you—although *invite* may not be a strong enough word—to adopt the thinking habits of a solo entrepreneur. As an indie business thinker, you will know that you are a business—that whenever you reach into your pocket for money, write a check, or slip out your credit card, you may be engaging in a business transaction. In the instant that you come to understand what it means to profess that you are a business, and that the work you do is blended

into every aspect of your life—well, that may well be the most important moment of your indie business life!

The Indie Business Mind-set

Developing this mind-set encourages you to take a new and different look at your business. Here's how you achieve it.

First, define your business as broadly as you honestly can. The more multifaceted and inclusive your field of endeavor, the more wide-ranging your expenses can be and therefore the less tax you'll end up paying!

- A photojournalist can deduct a more extensive variety of expenses than can a wedding photographer.
- A technological consultant's expenses will be more diverse than those of a computer repair person.
- A generalist writer—someone who might write about anything—has more assorted expenses than a sportswriter.

Second, take a look at all your activities from the vantage point of your new independent way of thinking. Don't be so sure that there is a well-marked difference between work and family and play and chores, or that you know what the difference is. The business life of an employee has clearly established boundaries, but the business life of a self-employed like yourself is intertwined with your personal life. If your business is broadly defined and your life is richly complicated, it can make for an intertwining that gets pretty tangled. If you're caring for your parents while running a day-care business, or dropping off several of your children at different locations while delivering products to clients, or struggling to find time for your new independent venture while holding down a full-time job, the interplay of your business and other interests can be intricate. On the other hand, if you live the life of a loner, without commitments or obligations, the boundary between business life and personal life might be remarkably simple.

Whether an expense is personal or business is often decided by the circumstances:

- A musician who is single and without children may do very little that is not considered ordinary and necessary to his business—travel, purchase entertainment system equipment and CDs, attend concerts.
- An alarm-system installer with four children who spends all his free time fishing, by himself, will have limited business expenses.
- A visual artist attends a Broadway performance and scrutinizes the sets and costumes. She deducts the cost of the theater ticket as a business **RESEARCH** expense.
- A structural engineer drives through Millionaires' Mile looking at the period architecture of the houses. Since this is research for him, the drive is a business event and the mileage there and back is a business **AUTO** expense.

- The proprietor of a shop that sells handmade clothes for children deducts as a **PUBLICATION** expense every magazine she purchases that has any clothing, children, or fabric industry trends in it.

Third and last, review your relationships. Your new indie business mind-set may present a different aspect to the link between what you do and the people with whom you do it. Anyone who has a connection with your business may be **primarily** a business associate even though in some cases he or she may also happen to be a college classmate, friend, parent, child, or spouse. Friendship with a business associate does not necessarily rule out a business deduction. You'll just have to show that the predominant motive for the activity that warranted the expense was business related.

- A dance instructor calls **his friend** to invite her to a movie and, also, to ask her to bring her workbook from the marketing workshop she attended so that he may borrow it for ideas for promoting his business. He deducts the business phone call.
- A carpenter deducts not only the tools that she buys but also the expense of dining out. Why? Because during the meal **with her husband,** an ad agency guy, she explains the timetable for her new business, gets his input on questions of scheduling, picks his brain about various proposals, and tests his reaction to her brochure. She could not have had this business discussion at the family dinner

table with her three children in attendance, and so the gift given to **her brother** as thanks for babysitting while she was at this dinner is also a business expense.

To Sum Up the Indie Business Mind-set

To achieve the best possible advantage regarding business expenses:

- Define your business as broadly as possible.
- Reexamine all your activities. It may be that many of them have a business element.
- Whatever you do, and whomever you do it with, consider the possibility of a business connection.

The next nine chapters discuss individual expenses. Each expense will be sufficiently presented to help you through just about every situation that may arise. This is a book of basics, and so there may be a complex event that takes place in your solo venture that is not covered here for which you will need special guidance. **Self-employed Tax Solutions** gives you such a strong foundation that you will know when you need special help. On the other hand, you may find that a particular expense has no bearing on anything you have encountered in your solo activity. If so, skip that sec-

tion of the book and move on. The information will always be there should a new circumstance come to pass. Don't burden yourself with information about situations that may never apply to you.

Part IV covers how to keep records, which records to keep, and for how long. However, if any expense calls for a unique kind of record-keeping, that will be explained when discussing the specific expense.

One more thing before we continue: There is one and only one directive in the Most Simple System. It will be thoroughly explained in Chapter Twenty-two, but for now you must accept it on faith. It is:

> From this moment on, get backup for everything you spend.

Pay for everything by check or credit card. If you must pay with cash, get a receipt. Everything? Yes, **everything**—from computers to toothpaste!

We'll now take a look at business expenses in a way you've never looked at them before. You are on your way to learning how to simply and easily miss not one business deduction and thereby pay the least tax legitimately possible. Let's take our next step keeping in mind a quote directly from the IRS: "There is no reason to pay more tax than the law requires."

CHAPTER SEVEN

Up and Running: Business Start-up Costs

Billy Bridesnapper was getting itchy about his job at Phil's Photos. He traipsed all around the county, in **his own** van, hauling **his own** equipment, getting shots that wowed everyone, yet he was earning only a small hourly wage and a small percent of each photo shoot he did while Phil made the big bucks. Over the course of several years, Billy had learned a lot, mostly through observation, about the management end of the business; via word of mouth he'd become known for his untypical black-and-white photos of typical family occasions. Friends and colleagues encouraged him to strike out on his own, but being a savvy businessperson (for a photographer, that is), he decided to first weigh the pros and cons by evaluating the market for his kind of photos and getting estimates of the cost to set up his business. Also, Billy didn't feel right going into direct competition with Phil, yet all his contacts were in the same geographic location. He'd have to do a lot of planning **before he started his own business.**

 Many of the expenses that Billy would incur in the organizing and planning stage of his new venture may be classified as **START-UP COSTS.** They might include items as diverse as a survey of potential markets, advertisements for his grand opening, or a legal fee paid for a review of his rental lease contract.

THE IRS SAYS ABOUT
Business Start-up Costs . . .

Business **START-UP COSTS** are the costs you incur when investigating the possibility of creating or acquiring a trade or business, or they are the costs of setting up a trade or business.

To qualify as **START-UP COSTS,** expenses must meet **all** the following guidelines:

1. The expenses have to be ones you could deduct if you were already in business, and
2. They must be paid or incurred for a trade or business that actually gets started, and
3. You must pay or incur the costs before you begin business operation.

Start-up expenses are many and varied. They fall into two types:

1. **Exploratory or General.** A person looking to go into business for himself might explore various fields of endeavor, as well as general questions of self-employment such as tax advantages, pension consequences, and work-space problems.

2. **Investigative or Specific.** After determining that self-employment is a viable and reasonable course for him to pursue, he might then investigate a specific business by traveling to a potential location or paying for a market survey.

The list of possible start-up expenses is as long and varied as a list of expenses for an existing business. The following is a small sampling:

- Survey of potential markets
- Analysis of available facilities, labor, and supplies
- Travel to look over business sites
- Fees for the professional services of accountants and lawyers
- Salaries and fees for consultants
- Training employees
- Office supplies
- Repairs
- Utilities
- Travel to find customers, suppliers, or financing
- Advertising for the grand opening

What's the big deal? Keep in mind that any expense that would qualify as a business deduction once you are in business qualifies as a START-UP COST if you incur it *before* you launch your new venture. That's pretty simple, isn't it?

You may be thinking: If it's that simple, and if the criteria for regular business expenses and start-up expenses are the same, whatever is the reason for classifying them as START-UP COSTS anyway? Why not just deduct them along with all the other business expenses?

Because the IRS won't let you, that's why. You can deduct all of your regular business expenses in the year they are paid or incurred, but to the IRS START-UP COSTS are not regular business expenses; they are considered *capital expenses.* Capital expenses cannot be deducted in the year you pay them; instead

they become part of the *basis* of your business. And because of that they have to be deducted in a different way: sometimes over a period of years, sometimes not until you sell or dispose of your business.

Before going any further, it will be helpful to look at three accounting terms: basis, capital assets, and capital expenses.

WHATTA**CONCEPT!**

Capital expenses and basis

Your **basis** in something is simply what it cost you. If you paid $200 for a bicycle, your basis in that bike is $200. If you paid $200,000 for a warehouse, your basis in that building is $200,000. The bike would be a **capital asset** of your messenger service business; the warehouse would also be a capital asset. Your business is a capital asset. Its basis is another way of saying how much your business cost you, and whether we're talking about a million-dollar widget-manufacturing venture or a $5,000 cookie-making venture, each entrepreneur who lays out money for capital assets has a basis in her business.

A **capital expense** is a cost related to the buying of a capital asset. The purchase of the bicycle is a capital expense, as are the snakeskin straps that you bought to attach to the pedals, thus becoming part of the basis (cost) of the bike. The warehouse is a capital expenditure, as are the legal fees associated with its purchase, all adding to the basis of the building.

START-UP COSTS are capital expenses. Other expenditures, even if incurred before you embark on your new enterprise, are not classified as START-UP COSTS. They are called business expenses and are deductible in a different fashion than are START-UP COSTS. The business expenses are:

- Loan interest
- Taxes
- Research and experimental costs
- Computers, machinery, or office equipment

You will learn more about these specific expenses in forthcoming chapters.

Now let's get back to Billy Bridesnapper. Although only twenty-seven years old, he managed to save up enough money to get started in his own business. (I told you he was unusual for a photographer.) When Phil announced he was going to sell the business to his brother Phineas, Billy really got busy, because he knew he did not want to work for Phineas. In a few months Billy spent $8,600 on locating and doing some repair work on a studio (with the help of his cousin, a carpenter) and printing high-quality promotional literature that stresses the merits of his exclusive use of black-and-white photographs for all his assignments, including weddings, bar mitzvahs, retirement parties, and so on.

His decision to concentrate exclusively on black-and-white photography sets him apart from and avoids competition with Phineas; he can send customers who want the color photograph treatment to Phineas, who can recipro-

cate by sending to Billy those interested in black-and-white prints. They shake hands, part company, and Billy heads out on his own.

Will Billy get to deduct all his START-UP COSTS? Because Billy's investigation and planning were successful and resulted in an up-and-running business, he can deduct **all** those pre-opening expenses—but because they are START-UP COSTS, the method of deduction differs from that used for most business expenses.

Billy may deduct up to $5,000 of his total START-UP COSTS in the year he starts his photo business even if his grand opening were as late as December 31.

The remaining $3,600 may be deducted over the next fifteen years (180 months). If Billy started his business on January 1, he would get to deduct one-fifteenth of his expenses every year for fifteen years. This is called *amortization.*

Here are the numbers: Billy's expenses total $8,600. If he deducts $5,000, he still has $3,600 left to deduct over the 180 months. If we divide $3,600 by 180 months, we get $20 per month. One year's worth is: Twelve times $20 equals $240, Billy's yearly deduction.

January 1 is a good day to open a photography business, because there are a lot of weddings in February. However, Billy had everything in place by November and was hoping to get some of the holiday trade, and so his grand opening was November 1. Billy may deduct the entire $5,000; however, since his amortization period begins with the month in which his business opened, he gets to deduct only an additional $40 in his first year (for two months' worth of START-UP COSTS, November and December). He gets a full twelve months' deduction the following year.

What if Billy sells his business? If Billy disposes of his business before the end of the amortization period, his leftover START-UP COSTS remain as part of the *basis of his business.*

Let's hope that Billy sells his business at a profit, in which case the remaining START-UP COSTS would help to reduce his gain. If, however, he gives up and walks away from the business, or sells it at a loss, the remaining START-UP COSTS would help to increase his loss.

What if Billy never starts his business? If Billy's business makes it past the starting gate, he gets to deduct all the START-UP COSTS involved in the launching of his new venture, albeit he has to follow the START-UP COSTS method of deduction. Now I'll show you what Billy is allowed to deduct if his undertaking never gets beyond the planning stage.

THE IRS SAYS ABOUT
Start-up Costs if the Business Never Gets Started . . .

If your attempt to go into business is not successful, the expenses you had in trying to establish yourself in business fall into two categories:

1. **Exploratory or General:** The costs you had before making a decision to begin or acquire a specific business. They include any costs incurred during a general search for or preliminary exploration of a new venture. These costs are personal and nondeductible.

2. **Investigative or Specific:** The costs incurred in your attempt to acquire or begin a specific trade or business. These costs are capital expenses and you can deduct them as a capital loss.

Looking at the IRS guidelines on START-UP COSTS for a business that never gets off the ground, it's quite clear that the agency wants to rein in people who have a notion to explore the possibility of going into business for themselves, but only as long as they can write off the search at the expense of their fellow taxpayers.

If a business never gets started, then *exploratory expenses* never can be deducted, but *specific expenses* always can be deducted one way or another. Be aware that when the IRS says "specific business," it means just that—that the costs are incurred trying to start a new business or buy an existing one. It does not mean exploring a specific *type* of business.

Therefore, an aspiring indie can be assured of getting a tax deduction if he settles on a business and makes concrete moves toward starting it up, whether the business actually gets started or not.

 Grace Granddaughter tried to start up one business but ended up in a different business. Let's see how her expenses get deducted.

Grace decided to start baking and selling Grandma's secret-recipe mouthwatering cookies. She put a nonrefundable deposit on professional bakeware and gave a month's security on renting a restaurant kitchen during its off-hours. But her plans were disrupted when Grandma became ill and Grace had to care for Grandma. Grandma died, leaving Grace no inheritance but with some experience in caring for the elderly. At that point Grace decided that the cookie-making business had crumbled. With her new skills she established herself as a home health aide for old folks.

START-UP COSTS for Grace's cookie-baking business were for a *specific* business and so can be deducted on her tax return—as a capital loss.

ALERT! If your clever friend—the one who always has a scheme up his sleeve—suggests flying to Hawaii to do some scuba diving and then flying back to Colorado to do some skiing, and he tells you that you can deduct everything by claiming that you were investigating the possibility of starting a scuba diving and/or a ski instruction business, tell him to forget it. The IRS is unyielding about allowing such deductions—unless, that is, you in fact do start one of those businesses.

Let's look at what would happen if Billy Bridesnapper had spent all his time, effort, and money and then decided *not* to go into the photography business. How and which START-UP COSTS can he deduct?

 At the last minute, Billy Bridesnapper got cold feet, deciding that the pressures of running his own business would be too much for him. Nevertheless, Billy's expenses for making ready the studio and printing promotional material, which totaled $8,600,

are deductible. However, the amount is not deducted as START-UP COSTS but as a capital loss, in much the same way as money lost in a bad stock market purchase is deductible.

If, instead of repairs and promotional material, Billy had purchased a computer, a copier, and a print dryer for a business that he never started, he could not deduct the cost of this EQUIPMENT *until he disposed of the items.*

For instance, if he sold the computer for $1,000 less than he paid for it, he would have a $1,000 capital loss, which has the same tax effect as having lost $1,000 on a stock market sale. If he sold the print dryer for $100 more than he paid, he'd have a $100 capital gain and would report it as such on his tax return. If he gave the copier to his cousin, he'd have neither a gain nor loss on the copier. If he gave the copier to the Community Teen Center, he may get a charitable contribution deduction on his tax return.

You're not alone if you find START-UP COSTS extremely complicated; they confuse many writers on self-employment, who then run out and publish misinformation. One addled writer of a well-known book on self-employment, for example, tells his readers that the expenses for an abandoned start-up business are investment expenses and should be itemized on Schedule A of your tax return. That's incorrect. Be careful.

The Smart Way to Deal with Start-up Costs

If you are planning to go out on your own, or maybe just thinking about going solo, here's a way to look at your situation to help you decide whether you're ready to spend some money on searching out your new indie business.

Depending on your choice of business, going out on your own could be an expensive proposition. I want to show you some ways to interpret the rules on **START-UP COSTS** that you can apply to your situation and perhaps lighten the tax burden of your journey into independent professionalism.

Run These by Your Tax Preparer

This book does not give advice on how to prepare your own tax return, but here I'd like to give you a few items to run by your tax preparer to make sure nothing slips through the cracks:

- If, when your tax return is prepared, you neglect to make the decision to deduct and amortize your **START-UP COSTS** (at IRS cocktail parties this is known as "making the election to amortize"), you may amend your tax return.
- A statement must be attached to your tax return itemizing the amortization costs, giving the date each cost was incurred, stating the month your business began operations.

As you've read in previous chapters (and it's worth saying again), just about every tax situation offers a variety of approaches. As my brother used to say, there's more than one way to skin a rabbit. That's where the tax professional comes in, to advise you on which approach makes the most sense in your particular financial situation. Your part of the work—let's speak of it as your job—as an indie, or as an indie-in-training, is to keep complete records of your business expenses. With those in hand you'll give your tax pro the raw material that she needs to construct a tax return that is best for you.

START-UP COSTS are a perfect example of the choices involved in deducting business expenses. Are you going to take the largest deductions in the quickest possible time— $5,000 plus amortization? Or should you stretch out the deduction and forgo the immediate $5,000 deduction? Are you living high off Aunt Ada's trust fund and in need of a big write-off this year? Or do you have so little income and so many deductions that you'd like to save the deduction until you sell the business?

Think Ahead

What if it's November when you leave your high-paying W-2 job to start your new independent venture? You have a high tax liability because of your wages for most of the year, and you are looking for a way to deduct all the expenses of setting up your new business. You want to take all the deductions right away. If only, you think, there were some way of turning your **START-UP COSTS** into regular deductible business expenses. Maybe there is. Depending on the business, it may even be easy.

Let's write a script for Billy Bridesnapper that illustrates my point. He's changed his mind again. Billy knows that he can't get along with Phil's brother Phineas, and so he is going full force into his own photography business after all. But he's really worried about being short of cash because the $8,600 he spent for his studio and on advertising has emptied his piggy bank. Well, here's a way out for him.

As you know, Billy has developed a reputation for his untypical black-and-white photos of typical family occasions, but did you know that his reputation developed over the years because he's been taking photos of family and friends and getting paid for it? The profit enabled him to buy his new Hasselblad and other photo equipment. This year alone he took photos at his sister's wedding and was paid for his work. A friend paid him for the photos he took of his bachelor party, and he was given an honorarium for the pictures he took of the school's PTA pet show. Well, if Billy's been taking photos for a profit, sounds to me like he's been a paid photographer, in business. His self-employed earned income is evidence that the IRS tends to accept as proof of being in business. If he dates the launching of his business from the day he first got paid for his photos—which occurred before he had the studio repaired—then the $8,600 for the studio and other projects are not **START-UP COSTS** but expenses of an *existing* business.

If you can credibly show that your business started some time ago, no matter how small that beginning may be, you can argue that later expenses are an expansion of your already-existing business, and those costs can be taken as deductions in the year that you incur them.

To Sum Up Start-up Costs

Let's look at three scenarios.

First scenario: Ken's company has informed him that he's being downsized. He begins to explore the possibility of self-employment in a general way. The company changes its mind and Ken abandons all plans of self-employment. Any general expenses incurred are not deductible; the IRS considers them personal expenses.

Second scenario: It begins the same way. But Ken, after generally exploring self-employment, makes plans to become a Web site designer. He incurs some expenses, including legal fees. The company changes its mind and Ken still has a job. He drops his plans for the Web site business. He cannot deduct the general exploration of self-employment; those are personal expenses. But he can deduct the expenses connected with his pursuit of the Web site operation. They are deducted as a capital loss.

Third scenario: Ken's job is terminated and he sets up the Web site business. He can deduct all of his expenses, both the exploratory look at self-employment and the specific focus on the Web site design business, including the legal fees. But all of those expenses are **START-UP COSTS** and thus capital expenses and cannot be deducted immediately. There is a limit on the amount that may be deducted each year; or the costs may be recovered when he disposes of the business.

CHAPTER EIGHT

An Indie Business Meets and Greets the World

In order to be successful, solos have to get themselves known, attract customers, entertain clients, develop networks, thank their colleagues, influence government agencies, and engage in a variety of activities that promote their businesses. Such activities are common to all business, however big or small, and most of the expenses incurred can be deducted if you follow the rules, however peculiar they may be. Let's take a look at how a solo makes his mark in the community.

Advertising, Promotion, and Marketing Expenses

What is **advertising?** It's attracting clients or customers, or showing that your service beats the competition, or getting out word that a sale is going on, or even nothing more than reminding the public that your business exists. Advertising executives may make distinctions between advertising, marketing, and promotion, but for tax purposes they are all the same thing. **ADVERTISING** expenses include:

- An ad for your service in the local paper, in trade journals, on radio, or on television
- The cost of a public relations consultant who puts out a press release about your business
- A Web site designer hired to present you or your product virtually to the universe

- An infomercial that expounds on the miracles performed by your product
- Brochures, flyers, or catalogs with your products or goods
- Advertising space in your child's yearbook or a friend's social club directory
- Contest costs and their prizes (not if open to your employees)
  - T-shirts printed with your business logo
  - Signs (If a sign will last longer than one year, then it is an **EQUIPMENT** expense.)

Even if people may not respond until next month, next year, or maybe five years from now, whenever you promote or advertise yourself—your business, your product, or service—your costs are deductible.

At one time the IRS insisted that deductions for advertising costs would have to be spread over several years because of the long-term effects of most advertising. But the IRS was taken to court on that and lost. Now the IRS allows advertising to be deducted in the same year that the advertising funds are spent.

THE IRS SAYS ABOUT

Advertising . . .

You generally can deduct reasonable **ADVERTISING** expenses if they relate to your business activities.

Expenses: Reasonable as Can Be

The IRS likes to insert a "generally" into just about every rule it makes as a hedge against exceptions. But you need have no fear of a disallowed deduction if your advertising expenses are reasonable and business related.

Business cards? Having them printed is a reasonable form of promotion. An advertisement in a community newsletter? That certainly is tied to business activities. Your name or product up on a billboard? A straightforward business expense.

Expenses: Use a Little More Care

Some brand-building endeavors aim at a result more indirect than business cards and billboards. Instead of being geared for an immediate result, they foster a warm, fuzzy feeling about your business, a positive image that promotes your business on a long-term basis.

Sponsoring your daughter's soccer team—which might include paying for uniforms or the cost of the away bus—is a valid promotional expense. But to ensure that the IRS sees it as deductible, establish a clear connection to your craft, trade, or business. See to it that the name of your business is on the uniforms and be able to show that your sponsorship will benefit your business in some material way.

Out-of-Bounds Expenses: Not Deductible

Then there are the expenses that will never make it past Uncle Sam, however hard you try. Every single person that Lorenzo Landscaper invited to his daughter's wedding was a business associate, client, or potential client. Can he deduct the cost of the wedding? No, that is a **personal expense,** not a promotional cost.

What if "Astrid Astrologer Tells the Future" is painted in fluorescent yellow on both sides of Astrid's car? Sure, that's a legitimate advertising expense and she can deduct it—the cost of having the lettering done, that is. But bright paint doesn't change her personal car into a business vehicle. (See Chapter Ten for more information on **AUTO** expenses.)

Foreign Expenses: Some Special Rules

If you plan to advertise on **foreign** radio, television, cable stations, or Web sites, check with your tax advisor before assuming the advertisements are deductible business costs. They might not be.

Expenses: Not What You Think

People in marketing may make distinctions between advertising, promotion, and public relations, but to the IRS they are all the same. On the other hand, what **you** may think of as promotion and therefore as a deductible **ADVERTISING** cost, the IRS may categorize as a different kind of deduction. **MEALS & ENTERTAINMENT** is one of those deductions. Regardless of your business reason for paying for the meal or the recreational event, the cost may not be treated as an **ADVERTISING** expense. You will see later in this chapter why the expense category distinction is important.

Advertising Expenses: In Hiding

As an indie business you're changing the way you think about what you do and the people with whom you do it. For instance, all those Christmas cards you bought and mailed. Did you send them to friends? Or did you send many of them to clients and prospective clients?

Also keep in mind that if you are engaged in an activity that is not in the normal course of your business but related to it, the **ADVERTISING** expenses are deductible. For example, if Lorenzo Landscaper, in response to many requests, teaches a Saturday-morning seminar "Tips for Winterizing," the cost of any advertisement, in any medium, associated with attracting people to attend the seminar is deductible. That holds whether or not there is a charge for admission.

There's more to advertising than meets the eye . . . and then there's even more!

Besides giving exposure to your business, there's another benefit to advertising: The very fact that you advertise your product or service helps to establish profit as a motive for doing what you're doing. It's evidence—even if you're not making any money—that you're not just indulging a hobby. And remember, if it's not a hobby, you get to deduct your expenses even if they far exceed your income.

Topics related to and sometimes confused with advertising are:

- Goodwill
- Lobbying expenses and political contributions
- Business gifts
- Meals and entertainment

Each will be covered in this chapter.

Spreading Goodwill: They Gotta Love Ya!

As far as the IRS is concerned, there is no such thing as a **goodwill** expense.

THE IRS SAYS ABOUT
Goodwill . . .

Goodwill is the value of a trade or business based on expected continued customer patronage due to its name, reputation, or any other factor.

What does the IRS mean by this? Well, they're not talking about peace on earth and goodwill toward men. What they are talking about is the worth of an intangible—putting a dollar amount on something that can't be touched or held or seen. Let me explain it this way.

If you were asked to put a dollar value on a friend's house—a house is a tangible—you might make a good guess. If you were pressed to be more precise, you could check on recent sales of comparable properties, make some calls, and come up with a more accurate appraisal. But if you were asked to put a dollar value on your friend's standing in the community—an intangible, his reputation—could you come up with an amount?

It's the same with a business. If Lorenzo Landscaper were to sell his business to a long-time, highly skilled employee, it would be possible to put a value on the assets of his business—the truck, lawn mowers, tools, computer, etc. But what value could be put on his business's reputation? How much is his name recognition worth? His dependability? His long-standing relationships with clients? In business circles these intangibles are known as goodwill.

As I noted earlier, the IRS makes no distinctions between advertising, marketing, and promotion. Many people think that goodwill is also in the same expense group—as a fourth item. That's not exactly so. Goodwill is a value that is only applied when a business is sold—but you create it as you go along.

Whenever a self-employed spends money working on her own image and the image of the business, fostering a favorable public impression of the business, she is creating goodwill. Although there is no such thing as a goodwill expense per se, the money spent to foster the image may be deductible as an **ADVERTISING** expense or as some other business cost, depending on circumstances.

Some examples of creating goodwill:

- If Lorenzo Landscaper services his customers promptly, efficiently, and with a smile, he is engendering a feeling of goodwill about his business—at no expense.
- If he gives workshops at a nursery on Saturday mornings about xeriscaping in the desert, he can deduct his costs as **ADVERTISING** expenses.
- If he takes a member of the chamber of commerce program committee out to lunch with the aim of being scheduled as next month's speaker, Lorenzo can deduct the cost of the lunch as a **MEALS & ENTERTAINMENT** expense.

- If Lorenzo gives landscaping advice on his Web site, that's a soft-sell approach that costs money now in exchange for name recognition that may attract customers in the long run. Those costs are **ADVERTISING** expenses.
- Graphic design costs for his new seed packets are an **ADVERTISING** expense. His costs for the seed packets that he mails out free with his spring newsletter—to promote goodwill—may be a **SUPPLIES** expense, or cost of goods sold as part of his **INVENTORY,** or an **ADVERTISING** expense. The costs of mailing would be a **POSTAGE** expense.

- If Lorenzo gives a $25 local restaurant gift certificate to Clyde Client in thanks for Clyde's sending him a customer, that is a **BUSINESS GIFT** expense.

So you see, when fostering goodwill you may encounter any number of different kinds of expenses. And although Lorenzo does not expect to see results from his goodwill efforts for many months or years down the line, he can deduct the costs as certain specific expenses in the year that he incurs them. But he can't deduct them as a goodwill expense because there is no such thing.

If Lorenzo's longtime employee did buy the business from him, and if part of the selling price were based upon Lorenzo's reputation and good customer relations, that part of the selling price is called goodwill—and that's what the IRS means by the term goodwill. In some parts of the country it's called "blue sky," possibly because the value set on these kinds of things is determined by looking up and pulling a number out of the blue.

If goodwill is a component of the sale price of a business, the purchaser must amortize—spread out—the goodwill amount and deduct it over fifteen years.

Giving It Away for Free

I want to mention one final point about goodwill: If a self-employed provides free services in order to promote goodwill, he cannot deduct the value of his time as a business expense.

If Lorenzo cut the grass of the local community center for free, his deductible costs would be his actual expenses only—for example, gas for the mower. If his usual fee for this service is $100, he cannot take $100 as a tax deduction; in other words, he cannot deduct anything for his time.

Although Astrid Astrologer promoted her business by giving away free astrological charts, she cannot take as any kind of deduction the value of her time in preparing the charts (although she could deduct the cost of the paper on which they were written).

On the same principle, in a recent case the tax court disallowed the deduction of a physician who took the value of his services as an **ADVERTISING** expense after providing free medical services to the public. The court ruled that the doctor's uncompensated services were not an expense.

You may think this is unfair. And you may not want to understand it. But here's the way it works out: You cannot take a deduction for something that did not cost you or someone else any money.

Lorenzo cuts grass, gets paid $100, pays tax on the $100 he earned. Then he donates the $100 to the Children's Society and gets a personal charitable deduction of $100 on his tax return. The contribution cost him $100.

Lorenzo cuts the grass around the Children's Society office building. His cost: not money, but time. He cannot deduct time on his tax return.

In the long run, though, goodwill may still be of value. Even though you cannot write off the value of your time as a tax deduction, remember that what goes around comes around, and by building up goodwill you may profit by getting new clients, or end up with more money in your pocket when you sell your entrepreneurial business because of the "blue sky" component, or it just may make you feel good!

Lobbying and Political Contributions

Lobbying is often thought of as a derogatory term. Stripped of its negative connotations, though, lobbying just means attempting to influence government legislation or policy. And there's nothing wrong with that—having access to government and being able to influence its officials is an important feature of a democracy.

Most of the tax guides are wrong about business deductions for lobbying. The source of the trouble is the official Internal Revenue Service tax code. And that brings me for a moment to a broader subject: One reason that many of the books, manuals, and columns that you read on the subject of taxes sound alike and offer the same advice is because by and large the authors just rewrite IRS material. That's why so much of it is wrong. Remember, one of the first things I told you was that the tax laws are not written with self-employeds in mind. So when I say that much of what you read is wrong, I don't mean factually incorrect. I mean wrong in the sense of being misleading and off target because the point of view is not that of a self-employed.

Lobbying is a case in point. Just about everything you read on the kinds of business deductions allowed for lobbying starts with the following opening sentence: "Generally lobbying is not deductible as a business expense."

That's a sentence taken right out of an IRS publication. Then follows a statement with a list of various lobbying expenses that cannot be deducted. They include such admonitions as you can't deduct your cost for contacting the president or your costs for trying to directly influence the views of the vice president. And so on. In writing this, the authors show more familiarity with the IRS manual than they do with the life of a sole proprietor.

Brilliant Deduction

But if you look at the genuine concerns of a self-employed, you'll find that a considerable amount of **LOBBYING** expenses can be deducted.

Most entrepreneurs and indie businesses—at least the ones who make up the bulk of my readers—have little to do with attempts to influence the president, the vice president, a cabinet member (the IRS tax code calls them

"covered executive branch officials"), or the speaker of the house. There are numerous occasions, however, when free agents and entrepreneurs are trying to be heard on a local level—at city hall.

And as far as the issues that come up at the mayor's office or at the city council meeting are concerned, you *can* deduct your **LOBBYING** expenses. If the local government is planning a zoning change that would be detrimental to your business, or if you want the city council to allow home businesses in the area in which you live, or if you're a restaurateur who's opposed to a proposed ban on smoking or live music, all your efforts in those areas are deductible. You can argue with the building inspector, attempt to be arrestingly persuasive with the police chief, and exchange heated

WHATTA**CONCEPT!**

Branches of government

For the sake of those who are not familiar with government, let me point out that at both the federal and state levels there are two separate branches of government that are lobbied—the executive branch, which runs the agencies and departments of the government, and the legislative branch, consisting of lawmakers called senators, congress members, legislators, assembly members, or other names depending on the state. The legislative branch makes the laws, the executive branch enforces them. The third branch of government, the judiciary, is not subject to lobbying.

views with the fire marshal, and you can deduct all the expenses incurred. So the stuff that the other guys write, while they may not be formally wrong, is highly misleading—because they're not in touch with the nitty-gritty of self-employed people.

Lobbying Expenses You Can Deduct

Local or County Government

You may deduct up to any amount for expenses of appearing before, or communicating with, any *local or county* council or governing body concerning its legislation, ordinances, or other official actions of direct interest to you. These governing bodies include boards of education, municipal or county planning or zoning boards, and local commissions. Your expenses, including travel, in meeting with any municipal or county official—from the mayor to the county clerk's secretary—are deductible if they involve your business.

Of interest to my fellow New Mexicans: An Indian tribal government is treated as a *local* council or similar governing body for the purposes of lobbying expenses.

My interview of an IRS attorney confirmed my reading of a peculiar loophole in the IRS regulations regarding LOBBYING expenses. You may deduct any expenses (you are not limited to the $2,000 maximum, see below) of communicating with *state* officials of the executive branch as long as your lobbying does not involve legislation. That means, as long as you are *not trying to influence the law.*

So although you are limited in deducting the costs of lobbying your state legislators about a piece of *pending* legislation, once a law is on the books you are not limited in deducting the costs of trying to influence a state agency *regarding enforcement of the law.* For example, you may deduct all costs of trying to influence your state environmental protection agency regarding an existing regulation that affects your business. The loophole demonstrates once again that you shouldn't look for logic in IRS tax code.

In-house Expenses of $2,000 or Less

You may deduct up to $2,000 in expenses at the *state and federal* level, including communicating directly with the president and the vice president, if the expenses are *in-house—*which means if it's done in your office by you or someone who works for you.

For example, if you wished to make your views known about a proposed state bill involving air pollution, you could deduct your expenses, including travel to the state capitol to attend legislative committee hearings. Since the deductions only apply to in-house expenses, you could not deduct the expense if you were to hire a lobbyist to do it for you, or if an organization to which you belong did it.

Lobbying Expenses You Cannot Deduct

These allowable deductions aside, it is true—just as the tax columnists and IRS publications say—that when you get to the upper reaches of expenses and the upper layers of government, much lobbying is not deductible.

The following in-house expenses cannot be deducted if they exceed $2,000:

- Influencing proposed state or federal legislation
- Attempting to influence the public about elections, legislative matters, or referendums
- Communicating directly with various federal high-ranking members of the administration, including cabinet-level officials and their immediate deputy directors, in any attempt to influence their official actions or positions
- Participating in any political campaign for or against any candidate for public office

Political Contributions: Sending a Check

Just to be clear about political participation, you cannot deduct direct financial contributions to political parties or candidates as business expenses, even if the contribution is under $2,000. A check flying out the door is not an in-house expense. (FYI: You cannot deduct political contributions as a personal itemized deduction either.)

Is It Lobbying or Promotion?

Because some self-employeds confuse lobbying with business promotion, I must add that you may not deduct **indirect** political contributions either. By which I mean things such as the following:

- Advertising in a convention program of a political party, or in any other publication, if any of the proceeds from the publication are for, or intended for, the use of a political party or candidate

- Admission to a dinner or program (including galas, dances, film presentations, parties, and sporting events) if any of the proceeds from the function are for, or intended for, the use of a political party or candidate
- Admission to an inaugural ball, gala, parade, concert, or similar event if identified with a political party or candidate

Let's explore deductible and nondeductible lobbying expenses through three Reality Checks:

 Fred Fixit **cannot** deduct that portion of his dues to the Santa Fe Handyman's Association that is used toward trying to convince state legislators to give handymen a special tax break. Reason: Fred is attempting to influence state legislation and his dues are not in-house costs.

 Lorenzo Landscaper **can** deduct that portion of his dues to the Landscapers' Association that is used to lobby the county government to try to dissuade the county from raising fees at the county dump. Reason: Lorenzo is lobbying at the local level and therefore there is no limit on his deductible expenses.

 Endie Naturopath, a naturopathic physician, is fighting to get licensing for naturopaths in New Jersey. She may deduct up to $2,000 per year of in-house costs for phone, travel, printing, and other items involved with her campaign to get favorable legislation enacted. Reason: Lobbying to influence legislation at a nonlocal level is limited to $2,000 of in-house expense.

Pretty complicated, wouldn't you say? Before putting any big bucks into lobbying, check with your tax professional. And ask her enough questions to be sure she really understands the fine points.

To Sum Up Lobbying

- You can deduct any amount for **LOBBYING** local or county government.
- You can deduct up to $2,000 for in-house **LOBBYING** of the state or federal government if attempting to influence pending legislation.
- You can deduct any amount spent on **LOBBYING** at the state level if attempting to influence enforcement of the law.

Of course, if you are a professional lobbyist, all business expenses that you incur in your business on behalf of a client are deductible for you (although not necessarily for your client).

Business Gifts

Rob Rolf has just about finished converting his garage into a two-room office where he intends to see patients in his massage therapy practice. Friday promises to be a crowded day— after meeting with a plumber first thing in the morning, he has to rush across town for an eight-hour workshop. Nevertheless, Friday is the only day that the truck will be in his area to deliver his new massage table. His next-door neighbor, Ned, also works at home, and they've been quite friendly since they helped each other dig out of a snowstorm. So Rob asks Ned if he would watch for the truck and let in the deliveryman with the table.

No problem, Ned says. Everything goes well, the table is delivered, and Rob buys Ned a bottle of wine as a thank-you present. Rob can deduct the cost of the wine as a **BUSINESS GIFT**.

Brilliant Deduction

THE IRS SAYS ABOUT
Business Gifts . . .

If you give **BUSINESS GIFTS** in the course of your trade or business, you can deduct all or part of the cost of the gifts.

Don't be too quick to rush out and buy that potential client a set of golf clubs. Sorry. A pack of golf balls is more like it. That's because *there is a $25 per-year per-person limit on* **BUSINESS GIFT** *deductions.*

No matter how much you spend on gifts for a particular business associate over the course of a year, you may deduct only $25 per individual. If Rob Rolf had bought Ned a bottle of Grand Marnier for $30, he could deduct only the $25 limit. If instead he bought Ned a $10 bottle of merlot, Rob could deduct the $10, could give Neighbor Ned another gift before the year was out, and could deduct $15 of the cost of the second gift.

The Soviet empire has collapsed, a new millennium has arrived, and yet the IRS gift limit was, is, and probably will be $25 until well into the future. Get used to it.

However, the IRS does allow you to deduct **related incidental costs** beyond the $25 limit—costs such as engraving on jewelry, or packaging, insuring, and mailing. A cost is incidental only if it does not add substantial value to the gift. For example, the cost of gift wrapping is considered incidental. The purchase of an ornamental basket for packaging fruit is not an incidental cost if the value of the basket is substantial compared to the value of the fruit.

Are you allowed to deduct a gift basket of fruit to Grandma? Of course you can—if Gram has some connection to your business. Did she show you how to hook up your printer? Make curtains for your office?

Your business relationship with Grandma brings up the recurring subject of how a self-employed needs to continue thinking as an indie business. This is particularly pertinent in gift giving. Of course, if you bought your client a basket of fruit as a birthday present, you would treat it as a **BUSINESS GIFT** deduction. But what about your friends with whom you have a business connection? You need to maintain an awareness of all the business connections between yourself and others. If your Web page designer, who is also a friend, invites you to her place for dinner and you bring a gift for the hostess, in this instance, is she primarily a business associate or primarily a friend? Be sure you're wearing your indie thinking cap. A gift to a business associate is deductible. One to a friend is not.

As with other business expenses, a gift may be deducted as a business expense when it is given in the **ordinary and necessary course of your business** to a business associate. Those associates include clients, customers, dealers, distributors, employees, Neighbor Ned, your Web page designer friends, Grandma—anyone who has helped to nurture your enterprise.

The gift counts toward the $25 per-year limit whether given directly or indirectly to a business associate. Therefore, if you send something over to the Callous Company—like a $25 cheese-and-nut sampler because Reggie Receptionist has been so pleasant and helpful to you—it's obviously intended as a personal gift for him. If later in the year you give him a box of chocolates on Secretaries Day, it's nice of you, but you've already used up your gift deduction to Reggie for the year. You can't deduct the chocolates.

The same holds for a gift to a spouse or child of a business associate. Finger paints for the child of a business associate are considered a gift to the business associate. If you've already given a client a gift that cost at least $25 and you are then invited to your client's daughter's wedding, you get no **BUSINESS GIFT** expense deduction, regardless of the value of the wedding present.

This rule does not apply if you have a bona fide, independent business connection with that family member—in this case, the bride (or maybe the groom).

If you and your spouse both give gifts to the same business associate, both of you are treated as one taxpayer and so together you can deduct gifts of only $25 per recipient. It does not matter whether the two of you have separate businesses, or whether each of you has an independent business relationship with the recipient. (There's IRS logic again.)

Gift Chronicles

When I was a child, one of my sisters-in-law kept a record of every gift she ever gave to anyone. (I think she is still compiling it.) You would do well to copy her careful watchfulness, but as I'll show you, there is a particular method you must use in keeping records of **BUSINESS GIFTS**.

If during an IRS audit you are unable to produce records of certain business expenses, in many cases the IRS will estimate the amount of your expenses and allow you to deduct them. The estimate is allowed if it is clear that the expenses have been incurred—as for example in the purchase of business equipment or telephone use.

That isn't the rule, however, with **BUSINESS GIFTS** or with business **MEALS & ENTERTAINMENT** expenses. Because the IRS suspects that such expenses are often invented or inflated, you are required to have records. If you have none, the deduction will be disallowed in an audit.

When you give a business associate a gift, to ensure that you will get the deduction, on the receipt write the following information:

- Date the gift was given
- Cost of the gift
- Description of the gift
- Name and business relationship of the person to whom you gave the gift
- Business reason for the gift, or the business benefit you expect to gain

Rob Rolf would have written on the receipt from the liquor store:

> *5/5/07, Neighbor Ned, let in table deliveryman. Thanks*

Gifts should always be documented and annotated. If a collection is taken for a baby shower for a business associate, for example, it's best to write a check. If that's impossible or inappropriate, and you contribute in cash, be sure to write the required information on a piece of paper that you will later use as your "receipt."

Entertainment or Gift? Does It Matter?

What if Rob had thanked Neighbor Ned by taking him to a Knicks game or to hear the Tony Trischka Band? Would that be a **MEALS & ENTERTAINMENT** expense or a **BUSINESS GIFT** expense for Rob? And why does it matter? It matters because it may affect the amount of taxes that Rob pays.

Let's look at the numbers in various scenarios.

First scenario: It doesn't matter how you categorize a $50 concert ticket for a business associate—as gift or entertainment. You end with the same deduction. Here's how:

- No matter what the cost of the gift, you can deduct only $25.
- As you'll see in the next section, you may deduct only 50 percent of a **MEALS & ENTERTAINMENT** expense. A little arithmetic here: 50 percent of $50 equals $25.

So in this case, the deduction is the same however you classify the concert ticket.

Second scenario: What if you treat your client to a ringside seat at the heavyweight championship fight for $400? Let's look at your choice then:

- No matter what the cost, if it's a gift you get only a $25 deduction.
- But as an entertainment expense, it's 50 percent of $400, which equals a $200 deduction.

Big difference in what you can deduct as the price moves up. At this point, how you classify the expenses—**BUSINESS GIFT** or **MEALS & ENTERTAINMENT**—does matter.

As you probably guessed, you don't have total leeway in choosing which kind of deduction you take. The IRS has set up specific rules to govern the **BUSINESS GIFT** versus **MEALS & ENTERTAINMENT** expense, as follows:

- If your client eats or drinks your gift of foodstuffs and liquor at a later time and without sharing them with you, that's a **BUSINESS GIFT** expense.
- Whenever you accompany your guests to the concert or game, you must deduct the cost of the tickets as a **MEALS & ENTERTAINMENT** expense.
- If your client attends the concert or game without you, the tickets you gave may be treated as either a **BUSINESS GIFT** expense or a **MEALS & ENTERTAINMENT** expense, whichever is to your advantage.

The Little Things That Don't Count

There is no $25 per-person limit for deductions on some things that you give away—as long as they're cheap, that is.

 Promotionally savvy Rob Rolf gives to potential clients small bottles of massage oil. In addition to information about the herbs used in the oil, the labels have his new address on them. These nominal gifts are not included in the $25 per-person limit.

There is no per-person limit as long as a gift item:

- Costs $4 or less, and
- Has the name of the self-employed or her business clearly printed on it, and
- Is identical to a number of others distributed to many clients or business associates.

You've all received pens, calendars, desk sets, magnets, baseball caps, and the like; now you know that they probably cost the smart entrepreneur no more than $4 each.

When a Gift Is Not a Gift

Free samples are not BUSINESS GIFTS. If you give samples of your merchandise to prospective buyers or to people who might review or publicize your products—whether it's a widget or a book—they are not subject to the **BUSINESS GIFT** cutoff amount of $25 because they are not considered gifts.

Your cost for the free samples gets deducted in another expense category, usually as **SUPPLIES,** or are deducted from **INVENTORY** as part of **COST OF GOODS SOLD.** These giveaway items will be deducted at your cost, not at the amount you would receive were you to sell them.

A gift to a charitable organization is not a BUSINESS GIFT. A sole proprietor cannot deduct as a **BUSINESS GIFT** money he has given to a charity. Such a contribution is a personal deduction.

Meals and Entertainment

Now let's see, does the dessert fork go to the left of the salad fork? Is it OK to eat a chicken wing with your hands? May you start eating before everyone is served? Do you pass to the left or to the right?

If you think the rulebook of dining etiquette is thick and complicated, wait until you get a load of the rules on the deductibility of dining and entertaining expenses for an entrepreneur. Believe me, it's not "Eat, drink, and be merry; we can deduct it."

However, life's ordinary guideposts can often lead us through the maze of IRS regulations. Think back to when you went to your first party all by yourself and your mama told you, "Now, just behave yourself, and everything'll be fine." Mama's early advice applies to your attendance at the mayor's dinner party as well as it applied to your friend's fifth birthday party: Follow the generally accepted rules of conduct that apply to all interpersonal relationships—like courtesy, attentiveness, and tact—

and even if you haven't mastered the finer points and myriad rules of elegant dining, you'll most likely not embarrass yourself or your host.

The same logic applies to **MEALS & ENTERTAINMENT:** Follow the generally accepted rules regarding business expenses and you'll most likely do OK.

The IRS says an allowable deduction is one that is (a) common and accepted in your field of business, trade, or profession; (b) not extravagant; and (c) helpful and appropriate, although not necessarily indispensable, for your business. As I said in Chapter Six, business expenses are the costs you incur to run your business—the money you must spend in order to make money. If you apply these principles to **MEALS & ENTERTAINMENT** expenses, you won't stray very far from what is an allowable deduction—unless, that is, your deductions get too creative.

What's Entertainment and Whom Can You Entertain?

Business meals or entertainment are deductible as a business expense if you talk business before, during, or after the meal or entertainment.

If Lorenzo Landscaper takes a client to lunch to discuss the plan for the client's patio garden, he gets to deduct the cost of lunch. But what if Lorenzo treats his brother-in-law Brian to the Packers game? And what if he then claims an entertainment deduction because during halftime Brian told him that he could get some great buys at a grand opening sale at Greg's Greenhouse? Nothing doing! That's a bit too creative for the IRS.

But don't assume that Packers tickets are not deductible. For many business occasions the ticket price can be deducted, and it is important for you to know how and when those occasions and situations come up.

What kind of activity is deductible?

Any activity considered refreshment, entertainment, amusement, or recreation

Where can the activity take place?

- At your place of business
- At a business convention or reception
- At a restaurant
- At bars, theaters, country clubs, social or athletic clubs, or sporting events
- At home
- On hunting, fishing, vacation, or similar trips

What kinds of expenses are allowable?

- Meals you provide to customers or clients, whether the meal is the whole deal or it's a part of an entertainment package (for example, refreshments at a football game)
- Tickets to sporting events, concerts, theatrical presentations, movies, etc.
- A meal expense including the cost of food, beverages, taxes, and tips
- Meeting personal, living, or family needs of individuals, such as providing meals, a hotel suite, or a car to customers or their families
- The costs you incur if a business associate visits and stays with you (cost of meals you serve, etc.)

With whom can you dine and party?

Any business associate, established or prospective. Broadly defined, this includes:

- Customer or client
- Supplier
- Employee
- Agent
- Collaborator
- Professional adviser
- Colleague

What kind of record must you have?

You must have a record of the activity that clearly shows:

- Amount
- Date
- Name of the place
- Type of entertainment, if not obvious
- Business purpose
- Business relationship

The easiest way of substantiating business meal expenses is to staple the business card of your associate to the restaurant receipt. See next page for a typical handwritten receipt.

 Tessie Tripp is trying to win a contract to handle travel arrangements for a major cable TV station. She invites the suits who will make the final decision to her mountain lodge for a weekend of negotiations. She pays all the bills for the weekend (maid, catered meals, etc.). Tessie gets to deduct the expenses.

Reality Nadine Novella has dinner with someone she is interviewing for a short story she is writing. She interviews during dessert. Nadine pays for the dinner. She gets to deduct the cost.

> 6/14/07 with Sally Source
>
> dinner @ Diners Delight
>
> $63.00 w/tip
>
> info re: 1920s fashions

Reality Charlotte Salesrep treats the local dentist to dinner, during which time she explains the instant access and lower radiation benefits of digital X-rays—hoping to get to make a sale. Charlotte's expenses are legitimate deductions.

The best way to ensure that the entertainment is directly related to business is to put it in a *clear business setting.* Like these:

- Billy Bridesnapper provides a hospitality room at a photography convention where he displays his unconventional black-and-white photos of conventional family events.
- Prudence Pas de Deux invites local civic leaders—none of whom has she ever met—to the opening performance of her dance troupe, "The Young Ones." She also provides the civic leaders with coffee, other beverages, and dessert during intermission.

Before you continue reading in this section, take a moment to think about your business. Sarah Sculptor spends all her time in her studio, she rarely dines out, and her agent does all the socializing necessary to sell her work. Sarah may skip the next few sections of this chapter and pick up on page 59 at *Travel Meals and Entertainment.* On the other hand, architect Frank Boyd White feels that more of his time is spent wheeling, dealing, and cajoling than designing. Frank needs to keep on reading about deducting the costs of the social distraction side of his business. Where does your business fit? Is there much business socializing? Is your home office not the best place to bring clients and so much of your work is done in town? There is a quick reference table at the end of this section. You be the judge of how much you need to know at this time about MEALS & ENTERTAINMENT deductions.

Some Finer Points of Dining for Deductions

Many self-employeds are convinced that the IRS tax code is arbitrary, but in the case of MEALS & ENTERTAINMENT deductions, the reason for the agency's beady eye is clear—the IRS is trying to weed out the invalid business deductions in an area that seems to invite abuse. And while taxpayers have the right to explain their honest differences of opinion with the IRS, guess whose opinion usually prevails?

Before taking a look at what the IRS says about MEALS & ENTERTAINMENT expenses, let me tell you a secret about that monstrous document, the IRS tax code. You've probably heard politicians orating about the thousands upon thousands of pages of the code that is reputed to be so formidable and intimidating. Well, it is. But the tax code that they are complaining about is a different animal from the numbered publications that are available to the public at the library or that can be downloaded from the Internet. These taxpayer-friendly IRS pamphlets—which explain how to do our tax returns and whether we can take Grandma as a dependent—are actually IRS employees' interpretations of the tax code, reorganized and put into plainer language to guide the taxpayer through the maze of tax regulations.

Does the official IRS tax code really exist? Yes, it does. It's about 10,000 pages long and it's published in very small print. Now for the secret: Many of the people who write about taxes haven't read the code. Like the general public they rely on those little IRS publications—interpretations of the tax code. They then interpret the interpretations or hastily rewrite interpretations of what others have written. The result can be something like the child's game that's played by whispering a story from one ear to another and another and another—what we end up hearing is often far from the original version.

Although it's a tiresome process and a strain on the eyes, I do read the IRS code, because I believe in going back to the source. That said, here's what the IRS presents in one of its interpretative publications:

THE IRS SAYS ABOUT
Entertainment Expenses . . .

You may deduct business-related entertainment expenses that you have for entertaining a client, customer, or employee if the expenses are both ordinary and necessary and meet *one* of the following two tests:

1. Directly related test
   or
2. Associated test

The amount you can deduct is usually limited to 50 percent of your meal or entertainment expense.

Most of the writers about taxes go on and on about how you can get a passing grade on one test or the other. If you can't show that the entertainment expense meets the directly related test, there's always the associated test. But my guess is you don't care a hill of beans whether you meet one test or the other test. Your only interest is to write off as much of your dining and entertainment costs as you legitimately can, and I'm going to show you how to do that.

Well aware that **MEALS & ENTERTAINMENT** expenses are a vital part of the conduct of business, the tax code gives the taxpayer considerable leeway in claiming legitimate expenses. The IRS gives you a reasonable series of alternatives:

Either

A. ***Business was the main purpose*** of the meal or entertainment,
   or

B. The meal or entertainment was ***associated with your trade or business.***

Either

C. *You engaged in business while entertaining,*
    or

D. The business discussion or event directly ***preceded or followed*** the entertainment.

Either

E. You had more than a general ***expectation of business benefit or income*** resulting from the entertainment,
    or

F. A ***substantial*** business discussion took place.

Let's take a look at each of these and see how they relate to a self-employed's business life and also how they differ from one another:

A. Business is the main purpose for the entertainment. Be careful when making this claim. Business as the main purpose seems unlikely when you're watching showgirls dance or Chippendales prance, or when you're sailing on yachts. Dinners with business as the main purpose are more credible.

Would you talk business at the opera? Between the acts of a play? For the most part, entertainment events are distractions that take you away from business, that make the mention of business an intrusion. To claim that business is the main purpose of an entertainment event raises doubts in the mind of an IRS auditor.

And although there may be time during hunting or fishing trips or while relaxing on yachts to talk business, the IRS has no reason to believe that business is the main purpose of such excursions.

Furthermore, if the attendees at your entertainment event include people who are not business associates, the IRS strongly doubts that the main purpose was business—especially if the wining and dining took place at a country club, cabaret, brewpub, vacation resort, or the like.

B. Associated with the active conduct of your business. If business is not the main purpose of the social event, then you must show that the event is associated with your trade or business. This simply means that you must be able to show a clear business purpose for the entertainment. The purpose may be to get a new client or to encourage the continuation of an existing business relationship. As I said in Chapter Six, anything you do that relates to your work, that stimulates or enhances your business, nurtures your professional creativity, improves your skills, wins you recognition, or increases your chances of making a sale is a business expense and therefore deductible.

 Raina Realtor's lunch with a potential home seller to settle on a sale price for the property clearly has "business as the main purpose." However, if that client is offended by an experience with Raina's assistant and if Raina takes the client to a dinner at La Elegante not to discuss business but to smooth her ruffled feathers, then that dinner is "associated with" Raina's business. The purpose was not to discuss business but to keep a client. Dinner is a deductible expense.

C. Engaged in business while entertaining. It's not the length of the discussion but its aim. If during the meal or entertainment you actively discuss business, then the business portion of the meeting doesn't have to be of any specified length. It is not necessary to devote more time to business than to entertainment. If you're a woman of few words, you will not be penalized for getting your point across quickly.

D. Engaged in business before or after the entertainment. Enjoy whatever you're doing or watching—an evening out at a restaurant, play, or sporting event—because it is not necessary to discuss business during the entertainment as long as the entertainment takes place *just prior to or immediately after* a business discussion.

Entertainment that occurs *on the same day* as the business discussion is considered to directly precede or follow business.

Time can be stretched when stuff happens. If the entertainment and the business discussion *don't occur on the same day,* you can still claim a deduction based on the particular circumstances. Perhaps there was a sudden change in schedule because of travel problems, someone fell ill, connections were missed. As even the IRS has to acknowledge, life is full of unforeseen things.

The rules about time sequence are not cast in concrete, as long as the full scenario—which includes the dimensions of the business discussion, the traveling schedule of the participants, and the time of the entertainment—makes sense. You can turn an expensive lunch check, or a dinner for eight at home, into a deductible business meeting—if you have a good sense of timing.

 Whoopi Happenin, a special events planner, invites a group of business associates from out of town to her place of business to present the wares of her Holiday Happy Happenings exhibit. If she entertains those business guests on the evening before the presentation, or on the evening of the day following the presentation, the entertainment is considered to be held directly before or after the discussion.

 Harry Hardseat owns a custom-made furniture business in Tacoma, Washington. Over the years he has selected furniture for homes designed and constructed by Frank Boyd White, an architect-builder for the rich and famous, and the two have become friends. Frank and his wife are in Tacoma for several days, and on Tuesday, Frank and Harry talked business while looking over plans and discussing furnishings for a new home Frank is building. On the day after their meeting, Mr. and Mrs. White dined at the Hardseat home. Harry can deduct the cost of entertaining the Whites at home as a **MEALS & ENTERTAINMENT** expense.

E. Great expectations. You don't have to seal the deal. You do not have to show that business income actually resulted from each entertainment expense, but you must show that some benefit had *reasonably* been expected. It's all right if the business discussion turned out to be fruitless, but you must be able to show some hoped-for, specific business payoff, not just a vague expectation of gain.

By the way, building goodwill is not considered a specific business benefit.

 Pat Personal Trainer invited another fitness professional to lunch to talk about jointly operating a fitness center at the mall. But his lunch guest, weighed down with problems, talked about nothing but his impending divorce and quarrels with his teenage daughter. They never did get to talk business. Can Pat take the lunch as a business deduction?

Yes. It is not Pat's fault that, for reasons beyond his control, he did not get to talk business at a lunch that was arranged for that purpose.

F. Something of substance. What's substantial to one may be trifling to another, so use your noggin. What is a substantial business discussion? The answer: It's up to you. The IRS says that a business discussion will not be considered substantial unless you can show that you engaged in it in order to win a specific business benefit.

Be careful if business is discussed only in passing, that is, "incidentally."

 Lorenzo Landscaper's brother-in-law Brian gave him a piece of incidental business information when he told Lorenzo about the sale at Greg's Greenhouse. That piece of information alone was not

enough to make the tickets to the Packers game deductible. But Lorenzo could deduct the Packers tickets if brother-in-law Brian had sketched out a T-shirt design or reviewed Lorenzo's marketing plan prior to the game.

The IRS considers that dining and fun activities that take place at a convention, trade show, or similar event are always associated with business, since the independent professional is there to further his entrepreneurial goals. But how much business do you think gets discussed in the schvitz, at the gym, at poolside, on a hike, or playing roulette? Nevertheless, if it's a tax break, we'll take it.

 If Tessie Tripp, at a trade show for travel agents, buys lift tickets as well as drinks and dinner for one of the speakers, or for one of her associates, the expense qualifies as deductible entertainment.

Business or Personal?

Be careful with deductions that mix business and personal expenses. The following situations need particular care.

Mixed Groups

If at the same event you entertain business associates as well as people not connected with business, you cannot deduct the entire cost as a business entertainment expense; you must separate the business expenses from the nonbusiness, or personal, expenses. If you cannot establish the exact expense for each person participating, allocate the expense on a per-person basis.

Reality Miles Mingus invites fellow musicians, promoters, and music critics to a party to promote his new CD. In addition to the twenty professionals attending, his immediate family of ten people also comes to help him celebrate. Only two-thirds (twenty out of thirty people) of the expense qualifies as a business entertainment expense. Miles cannot deduct the expenses for the ten family guests because those costs are nonbusiness expenses. But if his entire family were connected to the music business—hey, maybe.

Home Entertaining

You may entertain at home or, if your office is in your home, you may have business associates to your home for meetings during lunch, discussions over cocktails, or working dinners. You can deduct your costs for entertaining at your home the same as you can in any other setting. Be creative and clever in your substantiation. If you've sent written invitations, be sure to keep one along with your guest list or have the attendees drop their business cards into the micaceous clay bowl at the entrance. Better yet, make sure the invitation states the business purpose for the event.

Reality Dan Dapper is having a party to mark the first anniversary of the dating service he started a year ago. The guests at his apartment include couples he has personally introduced as well as others interested in using his service. He has a number of computers set up with questionnaires for the prospective clients to fill out as well as samples of several varieties of contracts that he has

with his clients. Dan kept a list of invited guests as well as a sign-in guest book. He has also invited his parents (who doubted this venture would be a success) along with a few other friends. The portion of the cost that applies to family and friends is not deductible.

Expenses for Spouses

You generally cannot deduct the cost of entertainment for your spouse or for the spouse of a business associate. However, you can deduct these costs if you can show that you had a clear business purpose, rather than a personal or social reason, for providing the entertainment to the spouses.

Reality Clarissa Clothier took an out-of-town client to dinner. Since the client's husband has made the long trip as well, it would be inappropriate for Clarissa to take the client without her spouse. In such a case, the cost of taking the spouse to dinner, as well as the client, is ordinary and necessary. If Clarissa's husband joins the party because the client's husband will be at dinner, the cost of entertaining both husbands is deductible.

Verboten! Prohibido! Not Allowed!

Watch out for these sensitive areas.

Family members as potential clients. You can no longer deduct the costs of a big party to which you invite people who might become your customers or clients. There has to be a more substantial basis for a deduction than the possibility of someone—and that includes your brother—becoming a client.

Taking turns. Expenses are not deductible when business acquaintances take turns picking up each other's meal or entertainment checks without regard to whether any business purposes are served. As with other tax matters: Be cool. Don't overdo it.

Entertaining yourself. Regular meals while working, but not traveling, are not deductible. Raina Realtor is always on the run from one showing or appointment to another and rarely eats at home. Instead, she grabs a bite on the road or in her office. She cannot deduct the cost of those meals.

Going over the top. MEALS & ENTERTAINMENT expenses that the IRS considers to be lavish or extravagant will be reduced if the taxpayer is audited. But expenses will not be considered lavish or extravagant just because they take place at deluxe restaurants, hotels, nightclubs, or resorts if the expenses reasonably fit the circumstances. In some cases a drive-through at Fast Finger Chicken might be suitable, while in others, if the deal is big enough, a $200 bottle of wine might be perfectly appropriate.

The 50 Percent Limit on Expenses

All right, you've figured out how to write off just about everything you eat and every place you play. Not so fast with the restaurant reservations. It is not a dollar-for-dollar-deduction.

You can deduct only 50 percent of your business-related MEALS & ENTERTAINMENT ***expenses.*** It doesn't matter whether you are:

- Entertaining customers at your place of business, a restaurant, at home, or at some other location

- Attending a business convention or reception, business meeting, or business luncheon at a club
- Traveling for business (whether eating alone or with others)

In each case you can deduct only one half the cost.

Meal or entertainment costs include:

- Taxes and tips relating to a business meal or entertainment activity
- Cover charges for admission to a nightclub
- Rent paid for a room in which you hold a dinner or cocktail party
- Parking at a sports arena

All of the above expenses are subject to the 50 percent limit. However, the cost of transportation to and from a business meal or a business-related entertainment activity, including parking, is 100 percent deductible as a **TRANSPORTATION** or **AUTO** or **PARKING** expense. However, parking at a sports arena is only 50 percent deductible. Does that make sense? If you are looking for consistency, you are searching in vain, for the IRS tax code does not often make sense. It's a patchwork quilt that's been sewn together, misaligned, and mismatched.

As you track your expenses, don't mix eating with sleeping.

Stella Sellit stayed several days at the Hilton, saw a number of clients, and took them out to dinner and to a jazz session in the hotel lounge. Some of her business expenses are 100 percent deductible: the room charge, phone and fax services, laundry. But the dinners and the lounge bill, which are MEALS & ENTERTAINMENT expenses, are 50 percent deductible. Although all the expenses are on a single hotel bill, she has to keep the categories separate for tax purposes.

Exceptions

There is no 50 percent limit on expenses in a few situations. You get to deduct your entire cost if you provide meals, entertainment, or recreational facilities to the general public as a means of advertising or promotion.

- Raina Realtor provides hors d'oeuvres and wine at an open house.
- Attila Atelier serves champagne at the opening reception for one of her artists.
- Whoopi Happenin has a "Come See How It's Done" event at her main office. The public is invited to taste, test, and view the inner workings of planning a gala. All food, drinks, supplies, and any other expense of the event are 100 percent deductible for Whoopi.
- Stan's Steam Train, a local amusement ride, offers free rides on Halloween for all children under age 5. Stan gives the kids chocolate pumpkins and candy corn. All his costs are 100 percent deductible.

Travel Meals and Entertainment

The deduction for MEALS & ENTERTAINMENT while traveling confuses a lot of people. All the information you need to get it straight is contained in Chapter Ten, Getting Around, but here's a summary:

Meals for yourself while you're away: When you are traveling for business you may deduct *all* your *own* meal expenses—breakfast, lunch, dinner, snacks.

Meals or entertaining for business associates while traveling: You may deduct the expenses for dining and entertaining business associates using the same guidelines explained in this chapter regarding nontravel MEALS & ENTERTAINMENT expenses. The deduction rules are the same whether you and your business associate are dining in London or in your home office.

When Is Entertainment Not Entertainment?

Your type of indie business may determine whether an activity is entertainment and thus only 50 percent deductible or some other category of business expense and thereby 100 percent deductible.

- Theobald Theater Critic is paid for his drama reviews. When he attends a theatrical performance in his professional capacity, it is not a 50 percent deductible entertainment expense, it is a 100 percent deductible RESEARCH expense.
- Nadine Novella is writing a feature story on life in the nightclubs of a small city. All expenses associated with her research at the clubs are fully deductible.
- Kristen Knockoff puts on a fashion show for a group of store buyers. Since she is a clothing designer, the show, a presentation of her new spring line, is not considered entertainment but an integral part of her business. It is a fully deductible

ADVERTISING expense. A party or lunch after the show, however, would be entertainment subject to the 50 percent limit.

Don't get the idea that just because you call something by another name you'll get to deduct the entire expense. If you take a Realtor out to dinner to promote your new territorial design homes, don't think that because you call it "promotion" it isn't really an entertainment expense. Yes, it's entertainment. And it's only 50 percent deductible.

Here's a quick reference table that summarizes what we discussed in this chapter.

BUSINESS MEALS AND ENTERTAINMENT EXPENSES:

When are they deductible?

WHY	For a business purpose	Present your idea, product, or service. Seek advice. Review a proposal, contract, prototype. Interview.
WITH WHOM	Business associate	Client, customer Potential client Professional advisor Supplier Employee Agent Collaborator Colleague

WHEN		
Directly related	Business took place during the meal or entertainment.	
Associated with	Business took place directly before or after the meal or entertainment.	

KINDS OF EXPENSES	Typical of your indie business	Meals Tickets to entertainment events Tickets to sporting events Accommodations Transportation

CHAPTER NINE

Staying in Touch: Communication Expenses

In this chapter we'll look at expenses incurred when communicating with your clients, suppliers, colleagues, and other business associates. Typical means of communication are:

- Telephone
- Cell phone
- Phone cards
- Personal digital assistant (PDA)
- Answering service
- Fax
- Internet service provider (ISP)
- Blackberry

If you've been reading **Self-employed Tax Solutions** straight through, this will be your first encounter with allocating expenses. Allocation becomes necessary when the same gadget (like your cell phone) or service (like your ISP) are used for both personal and business purposes. The IRS looks with a squinty eye at expenses that could have arisen from either personal or business use, citing them as "high-abuse items." To take deductions you are required to keep a record to show how much you use the gadget or service in the conduct of your business. It's an exasperating and irksome process. There are several ways to determine business versus personal use, and we will look at some of them in this chapter. By the way, "high-abuse items" include most means of communication as well as some other expense categories such as **MEALS & ENTERTAINMENT** and **AUTO**.

Even if you have set up parallel services, like two cell phones or two Internet access accounts, and strictly adhere to using one for business and the other for personal use, you may still need to prove your business use if you work from home.

The explanation of business **TELEPHONE** expense that follows will show you how to apply the business/personal allocation to most communication expenses.

Business Telephone Expense

Since 1989 no business deduction has been allowed for basic local telephone service for the first telephone line in a residence. This rule applies only to telephone service, not to other communication expenses such as ISPs. The IRS assumes that every American family has a telephone and uses it for personal communication—that a family or even a single person living alone would not have a phone for business purposes only. Therefore an indie who works out of her home and has only one telephone line cannot claim a business deduction for the basic local monthly telephone service charge even if she claims that that line is used solely for business purposes and even if the phone is listed as a business line in the name of her business.

If your only phone is a cell phone, the same disallowance of the basic monthly charge applies.

Nevertheless, even if you have only one line, you can still deduct for business long-distance service as well as charges for optional services such as call waiting, call forwarding, extra directory listings, or equipment rental. If these optional services are used exclusively for business, then you may deduct 100 percent of their cost.

How to Allocate between Business and Personal Use

The IRS wants a clear and specific designation of calls for business purposes versus those for personal use. Here is one method, which I call the *ideal way.* Then we'll look at those less-than-ideal methods that are not as meticulous but often pass muster with the IRS.

The Ideal Way

Keep a steno pad next to your phone and write the date on the top line. Then label one column "Phone #" and the other "Person / Reason." Every time you make a business call, write the phone number in the first column and the name of the person called or the reason for the call in the other column. At month's end compare your steno pad list with your phone statement. Tally the cost of the business calls plus any additional business options, such as call waiting. If you have only one phone line, then that tally is the month's business TELEPHONE expense.

If the phone line you use for business is not your basic line, then the arithmetic gets more complicated because you can also take part of the monthly charge as a business expense.

Here's what you do: Tally the cost of the business calls and compare that total to the cost of *all* that month's calls. Whatever that percent, take the same portion of the monthly charge as a business telephone expense.

For example: If $75 of the $100 in out-of-state calls is for business, then you can take 75 percent of your monthly service charge as a deduction as well as the cost of the phone calls.

Your business telephone expense will be a tally of business out-of-state calls and a portion of the monthly charge and any additional business phone options such as call forwarding.

I recommend that you use one line for personal calls and the other for business calls. This makes the monthly tally simpler.

More Practical Ways

Telephone calls for business purposes can amount to many thousands of dollars per month. If in an audit you cannot substantiate your business use, your deduction can be disallowed. However, in all my years in practice, I've come across very few indies who use the *ideal method* or even something close to it to record phone or Internet use. Here are some alternatives that have been used with varying degrees of success:

- Keep two months of ideal records—one month of the busy season and one month of the slow season. Calculate the average use of those two months, then take that percent of the entire phone bill (after excluding the monthly cost of the basic household line if this is your only phone). This method has been accepted in numerous audits. It's highly accurate.

- Make all calls and send all e-mails through the computer's database and use the database program's recording method as your record of business use to calculate actual costs or a percent of business use.

- Do not include as a business telephone expense any use of the home line but take 100 percent of everything else: business line, cell phone, phone cards.

- Save yourself some time by taking a somewhat smaller deduction than what you could probably take if you kept ideal records. Save all your phone bills so that if you are audited you can make a meticulous tally and come up with a deduction that exceeds the one you claimed in your return.

- Guesstimate a percent of use and hope for the best.

When keeping a record of personal use versus business use of the phone or e-mail time on your computer, it is best to use a method that you can credibly present to the IRS should your expense be questioned in an audit. For instance, if you and your teenage son are the only ones sending e-mail from your computer, you might calculate business use of your ISP this way:

2 parts for you:	1 part personal use
	1 part business use
4 parts for your son:	He's online twice as
	much as you.

6 total parts

In this example, business use is one-sixth. (Your one-part business use divided by six parts total). So if the monthly ISP expense is $48, then $8 is your monthly business expense.

If your indie business is not in your home, recordkeeping for the business communication expenses should be somewhat simpler, or at least more acceptable to the IRS.

Here are two of my actual IRS audit experiences that may help you decide which allocation method can work best for you.

 Like many musicians, especially those who compose, Miles Mingus tended to be better at recordkeeping than artists in other disciplines, so I expected this audit to go well. It didn't. (Audits are so subjective that I suspected the auditor's daughter had run off with a sax player.) When the auditor asked for the records for the telephone expense deduction, I showed her the phone bills on which Miles had circled all his business calls and had noted the initials of the business person he had called. Well, the auditor said, "Not allowed. This is what the taxpayer must do." I cut her off and told her this is the way I instruct all my clients: Keep a phone log; every time a business call is made, write down the phone number and the person's name—at which point she interrupted me to add "and a description of the phone conversation." I said many of my clients are reporters and psychologists, and by the dictates of their professions they cannot write a description of the phone calls. To which she replied, "Then they can't deduct it." We continued to argue it out. I asked what if this guy had another phone line in his house and just used it for business? "Oh no, as long as it's in his home, he's got to date, number, name, and describe the call because he might make personal calls from that line." I told her that I once worked at a design company and the employees would call home— wives calling their husbands, fathers checking on their children—and the company deducted those calls as a business expense. "Well, that's different," she sniffed. "That was a *real* business." The comment reveals the attitude of a significant contingent of the IRS and highlights the extreme arbitrary style of some auditors on these matters. I lost the argument. Could I have fought it? Yes. Would it have been worth it in time and expense to my client? No.

 The audit of another client, a business consultant we'll call Mike Manage, went quite differently. Mike simply totaled his twelve monthly checks made out to the phone company, took 40 percent of the total—estimating that was how much he used his phone for business—and the auditor accepted it!

I find recordkeeping for allocating a business/ personal use expense to be the most annoying and cumbersome of all the recordkeeping required by the IRS. My guess is that you'll feel that way, too, so somewhere along the way you will need to make a decision. Is it worth your time and effort to keep records the *ideal* way? What would it cost you if the IRS questioned your return and you couldn't back up your

claims for cell phone expense? Does your business involve a lot of time on the Internet? How much recordkeeping—and what method— makes sense for allocating phone card purchases? The answers to these questions may depend on the nature of your business, how many phone lines and cell phones you use, and the total amount of various communication expenses you have in relation to your total self-employed income or to your other expenses. Ask your tax preparer's advice on how best to handle these expenses in your unique situation. She should make suggestions suited to your circumstances in the context of all your other expenses and the accuracy of your records in general.

How Do You Categorize Communication Expenses?

There is no specific line on a tax return for communication expenses; different types of communication fall into different expense categories.

 Usually the IRS looks at business telephone expense as a **UTILITIES** expense. It will be up to your tax preparer as to how she categorizes it. She may combine it with the costs of your answering service as a **TELEPHONE** expense and list it under "Other Expenses" on your tax return.

Depending upon how you use the Internet, your ISP costs can be a **UTILITIES** expense or perhaps a **RESEARCH** expense. The costs of setting up and maintaining your Web site is an **ADVERTISING** expense. (Some tax preparers amortize the expense of Web site design over time.) Both a fax machine and answering machine are categorized as **EQUIPMENT.**

Some of the above expenses are explained from a different perspective in coming chapters. Keep this in mind: It is not necessary to know the category or classification of an expense. What you need to know is that these are all business expenses, and you want to take advantage of the deduction for every one of them.

Communication Chatter

Here are reminders and additional tips about communication expenses:

- If you're calling or e-mailing someone who is a friend and a business associate, if she is *primarily* a business associate and you discuss business, it's a deductible business call or e-mail.
- If you share a phone or ISP with another person, pay your portion by check, preferably directly to the phone or ISP company. If that is not practical, then pay your phone or ISP partner with a check made out to your partner. Note in the memo what the check is for. And keep a

copy of the bill. You will see in Part IV, Recordkeeping, how this way makes things easier for you.

- A phone line does not have to be listed with the phone company as a business line in order to be deducted as a business expense.
- Don't buy a stack of phone cards for your kids and then deduct them as a business expense. If the size of the deduction doesn't fit what the IRS has set as a "market guideline" for your profession, an auditor can disallow them in the absence of phone records.
- Telephone expense is not directly related to **OFFICE IN THE HOME** expense.

Brilliant Deduction

You may deduct for a phone used in your residence even if you do not have an office or studio in your home. If you do claim an **OFFICE IN THE HOME** deduction, don't think that somehow office size and phone use need to match. They don't. Your home office may take up 10 percent of your residence but you may use 88 percent of your household phone line for business. No correlation, no problem.

CHAPTER TEN

Getting Around: Travel, Transportation, and Auto Expenses

Travel expenses, transportation expenses, vehicle expenses—aren't they all more or less the same thing? No more so than trudging by mule pack in the Andes, taxiing through city traffic, or jetting to L.A. Let's look at them all.

Business Travel Expenses

Over the river and through the woods to Grandmother's house goes Pat Personal Trainer. Gram just bought a color laser and it's the cheapest way for Pat to print his new brochures. He leaves Friday afternoon. The bus gets him there in time for dinner. He works at the computer all the next day until the wee hours. (He's sure these new brochures will get him lots of customers.) Very early the next morning he kisses Grandma good-bye and heads back on the bus.

Brilliant Deduction

Pat was away from his home, for business, **overnight.** It was **business travel.** Therefore, he may deduct TRAVEL expenses.

Before I get into the rules and regulations of TRAVEL expenses, let me put your mind at ease. Travel rules are complicated. Don't expect to store them all in your memory for instant recall. **This is a reference chapter.** You'll need to refer to it often, whether you make trips biweekly to Florence or biennially to Philadelphia.

THE IRS SAYS ABOUT
Business Travel . . .

If you temporarily travel away from your tax home for business, you may deduct ordinary and necessary TRAVEL expenses. You may not write off "lavish or extravagant" expenses.

The IRS, you remember, says that an "ordinary expense is one that is common to your profession; a necessary one is one that is helpful and appropriate."

The IRS has written thousands of words on business travel. Here are the most important. Your trip is business travel if your business duties require you to be away from the general area of your tax home longer than an ordinary day's work so that you need to get some sleep or rest.

What is a **tax home?** Think of it as your main or regular place of business. It doesn't matter where you maintain your family home. Thus, if you stay away from your tax home overnight, your business trip would include needing to get some rest. But be careful: Don't go around telling people that you ordinarily work twenty-hour days or you'll miss out on deducting your business trips!

Simply stated, we can define business travel like this: If you are **away from your place of business, overnight,** for a purpose that benefits your business, then you have been on a business trip and your costs are deductible TRAVEL expenses.

Reality

What! You're an itinerant jester who doesn't have a regular or main place of business? Sorry, no **TRAVEL** expenses allowed.

Reality

Travis Truck Driver leaves the terminal at five in the morning. Three hundred miles later he's at the turnaround. While his truck is being unloaded, he has a big lunch and then dozes off outside the diner while waiting for the guys to finish the reloading. He then heads back to the terminal where the truck is again unloaded. He's home by midnight. Travis's lunch-break nap was just that, "a nap." It was not enough time to get adequate sleep. His trip is not considered travel. Therefore he cannot deduct **TRAVEL** expenses.

Travel or Transportation

A trip classified as business **travel** will get you a

Brilliant Deduction

lot more deductions than will one classified as business **transportation** (see the next section). If it's an overnight trip, it's **travel**. **TRANSPORTATION** expenses are solely the costs of getting from one business event location to another.

Reality

Albuquerque is about 70 miles from my office in Santa Fe. If I drive to Albuquerque in the morning to meet with a client, have lunch alone at a restaurant, drive to

Brilliant Deduction

a second meeting, then drive back to Santa Fe, my only deductible costs are my **AUTO** mileage there and back and parking.

Here's a different scenario. In the morning I meet with a client in Albuquerque and have lunch. Since my other client is not available to meet with me until 8:00 P.M., I do some shopping, have dinner with a friend at a restaurant, and then meet with the second client. The meeting runs much later than expected and I'm too tired to drive back to Santa Fe. I stay in an Albuquerque hotel and drive back to my home office in the morning. Because I was there substantially longer than an ordinary day's work, I can deduct my **TRAVEL** expenses that include my drive to, from, and around Albuquerque; my lunch and my dinner (not my friend's dinner); and the cost of the hotel.

Business Travel Expenses Are the Costs of the Trip

Business **TRAVEL** expenses can get tangled up in IRS jargon, so for easier understanding, think of them as falling into the following six groups:

1. Transport

This includes the costs of transporting you and your stuff, by any means, to, from, and while at your destination.

- Airfare
- Auto rentals
- Taxis, buses, subway
- Excess baggage charges
- Costs for separately sending your things, like your mock-ups, samples, or displays

2. Lodging

- Hotel
- Campsite fee

3. Other travel-necessitated expenses

- Telephone and other electronic communication
- Passport fees

4. Incidental expenses

- Laundry, cleaning, pressing of clothes
- Tips
- Fees for services such as secretarial assistance

5. Meals for yourself while you're away

When you are traveling for business, you may deduct the costs for all of your own meals—breakfast, lunch, dinner, snacks.

6. MEALS & ENTERTAINMENT for business associates

You may deduct the expenses for MEALS & ENTERTAINMENT for business associates using the same guidelines explained in Chapter Eight. The rules for MEALS & ENTERTAINMENT are the same whether you and your business associate are dining in Paris or next door to your home office.

If you are certain that your trip is entirely for a business purpose, then you may deduct all your TRAVEL expenses. It can be as simple as that. Or it may be as baffling as cashing a traveler's check in Gabon. Some of the complications are:

- taking another person with you on the trip
- a trip that is part business and part personal
- a trip outside the continental United States or
- both within and outside the USA

If none of the above complications apply to you, then **skip the rest of the travel section.** But do refer to it **before** the next trip if any of the above situations may apply.

Arrangements That Complicate Business Travel

Just as a midwestern storm that freezes up the national air traffic system can change a simple trip into a complex travel expedition, so too can certain situations befuddle your understanding of business travel deductions. Let's take a closer look at the complications we mentioned earlier.

Taking Another Person with You on the Trip

You may deduct TRAVEL expenses for your companion if that person fits **all** of the following three conditions:

1. Is a customer, client, supplier, agent, business partner, or professional advisor with whom you conduct or expect to conduct business, or your employee, and

2. Has a business purpose for the travel, and

3. Would otherwise be allowed to deduct TRAVEL expenses.

Bringing your best friend along because she'll type up your notes at the end of the day or help you charm the oldsters you're trying to sign up for your next senior cruise does not constitute a **business purpose.**

The old tax law allowed you to deduct expenses for your spouse if he served a business purpose. No more. If your husband is not your employee, it doesn't matter how much help he is on the trip. **No** deduction for him.

 Mary Motivate flies to Atlanta to give her biggest motivational presentation yet. She had a two-for-the-price-of-one airline coupon, so she brought along her husband, who makes sure the handouts, speaker system, PowerPoint presentation, and lighting go without a hitch. Mary's husband is not her employee. Mary may deduct the entire cost of the airline ticket because she would have paid for one full fare anyway. She does not have to divide the cost of the hotel room in half. If her double room at the hotel cost $200 per night and would have cost $170 for a single, she may deduct $170. The expense for the car rental may be deducted in full even though her husband rides in the auto with her. She may not deduct any expenses for her husband.

A Trip That Is Part Business and Part Personal

If you mix business and pleasure on a trip, deductions may depend upon whether you are traveling within the United States or outside the United States. Review the table on the next page to determine if your costs are deductible business expenses.

Special Rule for Travel Outside the USA

If you meet **one** of the exceptions below, you may treat foreign travel in the same manner as travel within the United States.

- You were out of the country seven consecutive days or less (don't count the day you left the USA), or

- You were out of the USA for more than seven days (count the day you left and the day of your return), but you spent at least 75 percent of your time on business activities.

Warren Wordsmith leaves Albuquerque on Monday (day does not count). Arrives in Frankfurt, Germany, on Tuesday (day 1). He attends the Frankfurt Book Fair for two days (days 2 and 3), then spends the rest of the time with his grandchildren; he even visits Strasbourg, France, with them. He leaves Frankfurt to fly back home on the following Monday (day 7, not counting the first travel day). Warren may not write off personal expenses, but he may write off all business expenses including all the airfare.

ALERT! If you have enough money to do your business traveling by luxury ocean liner (the IRS calls it "water transport"), I'm sure you'll be talking to your accountant about how to write it off. But since different rules apply to that kind of travel, do warn your friend Tracy Travel Agent that there are restrictions on the amount she can deduct for her New York-to-London business cruise. She'd better check with her tax advisor.

Also check with a tax advisor if you're heading to a convention outside the North America area.

BUSINESS TRAVEL EXPENSES

PRIMARILY, BUT NOT SOLELY, FOR BUSINESS PURPOSES

WHERE	MAY DEDUCT	MAY NOT DEDUCT	MUST PRORATE ON DAY-TO-DAY BASIS
All in the USA (includes 50 states and D.C.)	All business-related expenses that you would have incurred had you not taken any personal days Cost of transportation to and from	Personal expenses	
All outside the USA* *See the special rule for travel outside the USA.	All business-related expenses that you would have incurred had you not taken any personal days	Personal expenses	Cost of transportation to and from

PRIMARILY, BUT NOT SOLELY, FOR PERSONAL PURPOSES

WHERE	MAY DEDUCT	MAY NOT DEDUCT	MUST PRORATE ON DAY-TO-DAY BASIS
Whether in the USA or Outside the USA	Only directly related business expenses incurred while at your destination	Any other costs of the trip Cost of transportation to and from	

SPECIAL RULE FOR BUSINESS TRAVEL OUTSIDE THE USA

HOW LONG?	MAY DEDUCT	MAY NOT DEDUCT	MUST PRORATE ON DAY-TO-DAY BASIS
Seven consecutive days or less (do not include day left USA) or More than seven consecutive days (include day left USA); at least 75 percent time on business	All business-related expenses that you would have incurred had you not taken any personal days Cost of transportation to and from	Personal expenses	

Going on a Trip?
Establish a Business Motive

Using Alternative Travel Records

For most of your **TRAVEL** expenses you will have receipts of some sort—canceled checks, credit card slips, or cash receipts. Well, after its own fashion, the IRS has tried to make recordkeeping for **TRAVEL** easier by offering an alternative method of calculating allowable expenses.

The IRS has issued per diem (per day) charts. These charts list the maximum amounts allowed to be deducted without receipts for "lodging" and for "meals + incidentals." Self-employeds may use the amounts listed for meals + incidentals only. As you can see, it wasn't self-employeds for whom easier recordkeeping was set up but for employers and employees; the self-employed just happen to benefit from the crumbs that fall from the table.

Instruction on the use of these confusing charts is beyond the basics of this book, so if you do not have receipts for all of your travel meals, then be sure to ask your tax pro about using the alternative per diem method.

Grouping Travel Expenses

When **TRAVEL** expenses are deducted on your tax return, they are not listed separately as lodging or airfare or incidentals. All travel costs fall into one of two business expense categories. One is **MEALS & ENTERTAINMENT.** This includes all travel meals plus any expenses for business entertainment while traveling. The other category is **TRAVEL** expense, which includes everything *except* **MEALS & ENTERTAINMENT** while traveling.

There is a reason for the bifurcation. **TRAVEL** expenses get deducted at 100 percent of your outlay while **MEALS & ENTERTAINMENT** are deducted at 50 percent. See the Travel Work-

sheet in Chapter Twenty-three. And see Chapter Eight for a complete explanation of **MEALS & ENTERTAINMENT.**

Making Travel Arrangements: A Few Scenarios

Establish a business intent when you travel. Plan your business trips carefully and well in advance:

Sarah Sculptor is going from her studio in Ghent, New York, to Boston for five days of art study. She will not be enrolled in a formal course, but she wants to deduct the trip as a travel expense. So she establishes a clear business intent. She writes to the museums for their schedules and to the galleries she plans to visit. She keeps copies of her letters and e-mails. She wants to arrange for meetings with gallery directors, curators, or art professors, so she makes her requests to them in writing. Their responses—the letters **and envelopes,** whether positive or negative—are saved in her "Boston Trip—2007" file. When she is in Boston, she gets literature from every gallery or museum that she attends. Any sketches done on the trip are dated and placed. For example, "Boston Common, Sept 2007" is written someplace on each sketch or sketchpad. She keeps copies of all follow-up letters and thank-you notes that she sent to the directors—

if not for meeting with her, then for at least taking the time to read her request and respond. If Sarah stays an extra day because she ran into an old college friend (who is not in the arts and has no business connection to her), she cannot deduct the costs of that day, but she does not have to prorate her travel to and from Boston.

A business trip does not have to show a profit:

 Cindy Set Designer was very happy to land the contract for designing the sets for the Long Wharf Community Theatre. Even though it would be eleven straight hours of driving to get to Connecticut, at least she wouldn't have to rent a car while there. Her work would last for three weeks. The pay wasn't good, and she'd have to foot all her own expenses, but it would be a good career step. Renting two rooms from a local was cheaper than staying at a hotel and eating out. There was no refrigerator in the place, so she rented one. She figured that by the time she was done, her expenses would about break even with what she was paid or perhaps would exceed her income. But she knew that adding this prestigious theater to her résumé would get her more work. All her expenses were deductible—including rental of the refrigerator—even though this job may end up costing her money.

When on a business trip, be careful how much time you play when you could be working. If you play at least 25 percent of the time, you'll need to allocate costs:

 Shane Scriptwrite travels from New York to London ($300 one-way; day 1) to attend a three-day course in scene blocking for theater-in-the-round (days 2, 3, and 4). Before returning to New York he flies to France ($250) for a four-day vacation in Paris (days 5, 6, 7, and 8). He flies back (day 9) to New York from Paris ($500). He may deduct all his London expenses. He cannot deduct any of his Paris expenses. Shane was on a personal trip for four of the nine days. He must deduct from his total airfare (New York to London to Paris to New York) of $1,050, four-ninths of the expense he would have had in flying directly from New York to Paris and back. He should get something from his travel agent or a printout from the Internet to show what that cost would have been. Of course, the lower that airfare, the better for his write-off.

You'd think that Shane could deduct whatever the round-trip fare to London would have been. Or at worst that he could take five-ninths (five business days out of nine days total) of that fare. But what the IRS says to do is from his total fare deduct four-ninths of the cost of a round-trip to Paris. Shane found a $495 round-trip fare on the Web.

Total airfare: $300 + $250 + $500	=	$1,050
Paris round-trip: $495 x four-ninths	=	(220)
Allowed airfare deduction:	=	$ 830

It defies logic, but it's the IRS rule.

Are you supposed to know how to figure this out? No. So why am I telling you? Because with a little planning and consultation with your tax pro **before you take a business trip,** you may be able to get a bigger deduction. Also, I thought you might like another example of crazy IRS logic.

 P. R. Bernays mixes business and pleasure on his convention trip to Mexico. The industry convention is held in Puerto Vallarta. He spends five days at the convention and spends the following three days sailing and scuba diving at a resort. The two travel days—the day the trip began and the day it ended—are counted as business days. P. R. was out of the USA for a total of ten days. The allocation rules on foreign business travel apply; P. R.'s trip was primarily for business, he was outside the United States for more than one week, and spent less than 75 percent of his time on business (seven business days out of ten is 70 percent on business). He must allocate his transportation expenses. He can deduct only $700 of his $1,000 airfare because only 70 percent of his days were related to business activities.

 Samantha Semblance went to the same convention in Mexico as did P. R. But she limited her scuba diving to two days. Her foreign trip lasted longer than one week: Five convention plus two travel plus two scuba equals nine days, but less than 25 percent of the time outside the United States was spent on personal matters (two-ninths equals 22 percent). Samantha may deduct her entire round-trip airfare of $1,000.

Travel as a form of education is not a business expense:

 Jack Japanese Instructor may deduct a trip to Japan to take courses in Japanese and Japanese culture or history. He may not deduct the costs of a trip to Japan wherein he just travels around the country soaking up the culture.

If the trip is primarily a vacation, there is no deduction for travel costs to and from the foreign location:

 Just because Jack Japanese Instructor took a one-day haiku course during his ten days in Japan does not make the airfare or any of his other expenses deductible. Only the cost of the haiku course is deductible.

Things to Know before You Go

- While on a Vermont business trip, you buy maple syrup for your kid sister who lives in Texas? No business deduction there.
- Pat Personal Trainer ran out for lunch when printing his brochure at Grandma's? Yes, a **TRAVEL MEAL** expense.
- Pat gave Grandma a family tree program for her computer as thanks for the use of her printer? Yes, a deductible **BUSINESS GIFT** expense.
- Any expenses you incur while on a fun side trip while away on business? Nondeductible.

Whether you are traveling alone or with a group of friends, whether the trip is mandatory (your client insists that **you** supervise the equipment installation) or not (a chance to study with a ninety-eight-year-old master who may not be around next year), the matter of business travel shows how complicated and difficult it is for an independent professional to distinguish between personal life and business life. Therefore:

- Choose your business travel wisely. Plan ahead.
- Save all correspondence relating to your trip. Put it in a file folder labeled with the place and date of travel or some other label—"April Convention"—that makes sense to you.
- Keep a notepad log while on your business trip. Entries should show with whom you met and why.

Business Transportation Expenses

What if you sally forth on business and return without an overnight stay or a need for rest? Had Pat Personal Trainer—from several pages back—simply spent the afternoon using Grandma's laser printer and then hightailed it back to his home office in the same day, he would not have

had any **TRAVEL** expenses. However, he would have had **TRANSPORTATION** expenses. The distinction between **travel** and **transportation** is important because that distinction determines which of your costs are deductible. Before looking at the specifics of **TRANSPORTATION** expenses, let's review the distinction once again: **If you stay overnight or long enough to need some rest, then it's travel. If not, then it's transportation.**

If you've accepted the useful and tax-saving way of thinking like an indie business, then you're already aware that anything you do that is related to your work or makes you better at doing what you're doing is a likely business expense. Thus, going to or getting back from whatever you are doing for business is also a likely business expense.

Although there are no limitations on **what** mode of transportation is used, there are rules regarding **when** transportation is a deductible expense. In the following cases of Anton and Syd, you may be surprised to learn that you can't always deduct what you think of as business transportation—it depends on the situation. After you look at the two following circumstances, I'll thoroughly explain **TRANSPORTATION** expenses.

 Whether Anton Antique starts the day by taking a taxi, the trolley, or his own car from his apartment to his antiques shop in town, he cannot deduct the cost of his transportation from home to work. Even if Anton drove to his shop in his old (but not antique) Ford, laden with business papers, boxes of records, used coffee cups, and a battery-operated tape recorder (his car looks like a messy office), and even if Anton made business calls on his cell phone all the way, he cannot claim the drive as a business trip. Why not? The IRS says his drive is a *commute*.

 After Syd System gets his youngsters off to school, he takes his coffee into his home office. He checks his e-mail, then heads into town to meet with a client. Whether Syd takes a taxi, the bus, or his own car, his transportation costs from his home office to the meeting are deductible.

It wouldn't matter that Syd's trip was a $2 subway ride and Anton's was a two-hour commute into the city. Anton was commuting, Syd was not. The IRS does not allow a deduction for commuting to and from home and work. Whether you're Emma Employee or Indira Independent, you cannot take your first trip (your movement from a personal place to a business place) or your last trip (your movement from a business place to a personal place) as a business expense.

Anton's first trip was from home to his shop: no **TRANSPORTATION** expense. All of Anton's expenses for his additional business treks through the day are deductible **except** the one from his last appointment in town to his home. That is his home commute.

Syd's commute is from his kitchen to his home office. From his home office to his client's is not a commute but is business transportation, and so he gets to deduct his expense. All Syd's business trekking for the rest of the day until he gets back to his home office qualifies as **TRANSPORTATION** expense.

Work at Home to Increase Transportation Deductions

Let's take a look at how, by thinking like an indie, Anton could increase his **TRANSPORTATION** deductions and perhaps save some money on taxes.

A major reason for establishing a home office,

possibly more important than the home office expense deduction itself, is that it increases the possibilities for deducting **TRANSPORTATION** costs.

The IRS does not allow a deduction for commuting costs—that is, driving from home to work and back. But it does allow a deduction for getting from one workplace to another. No office in the home means no deduction for the miles from your home to your first work stop. However, if your commute is from your kitchen to your home office, where you perform administrative tasks like calls, e-mails, and billing, and then you drive to your *other* office, you are now driving "from one workplace to another." Without increasing any of your out-of-pocket costs, you have increased your business **TRANSPORTATION** deduction.

For just that reason the IRS fought long and hard to disallow using an office in the home for "administrative" (that means paperwork and phone calls) purposes only. But having lost the battle, the IRS has liberalized the rules on deducting office in the home expense. You can have an office or studio elsewhere and still deduct costs for the area of your home used exclusively and regularly for administrative or management activities for your business. (Be sure to read Chapter Twelve on home office deductions.)

Getting around the "Commuting" Limitation

Here are circumstances that allow you to claim part or all of your daily drive as legitimate deductions.

The Temporary Work Site

If you have a regular workplace, you may deduct the cost of getting to a **temporary work site** even if it is your first or last trip of the day.

 Anton Antique's shop is his regular workplace. Occasionally a client requires that Anton come to her site for a design consultation. Anton can deduct the cost of going from his home to the client's and back home. The client's home is considered a temporary work site.

Transportation Away from Your Tax Home

If you must leave your tax home, you may deduct the cost of transportation, even if it is your first or last trip of the day.

 One morning Anton began his workday by driving all the way from his home in Worcester, Massachusetts, to a little farmhouse just beyond Providence, Rhode Island. He took the 50-mile drive to look at a large cache of nineteenth-century silver spoons up for sale. Although he has no office in the home, he's entitled to deduct the mileage.

Had those spoons been in a home on the other side of Worcester, and had he started his day by driving there to see them instead of driving to the farmhouse outside Providence, Anton would not have been able to deduct his drive.

Tax home is another item in the quirky IRS jargon, and it has never been exactly measured in terms of distance. Some tax pros say your tax home is the 40-mile radius around your business. The IRS defines it as the "entire city or general area in which your business or work is located." In either case, Providence lies outside Anton's tax home, while the other side of Worcester does not.

In defining your own tax home, much depends on the geography and layout of your location. If your business requires these kinds of trips on a recurring basis, discuss your situation with your tax pro.

A Business Stop Close to Home

If your drive to your first appointment is a long one and circumstances rule out establishing an office in your home, then make your first trip of the day a short business trip. Let's say you go to your business post office box to pick up mail. You can then deduct your transportation from the post office to your first business appointment. But you can't deduct your return home unless you really must stop at the post office or maybe the local bank on the way home, in which case you'd only have to leave out the transportation from the bank to home.

The following are examples of valid business transportation deductions:

- Meeting with clients, customers, or colleagues
- Going from one work site to another
- Getting to and from a business entertainment event
- Attending seminars or study courses
- Doing errands or shopping for business supplies

For many self-employeds, an automobile is the chief means of business transportation. In the next section we'll examine business use of your car.

Business Use of Your Auto or Other Vehicle

Unless you live in Manhattan or some other major city, everyone you know owns a car. Maybe two. For most Americans, cars represent their second largest purchase (the first is a home). After mortgage payments, car expenses usually take the biggest bite out of income. With this in mind, it makes complete sense for a solo entrepreneur to look toward taking every possible deduction for business use of her car.

Police habitually speak of "vehicles" instead of "cars" or "autos," a practice that also makes sense when discussing business AUTO expense. Everything in this chapter pertaining to cars—except for some differences in depreciation, which I'll explain later—also applies to vans, SUVs, trucks, motorcycles, and other road vehicles. (An aside from the IRS: These rules do not apply to airplanes, boats, or snowmobiles). So I'm going to use "car," "auto," and "vehicle" interchangeably.

 Brilliant Deduction

Now mark the following carefully, because it's an exception to what I've been telling you in the last two sections.

Let's say that in a given week, you drive your car to numerous business appointments around town, for a total of 100 miles. In the same week you drive from Pennsylvania to

Ohio for an overnight business trip, a total of 300 miles. We combine these for a total of 400 business-use miles for the week. I know, I just got finished stressing the difference between TRANSPORTATION expenses and TRAVEL expenses. The reason for this seeming contradiction lies, as is so often the case, with the IRS. TRANSPORTATION is one category in IRS expenses, TRAVEL is a different expense category, and business-use miles for your vehicle is a third.

Therefore, if you took a taxi for your business appointments around town, it's listed as TRANSPORTATION expense. If you took a bus for your overnight stay in Ohio, it's listed as TRAVEL expense. But if you drove your car to all these appointments, the expenses are listed under business-use miles for your vehicle.

Calculating Auto Expense—Two Methods

Business AUTO expense can be figured in one of two ways. The first, the **standard mileage method,** simply multiplies your total business miles by a per-mile rate set by the government. The rate changes yearly. For 2007 it was 48.5 cents per mile. In 2008 it is 50.5 cents per mile from January 1 through June 30, then 58.5 cents per mile from July 1 through December 31. The other approach, the **actual expenses method,** multiplies your total auto expenses by the percent of business use, and adds to that an amount for depreciation of the business portion of the cost of the auto. (Depreciation is explained in Chapter Thirteen). Add to the total, with either of these methods, the business portion of auto finance charges, as well as all business tolls and parking.

Reality ✓ Lily Legal purchased a $20,000 auto four years ago. In 2007 she put 6,000 business miles on her car out of a total of 10,000 miles. Her total expenses for maintaining the car were $4,200, which included $500 in finance charges. Tolls and parking totaled $150. Here are the two methods of calculating Lily's **AUTO** expense:

The standard mileage method. Business miles for the year are multiplied by the per-mile rate for that year. The rate for 2007 was 48.5 cents per mile.

6,000 business miles x 48.5 cents per mile	=	$2,910
60% of finance charges of $500	=	300
Tolls and parking	=	150
Total expense	=	$3,360

The actual method. Business miles are divided by total mileage for the year to arrive at a percentage of business use.

Business miles	=	6,000
Total miles	=	10,000
	=	60% business use

Total auto expenses are multiplied by business use percentage.

$4,200 x 60%	=	$2,520
Tolls and parking	=	150
Depreciation	=	1,065
Total expense	=	$3,735

In Lily's case, the actual method produced a significantly higher deduction.

When using the actual method, in addition to information on the purchase date and price of your car, you will also need a tally of all the expenses for your car, such as:

- Gas and oil
- Repairs and maintenance
- Tires
- Insurance (including AAA or other road service coverage)
- Registration and license
- Car wash
- Garage rental
- Loan interest
- Lease costs

Parking tickets, speeding tickets, and fines are not deductible business expenses.

 The Vehicle Purchase Worksheet in Chapter Twenty-three (which repeats some of the items on the Auto Worksheet) is a reminder of information you'll need to provide to your tax preparer regarding deductions on your new vehicle.

Which method is better, standard or actual? It depends. High mileage on a car that's cheap to run may get a better write-off using the standard method. Low business mileage on an old vehicle with lots of expensive repair bills may get a better write-off using actual expenses. Let your tax preparer decide for you. She will calculate both ways and can switch from year to year to get the best advantage. There are some restrictions on switching that your preparer will take into consideration.

Of course, if for one reason or another you do not have good records of all your car expenses—say your forgetful brother borrows the car a lot and he simply cannot remember to get receipts when he buys gas—then you *must* use the **standard mileage method.** Another bothersome deduction problem for an indie occurs when several cars are used for business purposes. One of my clients has five cars in his family, and although he, his wife, and children each has his or her own car, for various reasons they often must switch cars. It is impossible for him to keep track of expenses separately for each individual car. He may use his car 85 percent for business but his sons' cars only 10 percent for business. So he simply keeps a record of his total business miles and we use the standard method.

How to Keep a Record of Business Miles

Regardless of which method you use to calculate **AUTO** expense, you will need to know the total business-use miles for the year.

If you use the actual method, you will need to do a little more work. In this case you'll also need to know the total mileage for the year for the vehicle. If you use more than one car for business, you will need these figures for each car used for business.

If you have any questions about what constitutes business use of your car, review the previous sections on travel and transportation.

The Easy Method of Recording Business Mileage

Let's start on New Year's Eve! Here's a little assignment before you head out to the party:

Get the mileage reading from your car odometer and write it in your calendar.

Next assignment: On the following New Year's Eve, **before** you go out (because you'll never remember in the morning), once again get the mileage reading and write it in your calendar. Completing those two assignments gives you a beginning and ending mileage reading for the year so you know how many miles you put on your car for the year. Now let's see what you do between parties.

As long as accuracy is your goal, the method used to figure out business miles is unimportant. Choose the routine that suits you and your business. Patti Partyplanner, who runs all over the state checking party and convention sites and prices of supplies and listening to bands, will have a very different method of calculating business mileage than will Rob Rolf, who rarely needs to leave his massage studio. Let's look at the different ways that they, and Lily Legal, figure out business miles.

 Rob Rolf uses his car for business only once a month to buy supplies. All he has to do is check the mileage from studio to supply house and back and multiply it by twelve. He's got his total business miles for the year.

 Lily Legal goes to the courthouse twice a week. She has an occasional trip to a client's office. Like Rob Rolf she does the multiplication thing to figure her courthouse appearances—two trips times forty-eight weeks (she takes off four weeks a year to go to Aruba). And she uses her appointment calendar to determine which clients she met with at their offices. Around early December she has her clerk figure the miles from her office to each client. He writes the mileage for each appointment in her appointment book and tallies them up. He adds the appointment mileage to her court appearance mileage for total business-use mileage.

 Patti Partyplanner spends much of her day in what she calls her "business" car. She was distraught at the cumbersome way her former tax preparer told her to calculate business miles. Sammy Segar told her to write down the odometer reading every morning (79,814.5) and then at the end of the day write down the new reading (80,013.6), and then subtract (199.1 miles). What a bother! By day's end she was so tired that she often made mistakes in arithmetic. Patti has another car—bigger, with a child seat, devoid of the clutter of her business car. She uses that one for just about all family errands. Patti came up with a much easier way of calculating business miles. She does her New Year's Eve notations in the calendar. But then instead of writing down all her business miles, she just notes in her calendar the few occasions she uses the business car for personal errands. She deducts her personal miles from her total miles to come up with a business-use figure.

As you can see from the above examples, there is no set way to keep a mileage record. Use a method that suits you.

The Calendar Method

Here's an easy, straightforward method to record business miles, based on the assumption that you use a calendar or appointment book to note your activities, appointments, and, possibly, errands. Your calendar clearly—but not necessarily neatly—shows things like: printer on Monday; Tuesday, town library; Wednesday, client presentation; Thursday at 2:00, meeting with C. Client; Saturday, marketing workshop; PTA meeting the second Monday of every month.

After a business appointment—driving to the printer and back—jot down the mileage on the calendar when you return to your office or home studio or workshop. Anyway, that's how it's supposed to work, but you know how it goes: At times it slipped your mind, or you hadn't time to make a notation because you had to get somewhere else. So in a week or a month or at year's end, with your appointment book or calendar in front of you, you'll see that you met with the printer on that day. If you don't know the mileage to the print shop, get out your map or log onto your computer or ask your wife, who knows the mileage to every place in the county. Then write the mileage in your calendar.

Any kind of calendar, appointment book, or computer date book will do. Whatever you are comfortable with. I don't recommend a separate mileage log. That's just another thing to keep track of, and it's double work to jot down your appointment in your calendar and a second time in your mileage log. Forget it! Write your mileage on the calendar that you use for all the other events and meetings going on in your life—that way you won't miss any business mileage.

At the end of the year add up the business miles that you noted or logged in your calendar, using a calculator that has a tape.

By the way, if you know that at least once a month you run to the office supply store, or that you visit the Quick-Send postal drop once a week, but you don't write these errands in your calendar, then multiply the trip mileage by the appropriate number of trips to come up with more miles to add to your calendar-logged totals. Many solos who work at home cheat themselves in business mileage. They forget that before picking up the kids at day care they went 5 miles in the other direction to pick up new business cards at the printer.

If your New Year's numbers showed a total of 20,000 miles and your calendar totals 15,000 business miles, then you know that 75 percent (15,000 divided by 20,000) of your car was used for business. That enables you to deduct 75 percent of your entire year's worth of car expenses and will also get you a 75 percent write-off of the cost of your car.

ALERT! A word of caution on where to keep your calendar. If your date book is stolen or mislaid forever, you've lost your entire year-to-date records. If you must carry it with you or you like to keep it in your car, then at the end of each month tear out that month and leave it back at the office or in your desk at home. In this way, if your calendar disappears, you've lost only the current month. If it's on computer, back it up.

In the event of an audit, the IRS will want to see your appointment calendar. For psychologists and reporters and other professions where confidentiality is a concern: Should you be audited, photocopy your calendar and black out all confidential information on the copy you show to the IRS.

What if you missed getting the mileage reading on New Year's Eve? Can you make it up? How does the IRS check the mileage figures you use? Well, in an audit they'll ask for repair receipts. Most repair receipts have the odometer reading at the time of the repair written on the receipt. If you forget to check your mileage reading on New Year's Eve, check a recent repair slip and make a guesstimate.

More Than One Vehicle Used for Business

If you use more than one car for business, and you use the actual expenses method to calculate your business AUTO deduction, then you must segregate the expenses and mileage for each vehicle. If for instance you use the van as your business vehicle but on rare occasions you use your husband's car, you must keep the same records on your husband's car as on your van. Tally his expenses at year-end and, though it may be tiny, take your business percent.

Spreading your business driving between both (all) your cars will increase your AUTO expense deduction. If your policy has been to use only the old clunker to cart around your supplies and drive from your office to clients, change your ways and put some business miles on the new Volvo as well. For instance, if 3,000 of the Volvo's 10,000 miles per year are for business, you will get a deduction of 30 percent of all Volvo costs. That means 30 percent of the $40,000 purchase price as well as things like insurance, gas, etc. This is in addition to the deduction for 90 or 95 percent of the costs of the old clunker.

Using a borrowed car? No matter. Keep records just as you would for any other vehicle you use for business.

What if you lease or rent a car? Same thing. Keep the same records as you would for a car you owned. Have your lease or rental agreement available for your tax preparer, because you are required to reduce the amount of **AUTO** expense deduction by a small percentage of the fair market value of the leased car. Your preparer will need to get that figure from your lease agreement.

If you rent a car while on a business trip, the entire cost of the car rental is a travel expense. If, however, your trip is mixed business and personal, you'll have to keep a mileage record.

WHATTA**CONCEPT!**

Lease versus own

Should you lease? If your business requires you to wow clients with glitter, a new car every two years is imperative, and leasing is probably the better way for you.

Leasing versus owning, however, is generally based on how good a deal you can get, with tax considerations secondary. If tax savings are a key factor in your purchasing decision, then run it by your tax pro. (Try to time your purchase so that you're not questioning her at the height of the tax return season.) Any savings in tax deductions must of course be balanced against purchase price, operating expenses, and other considerations.

To Sum Up Getting Around

For all **TRAVEL** and **TRANSPORTATION** and **AUTO** expenses, all you need do is complete the worksheets in Chapter Twenty-three for your tax preparer. Here's a wrap-up.

- **TRAVEL** is overnight. **TRANSPORTATION** takes place in the same day.
- Your means of getting from one place to another, whether for **TRAVEL** or **TRANSPORTA-TION,** may be the same.

  - If your stay is overnight, then the expenses go on the Travel Worksheet.
  - If not overnight, the expense is listed on the Transportation line of the Summary C Worksheet.
- If you use your own vehicle, whether for **TRAVEL** or **TRANSPORTATION,** all information goes on the Auto Worksheet.

CHAPTER ELEVEN

Learning the Ropes: Business Education Expenses

Learning can be fun, useful, profitable—and tax deductible. In this chapter I'll show you how to reduce your taxes while learning, whether learning takes place in a classroom; at a workshop; in the field or the theater; via the Internet, podcast, or DVD; or by means of the most ancient of learning tools, the book.

 Reality

After almost a decade in business, Caitlin Caterer is prospering. Never having specialized in any specific type of food, her catering service has always done its best to fill requests for all sorts of cuisine. She has noticed that many of the young professionals moving into her neighborhood are vegetarians. They are prosperous and entertain frequently. She doesn't understand how they can pass up *veau orloff,* but for the sake of her business she wants to be ready, willing, and able to cater to their tastes, and she has concluded that it would benefit her business to be more versed in the art of vegetarian cooking. A chef who accepts very few students has been recommended to her, but his course in meatless cookery is a big-ticket item. After checking with her tax advisor, Caitlin decides to take the course. She has learned that she can deduct the course and the materials required for the course, as well as her transportation there and back. So her out-of-pocket costs will be less than she thought.

THE IRS SAYS ABOUT
Business Education Expenses . . .

You *can deduct* your EDUCATION expenses (including certain related travel expenses) if you can show that the education *maintains or improves skills* required in your trade or business, or it is *required by law* or regulations for keeping your pay, status, or job.

You *cannot deduct* EDUCATION expenses you incur to *meet the minimum requirements* of your present trade or business, or those *that qualify you for a new trade or business.*

 Brilliant Deduction

Let's look at the IRS language from the viewpoint of self-employment. In order for an indie to deduct EDUCATION expenses, he must determine the following:

Part One: Does the course qualify as business education?

Part Two: If the course does qualify, which of the costs related to the education are deductible as business expenses?

Part One: Does It Qualify as Business Education?

As we've just seen, the indie's first step is to determine whether the course, seminar, convention, or workshop qualifies as business education.

Can Harvey Housesitter deduct the expenses of a course on how to care for indoor plants? Can Syd System (who works in his home office and whose misbehaving dog is driving him crazy) deduct the cost of dog obedience training, so that he can work without interruption in peace and quiet?

Qualifying Education

Not all courses qualify as business **EDUCATION** expense. According to the IRS, courses must meet at least **one** of the following tests in order to qualify:

1. The education must be *required by law* in order to keep your present income, status, or job, or

2. The education must be *required by your employer* to keep your present income, status, or job, or

3. The education must *maintain or improve skills* needed in your present work.

Let's look at each of these requirements.

1. **Education required by the law.** Once you have met the minimum educational requirements for your business, you may be legally required to get more education in order to hold on to your present position or status.

Stacy Stockbroker works out of her home office. She has satisfied the minimum requirements for a Series 7 license. To maintain her licensed status, she has to take continuing education courses required by the Securities and Exchange Commission and the National Association of Securities Dealers. Her courses are deductible.

2. **Education required by your employer.** The IRS allows deductions for education required by your employer. Since you are a self-employed and thus your own employer, you have to decide for yourself (and with the help of your tax consultant) whether the deduction will meet the criteria.

   Furthermore, many self-employed professions and businesses are not licensed, and for many no certification is necessary, which means that the education you require of yourself is even more of a judgment call.

   So what do we have to go by? For one thing, the IRS admonition, "in order to be deductible, a business expense must be ordinary and necessary to your profession." What you require of yourself as your own employer is determined by the next criterion, number 3.

3. **Education to maintain or improve your skills.** Education not required by laws or regulations may qualify for deduction if it maintains or improves skills or knowledge required in your present work.

   It doesn't matter whether a course or workshop is academic or vocational in nature; refresher courses, seminars on current developments, and correspondence courses can be included.

Rebecca Repair fixes TV sets, DVD players, radios, and electronic music systems. These technologies are changing so fast that she has subscribed to a service that keeps her up to date by e-mail. She also takes seminars and workshops whenever her schedule permits. The e-mail service and the seminars maintain and improve skills required in her work. She can deduct them.

 Angelo Automend has been fixing car radiators, mufflers, electrical systems, and fuel systems for several years, but he has always sent potential customers elsewhere for accident collision repair. Now Angelo has decided to expand into collision work, but he has to take a course on it at the community college. Would Angelo shock his friends by announcing that he's going to straighten out bent fenders and twisted frames? Of course not—it's a logical development of his business, and he can deduct the cost of the course.

 Sally Shrink, a practicing psychiatrist, is studying at a fully accredited institute to become a psychoanalyst. Since the study maintains and improves skills required in her profession, Sally can deduct the cost of her studies.

You can see that Dr. Sally Shrink and Angelo Automend were able to deduct the cost of their education because it was closely tied to or an expansion of their present work. Even if a freelancer attends a workshop because his business has changed its focus, as long as he's not going into a new trade or business and if the new focus involves the same general work as he's been doing, then the cost of the workshop is deductible.

Caitlin Caterer can deduct the cost of her course in vegetarian cookery, and Harvey Housesitter can deduct the course in indoor plants, but Syd System cannot deduct the cost of sending his rambunctious dog to obedience school.

You are also allowed to deduct the cost of education to maintain your skills while you are temporarily absent or on leave from your business. The IRS defines **temporary** leave of absence to be **a year or less.** For the deduction to qualify, however, you must return to the same general type of business.

 Ned Nutritionist likes children and wants to add more day-care centers to his client list. He leaves his nutrition counseling business to become a full-time graduate student in children's nutrition for two semesters—less than a year. Then he'll pick up his business where he left off. He can deduct the costs of his education.

Eddie Electronic worked as an employee for TV Quick Fix, Inc., where he was assigned to fixing TV sets, though he was qualified to do a lot more. He left the job and took a monthlong course, "Twenty-first-Century Electronics." Shortly after that he started his own business. He may deduct the costs of the course because it was related to his present work, and he returned to work in the same field. Since the IRS has no problem with a switch of employers, Ed's becoming his own boss was OK, too.

If you are absent from your work longer than a year, you cannot deduct the expense of any work-related education.

 Nat Newdad loved his work as advisor to small corporations on how to avoid hostile takeovers. As an independent consultant he enjoyed total flexibility in his work schedule. He wanted to be a full-time father when his first child was born, and he was successful enough to have the wherewithal to take off a year. He finished up his contract with Innovative Ideas Corporation just before Christmas, only days before his daughter was born. He is planning to return to his consulting business after her first birthday. Because the IRS defines temporary absence as one year or less, any seminars that Nat attended to keep current with the corporate community would not be deductible because he's away from his business for more than a year.

Nonqualifying Education

Certain education costs do not qualify for deductions even though they meet some of the criteria we have examined. For example, even if the education is required by law or needed to maintain or improve skills, you *cannot deduct* the costs if:

1. The education is needed to meet minimum education requirements, or

2. The education qualifies you for a new trade or business.

Let's look at these two barriers to qualification.

Disallowed expenses 1: education to meet minimum requirements. You cannot deduct the costs of pursuing the minimum requirements necessary for your profession, trade, or business. It doesn't matter whether these minimum requirements are mandatory because of laws, regulations, or industry standards.

 Raina Realtor quit a dead-end no-future job. She took the six-week real estate course required to get a Realtor's license. The costs of the course are not deductible.

Here's the first exception to the minimum requirements exclusion: If the minimum requirements change while you're in the field, any education costs incurred to meet the new standards are deductible.

 If state law changed and required all Realtors to take an additional course on mortgage financing, Raina would have to take the course before she could get her license renewed. Because she had already met the minimum requirements when she originally got her license, the cost of the course would qualify for deduction.

However, a new applicant for a Realtor's license would have to satisfy the new minimum requirements and could not deduct any of the schooling.

Watch out for the definition of minimum. Just because you are doing the work does not mean that you have met the minimum educational requirements of your trade or business.

Annabelle Architect is attending college with the intention of becoming an architect. To help pay her college expenses, Annabelle freelances for several local architectural firms. She prepares architectural drawings and researches the cost and availability of new materials. Although her college courses in architecture improve the skills she uses in her freelancing, she has not met the minimum job requirements of an architect. Her college education does not qualify for a business expense deduction.

And here's the second exception to the minimum requirements exclusion: Once minimum educational requirements have been met, an indie can deduct the costs of education if he transfers the business to another state where additional testing or more advanced education is necessary for certification.

 Dr. Endie Naturopath's practice was in Connecticut. When she moved to Hawaii, she had to take an exam in order to get licensed in that state. Because Hawaii's exam included a test on homeopathy, an area in which Endie had not concentrated while a doctor in Connecticut, she had to take a refresher course before she took the exam. Endie can deduct the costs of the course.

The IRS considers that once you have met minimum educational requirements in any state in which you practice, any courses you might have to take upon being certified in a new state qualify for deductions.

Disallowed expenses 2: education that qualifies you for a new trade or business. EDUCATION expenses not related to your present trade or business are not deductible.

 Thomas Twocareers, a real estate agent, has decided to become a massage therapist, so he enrolls in an intensive—and expensive—six-month course in his new chosen field. The cost of the course does not qualify for deduction. His career has veered off in an entirely new direction.

Also, courses to prepare for a bar examination or a certified public accountant examination cannot be taken as educational deductions.

Bones of Contention

Whether certain courses or workshops qualify for deduction can be a judgment call.

 After becoming a psychoanalyst, Dr. Shrink decides that the key to understanding the mind lies in computer theory. She takes an intensive course in cybernetics to discover the sources of reason.

Dr. Shrink decides that mind and body are so closely linked that she wants to combine and incorporate both in her work, so she undergoes training in Rolfing, a form of physical therapy that attempts to explore manifestations of neurosis that show up in physical problems.

After the training in Rolfing, she takes a course in nutrition and its effect on behavior psychology.

In all these instances Dr. Shrink and the IRS might each have cause to argue about whether such courses qualify for deduction. My vote goes for a deduction in all three situations.

To Sum Up Qualifying Education

So what have you gleaned from this extensive look at what qualifies as business **EDUCATION?** You know that in order to deduct education costs as a business expense, it is necessary to get beyond the minimum requirements of your field, that you are actively working in or returning to your field, and that the education must be demonstrably related to your field.

Part Two: Which Education Costs Are Deductible?

OK, you've determined that your proposed course, seminar, convention, or workshop does qualify as business **EDUCATION.** But which of the costs related to the education are deductible as business expenses?

The IRS says that if the education qualifies as a deduction, then the following educational expenses are generally deductible as business expenses:

- Tuition, books, supplies, lab fees, and similar items

Brilliant Deduction

  - Other educational expenses such as costs for research activities
  - **TRANSPORTATION** and **TRAVEL** costs

Tuition and supplies, other direct costs

such as paying someone to type your term paper, or admission fees to a presentation where attendance was required by your instructor are all unquestionable **EDUCATION** expenses. However, expenses for transportation and travel can get complex.

TRANSPORTATION costs related to **EDUCATION** expenses include:

- Bus, subway, cab, or other fares
- Use of your own car (See Chapter Ten.)

TRANSPORTATION expenses *do not include* amounts spent for travel, meals, or lodging while away from home overnight. Those are **TRAVEL** expenses. (If you haven't read Chapter Ten, which explains the difference between travel and transportation and travel for educational purposes, be sure to do so.)

The following explains what you can deduct as business **TRANSPORTATION** when getting to and from classes. If the class you're attending is a mile away, you may not want to be bothered with these complicated rules. But if you drive 40 miles each way or your train fare is $30 round-trip to attend class, you might be interested. You decide how well versed you want to be in this area. If it's going to save you a bundle of money, then read on. If not then skip forward ten paragraphs to the discussion of **TRAVEL** costs related to **EDUCATION** expenses.

What the IRS allows for local costs of transportation depends on whether your education is on a temporary or regular basis.

For *education on a temporary basis*—to the IRS that's one year or less—you can deduct the *round-trip* costs of transportation—that is, transportation from your place of business **or from your home** to school and then back. You can deduct the entire round-trip cost regardless of the location of the school, distance traveled, or whether you attend on work or nonwork days.

Here are a few scenarios:

Let's say that your pet-grooming service is your full-time occupation and that you go directly home from your shop every evening. If after arriving home you attend poodle-cutting class nightly for three weeks, you can deduct your daily round-trip **TRANSPORTATION** expenses between home and school.

If on some nights, or every night, you go directly from your shop to school and then home, you can deduct your **TRANSPORTATION** expenses from the shop to school and then home.

If the course were given on six consecutive Mondays, a day that your shop is closed, you can still deduct your round-trip **TRANSPORTATION** expenses in going between home and class.

If you **attend class on a regular basis** rather than on a temporary basis—that means for more than a year—then the IRS will not let you deduct the round-trip costs of your **TRANSPORTATION.**

Instead you may only deduct one-way transportation expenses from your shop to school. If you return home after work and then go to school, your transportation expenses cannot be more than if you had gone directly from your place of business to school.

The same one-way versus round-trip rules apply if you drive your car to class. Be sure to see the previous chapter on business use of **AUTO.**

TRAVEL costs related to **EDUCATION** expenses include:

- Getting to and from the location of the course, seminar, or workshop
- Lodging while going to, coming from, or while at the location
- Meals (subject to the 50 percent limit) while going to and from and while attending the course

Remember the difference between **TRANSPORTATION** and **TRAVEL** is that **TRAVEL** *is overnight.* Travel expenses for qualifying education are treated the same as travel expenses for other business purposes. Many rules and regulations apply to business travel deductions, so once again I urge you to read Chapter Ten on business travel for specifics on deductions. Keep in mind that:

- You cannot deduct expenses for personal activities, such as sightseeing, visiting, or entertaining.
- If you mix business with pleasure, you will have to prorate or exclude certain expenses depending upon where you traveled and for how long.

The following examples illustrate how and to what extent business travel is deductible when it is mixed with personal travel on the same trip.

 Patti Partyplanner's business is in Boston. She traveled to Philadelphia to take a deductible one-week course on security measures for large events. While there, she entertained friends and took a one-day trip to Valley Forge. Since the trip to Philadelphia was mainly for business, she can deduct her round-trip airfare, the transportation related to the course, and meals and lodging for the days of the course. She cannot deduct the transportation or other expenses of her visits with friends or her trip to Valley Forge.

Reality ✓ Estelle has really made a go of her estate sales business in Seattle. She flew to San Francisco for a two-week seminar on new trends in tracking down and marketing antiques. While there, she spent an additional four weeks visiting her mother. Given these facts, her main purpose was clearly not business. Therefore she cannot deduct her airfare or any other expenses during her four-week visit with her mother. She can deduct only her expenses for meals and lodging for the two weeks she attended the seminar and any other seminar-related expenses.

ALERT! Heed not the siren call of certain cruises and conventions that offer seminars or courses as part of their itinerary. Even if these are work related, your deduction for travel may be limited if the travel is by ocean liner, cruise ship, or is held outside the North American area.

ALERT! You may no longer treat travel as a form of education even if it is directly related to your business.

In Chapter Ten I explained that Jack Japanese Instructor may deduct a trip to Japan to take courses in Japanese and Japanese culture or history. He may not deduct the costs of a trip to Japan if he just travels around the country soaking up the culture.

If the trip is primarily a vacation, there is no deduction for travel costs to and from the foreign location. Just because Jack Japanese Instructor took a one-day haiku course during his ten days in Japan does not make the airfare or any of his other expenses deductible. Only the cost of the one-day course is a business expense.

Which Education Records to Keep

You may at some time be called upon to prove that your **EDUCATION** expenses are legitimate business deductions. In addition to canceled checks and receipts that show your expenses, you may also need to prove that the course or workshop itself was a valid business deduction. Therefore, you should also keep papers such as:

- College transcripts
- Course descriptions
- Seminar agenda
- Workshop speaker lists
- Catalogs or brochures
- Scholarship information

If you have attended a workshop that you believe qualifies as **EDUCATION** expenses, keep—in addition to records of the expenses—evidence of the workshop's connection with your business, especially if the connection is a bit wacky or sounds just a trifle too imaginative. If at a later date you can show how that course figured in your business, also put that information in your tax file of the year that you took the expense. For instance, if Dr. Shrink is written about in the local paper as an innovative psychiatrist who incorporated Rolfing into her diagnostic technique, the clipping should be saved for the IRS.

Taking Credit Where Credit Is Due— and Other Tax Benefits

A movement began in the early 1990s to smarten up America—to train, to educate, to teach old dogs new tricks. Self-employeds are included.

Changes in the tax code were made at that time that have given many tax benefits for higher education or vocational school expenses to those who qualify—for the most part, lower- and middle-income Americans. You may not claim more than one type of tax benefit from the same expense. Therefore, you are not allowed to deduct your education costs as a business expense and then use the same expenses for another tax benefit. This is where the knowledge of a tax professional is direly needed, because many calculations may be required to determine which tax treatment does you the most good.

Many education incentives are in the form of *tax credits.* Even though your tax preparer will advise you on and calculate which benefit suits you best, it is important for you to have a grasp of the difference between a business expense deduction and a tax credit and how each may save you some tax money.

Deductions versus tax credits

There is a big difference between a *tax deduction* and a *tax credit.*

A tax **deduction** is subtracted from your income, a benefit to you because your tax is calculated on the amount of your income. A $1,000 deduction reduces your income by $1,000 and, depending upon your tax bracket and state taxes, could save you from zero up to $500 in taxes.

A tax **credit** on the other hand is an amount subtracted directly from your tax. A $300 tax credit reduces your tax by $300; a $1,000 tax credit saves you $1,000 in taxes.

EDUCATION COSTS: Are They Deductible Business Expenses?

Is the education needed to meet the minimum educational requirements of your trade or business?	**YES**	Your education does not qualify.
	NO	Your education qualifies.
Is the education part of a study program that can qualify you in a new trade or business?	**YES**	Your education does not qualify.
	NO	Your education qualifies.
Is the education required by law to keep your present income, status, or job?	**YES**	Your education qualifies.
Does the education maintain or improve skills required in doing your present work?	**YES**	Your education qualifies.

When you have deductible business education expenses, your tax preparer will compare the tax savings of a **deduction** against the tax savings of a **credit.** There are often income limitations on tax credits. That means if your income is over a certain amount, you are not eligible for the tax credit.

Be sure to categorize your **EDUCATION** expenses carefully so that your tax pro can get you the best tax savings for your educational dollar.

Research or Not, It's Deductible

When you become involved in any dealings with the IRS, keep in mind that the agency is a self-contained and distant realm, with its own special terminology and its own arcane definitions for everyday words. Take for instance the meaning that the IRS attaches to the word **research.**

In ordinary English, research is the common element in the following four examples of valid business expenses. In the **MEALS & ENTERTAINMENT** section of Chapter Eight, I used these two examples:

Nadine Novella is writing a feature story on life in the nightclubs of a small city. All expenses associated with her research at the clubs are fully deductible.

Theobald Theater Critic is paid for his drama reviews. When he attends a theatrical performance in his professional capacity, it is not a 50 percent deductible **ENTERTAINMENT** expense, it is a 100 percent deductible **RESEARCH** expense.

And in Chapter Six I gave you two other examples:

- A structural engineer drives through Millionaires' Mile looking at the period architecture of the houses. Since this is research for him, the drive is a business event and the mileage there and back is a business expense.
- Ivan Inventor—of computer games, that is—shouldn't assume that buying someone else's computer game can't be a business expense. Even if he stayed up half the night fighting invaders from another galaxy, he was researching the competition. The purchase of the game is a business deduction.

In each of these examples, my use of the word **research** describes quite clearly the activity that has led to a business expense deduction. But the IRS attaches its own particular meaning to **research.** It speaks in a special language that classifies expenses in its own way—and as far as that agency is concerned, only one of these examples (Ivan Inventor) is categorized as a **RESEARCH** expense. All the other expenses are deductible business expenses, but by IRS definition they are not **RESEARCH.**

THE IRS SAYS ABOUT
Research and Experimental Costs . . .

They are the reasonable costs you incur for activities intended to provide information that would eliminate uncertainty about the development or improvement of a product.

The term "product" includes the following as well as items similar to these:

- Formula
- Invention
- Patent
- Pilot model
- Process
- Technique

In the IRS realm, **RESEARCH & EXPERIMENTAL** costs do not include expenses for any of the following activities:

- Advertising and promotion
- Consumer surveys
- Efficiency surveys
- Management studies
- The acquisition of another's patent, model, or process
- Research in connection with literary, historical, or similar projects

The IRS does consider the costs of developing computer software to be a **RESEARCH & EXPERIMENTAL** cost. Thus, in our above examples, only Ivan Inventor can call his expense **RESEARCH.**

That doesn't mean, however, that the expenses of Nadine Novella, Theobald Theatre Critic, and the engineer who took a drive through Millionaires' Mile cannot be deducted. They are perfectly legitimate deductions—but to the IRS, they are not **RESEARCH** deductions.

If all these other expenses are deductible, does it really matter what we call them? Well, here's an answer you won't like: Sometimes.

For instance, there's a big difference for Theobald Theater Critic. Because were he in a different line of work, going to the theater for business would be an **ENTERTAINMENT** expense and so only 50 percent deductible.

If something by IRS definition is a **RESEARCH** expense, then your tax preparer will have several ways by which she can deduct that expense. Her choice would be determined by your tax situation. This choice of tax treatment is not available for other kinds of expenses.

The IRS provides no guideline as to what to call those other expenses that we call "research." The drive through Millionaires' Mile will show up as an **AUTO** expense deduction when the mileage is added to the rest of the business miles. But what about the others? Over the years I have called them a number of different things and they've never been disallowed for being misnamed. Nadine's nightclub expenses I label as "research" and Theobald's theater ticket I comfortably call "performance admissions." It really doesn't matter what we call them (your tax preparer will make her own choice)—the important point here is for you to know that they are legitimate business expenses and be sure that your preparer understands what may be your unique situation in incurring that expense. Be sure they make it to your tax return, uncut.

Because **RESEARCH** expenses (in the IRS terminology) have a special character, they can be treated in a variety of ways on your tax return. Your tax preparer will want them set apart from other expenses so that she can get you the biggest tax write-off on your return. You might be able to claim a research tax credit. Remember tax credits? A direct write-off against your taxes! If you think you will have **RESEARCH** expenses, it's smart to contact your tax pro *before* you start spending money. She may have some tax-saving advice that works only if you do your spending in a certain way.

CHAPTER TWELVE

Where You Hang Your Hat or Plunk Your Computer

As an indie business, you may work anywhere you want. You may rent an office or studio, purchase an entire building in which to set up shop, or work out of your home—whatever suits your situation. As you'll learn in this chapter, you may also work out of all these locations and deduct expenses for all of them.

Renting Work Space

Renting an office or studio or workshop gives you clear and unchallengeable deductions.

RENT, UTILITIES, cleaning service, parking lot snow removal, **REPAIRS,** etc., are 100 percent deductible business expenses.

Deducting **INSURANCE** payments may be a little tricky, and you'll want to have your insurance bill available to show your tax preparer. This is because you can only deduct the portion of your insurance payment that is for the current year. If your payment covers part of next year, the deduction will have to be prorated. Also, you may not deduct your rent security payment. (It's not an expense because you're going to get it back. But it is an expense if you

don't get it back.) Except for insurance and security deposits, rented office, studio, or workshop deductions are clear-cut.

Owning a Business Building

If you purchase a building for your business, the deduction is more complicated. In addition to all the typical expenses such as **UTILITIES, REPAIRS, REAL ESTATE TAXES,** etc., you get to write off the cost of the building—but not all at once. A commercial building is a capital asset, and its cost must be depreciated over thirty-nine years. Let's say you purchased a $39,000 building in an office park (no land came with the purchase) and you gave the seller a check for $39,000; your deduction for the year of purchase and for the next thirty-eight years would be $1,000 per year. That deduction is called a *depreciation* expense, and your tax pro will calculate the amount based upon the purchase information that you provide to her.

If you purchased an old ranch, with a large shed that you could use for a workshop and great fields where you could roam while sweeping the cobwebs out of your brain, it would work like this: You cannot deduct the cost of the land. Assume you paid $104,000 for the ranch. A real estate tax bill shows that 25 percent of the cost is for the fields and meadows and 75 percent is for the building. Because you can only deduct the cost of the shed and not the cost of the land, the cost of the building must be calculated. In this case the cost of the building (75 percent of $104,000) is $78,000. Depreciating that over thirty-nine years—you can think of it as dividing the cost by thirty-nine—gets you a whopping $2,000 per-year depreciation deduction.

Whether you pay for the entire building when purchased, which is highly unlikely, or you obtain a mortgage to finance your purchase, you still get the same one thirty-ninth of the cost of the building as a depreciation deduction. When you have a mortgage, you also get a deduction for the mortgage interest paid for the year. That gives you a two-part deduction: One part is the one thirty-ninth cost of the building, the other part is the mortgage interest paid. These two parts do not—unless coincidentally—equal your monthly mortgage payment. Many indies mistakenly think that the mortgage payment is the deductible amount.

WHATTA**CONCEPT**!

The impact of taxes on a mortgage rate

Deducting mortgage interest as a business expense reduces the cost of a mortgage considerably. Here's some arithmetic on a 10 percent and a 5 percent mortgage to show the tax savings:

Mortgage rate:	10%	5%
Mortgage balance:	$100,000	$100,000
Finance charge for the year	$10,000	$5,000
Combined tax rate (federal plus SE tax plus state)	30%	30%
Tax savings from mortgage deduction		
(30% x $10,000)	$3,000	
(30% x $5,000)		$1,500
Actual mortgage rate paid		
($10,000 - $3,000 = $7,000 / $100,000)	7%	
($5,000 - $1,500 = $3,500 / $100,000)		3.5%

Unconventional Work-space Arrangements

- A speech therapist gets to use his mother-in-law's casita in exchange for taking care of the grounds.
- Nancy, of Nancy's Nuts, uses a local bakery's oven to roast nuts at night in exchange for providing the bakery with little bags of nuts to sell as point-of-purchase items at the register.
- A photography designer has the use of a business's darkroom in exchange for recommending clients.

Many indies make creative arrangements to obtain work space for no outlay of money. For others, there may be a cost—Nancy pays for the nuts and spices that she gives to the bakery. But she has no deductible **RENT** or **LEASE** expense. These are all legitimate arrangements.

Office or Studio or Workshop in the Home

Here we run smack into one of the most persistent old husbands' tales: Don't take the **OFFICE IN THE HOME** deduction; it's a red flag and the IRS will be at your door.

THE IRS SAYS ABOUT
Office in the Home . . .

In recent years the IRS "has uncovered a number of abusive home-based business tax schemes that erroneously assert that individuals can operate any type of unprofitable 'business' out of their homes, and then claim personal expenses as business expenses." The IRS "will continue to focus . . . enforcement efforts in this area."

So what's an indie to do? I'll tell you what to do: If you use your home for your self-employed business, then, by golly, don't be afraid to take the deduction. By deducting expenses for your home work space, you'll pay less tax. The only caveat: Play by the rules.

The IRS has relaxed the rules in recent years, and they are simpler than you may have been led to believe. There are now only three home office rules.

Rule 1: Exclusive Use

The part of your home used for business must be used exclusively for business.

Lily Legal writes her briefs at the dining room table but also has dinner parties there. She has to forgo any deduction for the dining room.

Victor Visual and his wife, Faye Fabrique, a textile designer, share the same studio in the home. Neither gets the deduction because neither has exclusive use. (It's unfair, but it is correct.)

Exceptions to Rule 1

The IRS allows a few exceptions to the rule that requires that home work space be devoted **exclusively** to business.

An indie who needs *a place to store inventory or product samples* and whose home is the only *fixed* location of her business can deduct that storage space even if it is also used for other purposes.

 Betty Bestow sells most of her gift baskets at Christmas, Easter, and Mother's Day, often at flea markets, home parties, and via her Web site. Just before the holidays, her inventory is very high. She stores it all in her basement. But Betty has two teenagers, and a lot of their personal items end up in that part of the basement. That's OK. Although the kids throw their stuff in there, Betty can deduct the portion of the basement used for storage as long as she has no other storage facility.

Entrepreneurs who run day-care centers are also exempt from the exclusive use rule. If the area is used as a service business involving the care of children, the elderly, or the sick, it can also be used for personal purposes without forfeiting a deduction. However, the deduction is allocated based on how many hours out of a twenty-four-hour day the area is used for these business purposes.

ALERT! If your state requires licenses or certification for daycare, you must have obtained that license or other certification or you cannot deduct home expenses.

 Sophie Soccermom watches her neighbor's children in her home and charges the going day-care rate. She's saving the money she makes for her daughter's college costs. Although Sophie is a bona fide self-employed, she does not, alas, have the required license approval by her state and so she cannot deduct any home office expense for her day-care business. She may deduct all her other expenses.

Rule 2: Used on a Regular Basis

The part of your home used for business must be used on a regular basis for business.

 Clement Creator has a rented studio in town. He also has great light in a back room of his house. The room is always locked and seldom used. Once in a while he brings a potential buyer to his home to look at a painting and he uses the back room for the viewing. This is not regular use, so he cannot deduct the use of that room as a business expense.

Rule 3: Principal Place of Business

Your home office or studio or workshop must be your principal place of business. For some indies, that needs no explanation.

 Bulky Benjamin runs his watch repair business out of his basement and only out of his basement. There's no question that the basement is his principal place of business. He can deduct.

But for many indies, the IRS term *principal place of business* is misleading. If you have more than one place of business, one of them may qualify for home office status if it fits *any* of the following three criteria:

- It is where you perform *administrative tasks.*
- It's a place where you *meet* *clients or patients or customers.*
- It's a *separate structure.*

The Place Where You Perform Administrative Tasks

The IRS says that for your home to qualify as a "principal" place of business, in addition to the room or area in your home being used *exclusively* (rule #1) and *regularly* (rule #2) for your business, it merely has to be *the place where you conduct substantial administrative or management activities.*

The operative word is "substantial." It connotes activities like bookkeeping, phone calls, e-mailing, ordering supplies, or setting up appointments. Not a phone call now and then, or every once in a while bringing your laptop into the den to do some e-mailing.

 Dr. Endie Naturopath runs a successful holistic health practice. Bob, her bookkeeper, does all the recordkeeping at his home office. Endie often sets up patient appointments on her cell phone while on the road. She does minimal paperwork at her rented office in the city, where she meets with patients and presents a "professional face." She has three children and likes to spend as much time as possible around the house, so she does most of her administrative and management chores at her home office, including patient callbacks, supplement supplies ordering, patient chart reviews, and notes. Endie can deduct her home office.

The Place Where You Meet Clients or Patients or Customers

 Celia Ceramist rents a neighbor's garage as her work studio. It's always a mess. She has set up the small sunroom in her home as her showcase studio. Potential buyers come there by appointment to view her work. Although her works also show at a number of galleries throughout the United States, Celia can deduct the sunroom as a home office.

A Separate Structure

 Kyla Chiropractor shares an office with an acupuncturist. They alternate days. Kyla does not keep patient records at the office. Each morning she brings from home that day's patient folders. She keeps all her patient records, and her professional library, in a small barn on her farmland home. Kyla can deduct the barn.

Office in the Home Deductions: What, How, and When

Let's look at the various aspects of an actual home office deduction.

What's a home? Your home may be any kind of residence: house, apartment, condominium, cooperative, houseboat, mobile home.

What portion of your home and which expenses can you deduct? All expenses for the portion of your residence used for business are deductible. That includes rent, repairs, utilities, security system, and upkeep expenses. If you own the home, deductions include mortgage interest and real estate taxes. If for instance 20 percent of your home is used for business, then you can deduct 20 percent of all these expenses.

How do you calculate the business-use portion of your home? There are two ways to calculate the business space as a portion of your home.

First method: Measure square feet. What is the square footage of the area or areas used for business? You calculate square feet by multiplying the width of the room or business-use area by the length of the room. A 15-foot by 20-foot room is a 300-square-foot room. You calculate the percentage of business use by dividing the business square feet by the total square footage of your home. If the office space is 300 square feet and the entire apartment is 1,500 square feet, the business use is 20 percent (300 / 1,500 equals 20 percent). You must include attic, basement, and garage in your calculation of total square feet if these areas are heated and used as general living or storage quarters.

Second method: Count the rooms. If rooms are of approximately the same size, then you can divide the rooms used for business use by the total number of rooms. One room out of four would be 25 percent. Even if rooms are not the same size, you can still use this method. For instance, two bathrooms may equal one regular-size room, or a large living room may count for two rooms. Remember the attic and basement in this method, too.

A business area doesn't have to be an entire room. A part of a room can be taken as a deduction, if it is used only for business. In your calculations remember to include closet space where you store office supplies or the shelves in the living room that stack only your business books. A 12-inch-deep shelf that runs for 6 feet is another 6 square feet of space. (1 foot times 12 feet equals 12 square feet.)

If you take an **OFFICE IN THE HOME** deduction, I recommend to you as I do to my clients: Take photos of the business area. The space you use this year may be different than the space you use next year after the baby arrives or Grandma moves out. If your tax return is questioned, your photos will provide proof of business use for the year in dispute. A calendar or newspaper in the photo showing the date adds to your evidence. Keep the photos in your tax file for that year.

What costs can you deduct? Expenses are broken into three groups. The first I call *entire* (the IRS calls them indirect expenses). These are costs that pertain to the entire residence: rent or mortgage interest, real estate tax, utilities like heat and water, repair of a roof. The next group is for expenses related to the *business area only* (the IRS calls these direct expenses), like the repair of a window in the studio, or the purchase of a lock for the office door. The third group includes *personal expenses* you cannot deduct, such as plumbing repairs in the master bathroom or a chimney sweeping of the family-room fireplace.

You cannot deduct lawn care unless there is an area that is for the exclusive use of your business. The housekeeper that you have agreed to pay "off the books"—the one who takes cash only—cannot be deducted as an expense. You can deduct the costs for a legitimate cleaning service or a housekeeper for whom you pay all payroll taxes.

What about the price of the residence itself? Just as you may deduct the cost of a commercial building that you own for your business, you may also deduct the cost of the business portion of your residence. First the cost basis of the entire home must be established, then the business portion of that basis must be calculated. This would be a good time to go back to Chapter Seven, Up and Running, and reread the Whatta Concept! about capital expenses and basis.

A home purchase includes more than the price of the house. The other charges, often called closing costs, add to the cost—also known as basis—of the house. These include things like attorney fees, inspection costs, title insurance, etc.

Your tax preparer will need to calculate the total basis of your house in order to determine the

basis of the business portion of your residence. In Chapter Twenty-three you will see a Residence or Real Estate Purchase Worksheet and a Capital Improvements Worksheet. Your information on both worksheets will aid your tax preparer in calculating the basis of your home office.

Every capital improvement also increases the home's basis. A capital improvement is something new, something beyond a repair, something that becomes part of the structure. A new roof, a new bathroom, adding windows in the attic—these are capital improvements.

Repair of a broken attic window or a bathroom faucet is not a capital improvement.

As a tax deduction, **REPAIRS** are more beneficial. The entire cost of a repair is deductible in the year paid. The business-use portion of a roof repair is an immediate deduction, whereas the business portion of a new roof must be written off over thirty-nine years.

 Miles Mingus's CD went gold and he got a sizable recording contract. He decided to spend the contract money rather than send it to Uncle Sam. Boy, was he sorely disappointed upon finding out that the $20,000 studio remodeling job wasn't going to get him a big tax write-off.

 Karen Coolcuts spent her summer patching plaster and sanding floors, part of the overhaul of what was once a bedroom and master bathroom that would soon serve as her new hair-styling salon. Just because some of the work was more "repair the old" than "install the new" doesn't make it a **REPAIRS** expense. That Karen also installed new wiring and plumbing and gave **new use** to what was once part of a residence makes the

 entire remodeling job a **CAPITAL IMPROVEMENT.** The $80,000 cost will have to be depreciated over thirty-nine years.

ALERT! Deducting **OFFICE IN THE HOME** expense for a residence that you own may have an impact on the amount of taxes you pay when you sell your home. The impact has been minimized by new regulations regarding depreciation of a home office, and almost always the home office deduction outweighs any capital gains tax it may trigger when the home is sold. Even so, be sure your tax pro takes the sale consequences into consideration when preparing your return.

To Sum Up Office in the Home

Forget the old husbands' tale. You're thinking now like an indie. Yours is an honest, serious business, and it is your obligation to take every deduction you can. Whether you rent, own, or use a home office for your independent venture, take the deduction.

CHAPTER THIRTEEN

Here to Stay or Gone Tomorrow: Equipment, Inventory, and Supplies

Things used in your business. This area of expenses always stumps an indie. Is it an office supply? Or is it equipment? And what's this thing called COGS? The stapler you bought will last more than a year. Does that make it "equipment"? And your brother said you'd better have a year-end inventory amount before you go see your accountant, but you're not sure what inventory is.

Well, don't fret. All you must know is this: If you use it in your business, it's a deductible business expense. The tricky part is how the expense gets written off on your tax return—all in one year, over a period of years, or perhaps when you sell the business. But you won't be making those calls; leave the fretting to your tax professional.

Nevertheless, the better you understand the distinctions, the better will be your records and the easier will be your tax return preparation (thus reducing your tax prep fee) and the likelier that you will not miss any deductions. So let's take a look at how to group the things you use in your business.

Equipment

The **EQUIPMENT** expense may be the easiest to understand. If you purchase a tangible item (that means something you can touch and, very likely, that you, or you and some friends, can actually pick up), and if this tangible item will last longer than a year, it's probably a piece of **EQUIPMENT.** When is it not **EQUIPMENT?** Different tax preparers answer this question differently. A desk, a copier, a massage table, a drafting board, a display case, a computer are all considered **EQUIPMENT.** Some years back I delineated **EQUIPMENT** as something lasting longer than a year and costing more than $100. Now I

say it's something that lasts longer than a year and costs more than $200. By that definition, a stapler is not **EQUIPMENT,** it's a **SUPPLY.**

EQUIPMENT is also called a "business asset." It's an asset because it adds value to the worth of your business. If you are a public relations consultant, let's say your business is you, on the phone. That's all there is. When you buy a desk on which to put your phone and lean your elbows, you now have some tangible thing of value that is part of your business. The desk is a business asset. Using my definition of **EQUIPMENT,** if you bought the desk at a garage sale for $20, it's not **EQUIPMENT**—it's a **SUPPLY.**

EQUIPMENT, unlike **SUPPLIES,** gets deducted over a period of years. This is called depreciating the asset. The number of years for depreciating is called the asset's useful life and is determined by IRS classification on the type of equipment. For instance, a computer gets written off over five years because that's how long the IRS says it will be used in a typical business setting. Yeah, right, five years. Do we know any solo who has used the same computer in his business for five years if he could afford to buy a new one? A desk is depreciated over seven years.

Depreciation is complicated, arbitrary, and not a good conversation starter at a cocktail party. Do not try to figure it out unless mastering it is part of your total career plan. Here are the main points you need to know about **EQUIPMENT** and depreciation:

- If it lasts more than a year and costs more than $200, it's **EQUIPMENT.**

- Be prepared to give your tax preparer the date of purchase.

- If you use the **EQUIPMENT** for personal as well as business use, you can only deduct as a business expense the portion used

for business. You will need to present your preparer with a use breakdown. (I'll explain how to do that a little later.)

- Even though **EQUIPMENT** gets depreciated over a specified number of years, there are special allowances that permit 30, 50, and 100 percent deductions in the year of purchase. This can be a huge tax savings! If you will spend a substantial amount on **EQUIPMENT** in any one year, discuss your purchase with your tax pro *before* your purchase. What's a substantial amount? Depends on your business, your income, and your other expenses. If in doubt, call your professional.

Sometimes a **REPAIR** to a piece of equipment or business asset is classified not as a **REPAIR** but as **EQUIPMENT.** If the repair is not ordinary maintenance but is an improvement to the equipment and adds to the value of it or prolongs its useful life, then the cost of the repair will have to be depreciated. If you took the $20 desk that you bought at the garage sale and had it reglued and refinished and set off with a custom-cut glass top for a cost of $800, then the entire $820 would be depreciated as the cost of the desk.

Both Business and Personal Use

In the beginning of Chapter Nine, I go into detail on how to handle something you use both in your business and personally. Typical mixed-use expenses are telephone, Internet service, car, DVD player, and computer. If you or someone else uses a piece of business **EQUIP-MENT** for personal reasons, the cost of that **EQUIPMENT** will have to be allocated. If you get to use the family computer for business only after the kids are asleep, and that usage amounts to three hours of the computer's nine-hour work-day, then your business use is only one-third (three-ninths). If the computer cost $2,700, then your **EQUIPMENT** expense will be $900 (one-third of $2,700). In situations like this the IRS expects a log of computer use, such as a pad next to the computer showing name, purpose, date, time in, and time out. This is a very difficult or, let's be frank, just about impossible procedure to fol-low. If you cannot have a computer for business use only—which is the easiest solution—then you'll have to make prorating calculations. You can try tracking use for one day a week for a couple of weeks, then use that percent for the entire year. Or maybe just clock in when you use the computer for business and take that percent of an eighteen-hour day. That assumes the entire family sleeps a minimum of six hours. If there are four users, then maybe you'll want to simply take one-fourth as business use.

And what if you have a *business* computer? There's little doubt that at some time it will be used for a personal reason. Whether it's finding an old schoolmate or researching the price of a refrigerator or keeping your bookkeeping—both business and personal—on computer, you will need to come up with some arguable percent of business use. If you decide 5 percent personal use, well then, other than throwing the I Ching or the dice, you need to be able to show the IRS how you came up with that figure.

While we're on the subject of personal and business use, there are many typically personal or household items you might not think of as business equipment. Think again.

Rob Rolf washes and dries all the sheets and towels that he uses in his massage business in his home appli-ances. That means a percent of the cost of his washer and dryer is a business **EQUIPMENT** expense.

Musician Miles Mingus has a superb music system set up for listening and recording. Of course, it's a business deduction.

Tessie Tripp bought a DVD player and a camcorder. She views travel DVDs and makes videos of events on some of her tours. If she also uses the camcorder to tape family events, she'll have to allocate some of the cost of the **EQUIPMENT** to personal use.

Converting from Personal to Business Use

Many independent professionals migrate to self-employment from the joys of hobbyland or from work as an employee. Caitlin Caterer came to her profession when her kids entered school and by turning her joy of cooking for friends into a profitable business. Eddie Elec-tronic went from selling himself short while working for someone else to selling his service for himself and keeping all the profit. Both these indies started their sole proprietorships with equipment and supplies that they had purchased for private use. Caitlin had a significant culinary library that she began accumulating before she went into the catering business. Eddie had more electronic testing equipment and software than many who had been in business for years. Both Caitlin and Eddie used these things in their new business venture. And they could write off the costs of their personal-to-business-use equipment and supplies. Here's how:

They need to look at each thing as they would were they buying it used from a thrift shop or on the Web, for example. If Eddie, over the years, paid thousands of dollars for his equipment and software but could now sell it all at a flea market for $900, then he treats these items as a $900 purchase for his business. If Caitlin, over the years, paid $2,000 for her book collection but now, because many of the books are out of print, could sell her culinary library online for $2,800, she would get a library deduction for her new business in the amount of $2,000. Why less than it's worth? Because you get, as a deduction, the lower of your cost or fair market value at the time it went into use in your business.

 If you are moving your equipment from the family room to your new office, be sure to use the Equipment Worksheet as an aid in calculating your deduction.

Inventory and Cost of Goods Sold

The word "inventory" is often used when what is really meant is "cost of goods sold." **COST OF GOODS SOLD,** or **COGS,** is just that: your cost for

 the items or materials that went into the items that you sold. An **INVENTORY** is a record or accounting of things on hand. If you're having a party and want to know if there's enough soda or paper plates, you might check the pantry and get a list of the number of plates and the number of cans and flavors of soda. This list would be an **INVENTORY** of party supplies.

 Anton Antique frequents estate sales, where he buys much of what he sells. If he pays $200 for a vase that he then sells for $450, his **COGS** is $200.

 Wooly Weaver buys all the wool that goes into his rugs from a local shepherd. He may buy $2,000 worth of wool, and although his sales ran around $10,000, he still had about half the wool he'd purchased stored in the bin. Wooly's **COGS** for that year was $1,000 (one-half of $2,000).

 Clarissa Clothier purchases one hundred fuzzy bunnies at $2 each to give away with each pair of children's pajamas she sells. The $200 purchase (one hundred fuzzy bunnies times $2) becomes part of her **INVENTORY.** If she gives away twenty-five bunnies, then her **COST OF GOODS SOLD** is $50 (twenty-five fuzzies times $2).

INVENTORY is an accounting of the cost of supplies on hand. In Wooly's case it was zero at the beginning of the year. He then added to his inventory by a $2,000 purchase of wool. At

year-end his **INVENTORY** balance was $1,000.

Anton keeps an accurate list of all purchases. As he sells each piece, he notes it as sold on his "in-house" list. At the end of the year he adds up the cost of all the pieces sold to come up with his yearly **COGS.**

The only items that become part of **INVENTORY** are those items that will eventually be sold as a typical function of your business. Sometimes packaging is included.

THE IRS SAYS ABOUT

Inventory . . .

An **INVENTORY** is a thoroughly detailed and itemized list of all material goods you have on hand to sell, or what will become part of the merchandise you will sell, with the values indicated.

There are many ways to calculate inventory. It depends on your kind of business, the amount of your gross receipts, whether you are a cash basis or an accrual basis taxpayer (see

the Whatta Concept! about cash versus accrual recordkeeping in the next chapter), and what kinds of recordkeeping suits your style. This is an area that you must discuss with your tax professional. You need guidance on this from the very beginning.

Supplies

So, if it's not **EQUIPMENT** and not part of your **COST OF GOODS SOLD,** the only thing left is **SUPPLIES.** There are **OFFICE SUPPLIES** and then there are just plain business **SUPPLIES.** Don't get hung up on the distinction between these two because they get deducted in the same way on your tax return.

 Brilliant Deduction

OFFICE SUPPLIES are those items that typical offices use: paper, ink, CDs, staplers. Business **SUPPLIES** are those items specific to your business: sheets to a masseur, tissues to a psychologist, maps to a tour director, seed and fertilizer to a landscaper.

CHAPTER FOURTEEN

Write-off Wrap-up: Business Expenses with a Twist

Thus far in Part II, we have examined a broad range of business expenses. In this chapter we look somewhat more briefly at other expenses not previously covered. There are also guidelines for distinguishing between a few valid and invalid deductions.

On federal Schedule C: Profit or Loss from

Business, in the expenses section, the IRS lists expenses that it regards as typical of sole proprietors. The final line in that section is labeled "Other Expenses." Among my clients—and my guess is that for you as well—many business expenses fit nowhere else.

Of the expenses I haven't yet presented, I'll

first go over those specifically listed on Schedule C. Then we'll look at the ones that end up on the Other Expenses lines of the tax return.

Expenses that appear specifically on Schedule C:

- INSURANCE (does not include medical insurance)
- INTEREST
- LEGAL & PROFESSIONAL SERVICES
- REPAIRS & MAINTENANCE
- TAXES AND LICENSES

And the others:

- BAD DEBTS
- BUSINESS BANK ACCOUNT FEES AND CREDIT CARD FEES
- CLOTHING/UNIFORMS/COSTUMES AND THEIR CARE; HAIR AND MAKEUP
- DUES, MEMBERSHIPS, ADMISSIONS, AND FEES
- PUBLICATIONS

And then there are the "other" expenses that the IRS doesn't allow at all—with rare exception:

- Penalties, fines, bribes, and kickbacks
- Contributions

Schedule C Expenses

Let's look at some of the expenses listed on Schedule C that I have not covered elsewhere in the book.

Insurance Premiums

You cannot deduct personal insurance, such as life insurance on yourself. Nor can you deduct the premiums for insurance that pays you for lost earnings due to sickness or disability. This is usually called disability insurance. Sometimes a disability policy will include as part of the premium a portion for business overhead expenses—rent, utilities, etc.—that continue during a period of illness or injury. That portion of the premium is a deductible business expense.

All *business* INSURANCE is deductible and includes the following:

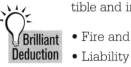
Brilliant Deduction

- Fire and theft
- Liability
- Malpractice
- Business interruption
- Coverage for a business vehicle
- All insurance for employees

What about deducting *health* insurance premiums? We're talking about premiums for medical, dental, and long-term care for self-employeds and their families that is paid by the self-employed and not paid through an employer's plan (for instance, via a spouse's job).

They are not business expenses. You may deduct 100 percent of the cost of health insurance (there is a limitation on long-term care premiums) paid by you, but not as a business expense. Premiums are deducted as an **adjustment to income.** An *adjustment to income* provides a much smaller tax advantage than a direct deduction against business income.

That tax advantage—a direct business deduction for the cost of health insurance—is currently enjoyed by the Callous Corporation and other big guys, while it's denied to indies. That's unfair, of course, but federal and state tax codes generally treat self-employed people unfairly. However, there's renewed talk in Washington about allowing indies to deduct health insurance as a business expense. It hasn't happened yet, but it's possible that the tax laws and regs might be changed before this new edition is in the bookstores. So check with your tax pro.

Finance Charges

You may deduct as **INTEREST** expense all finance charges on business loans, or personal loans if used for a business purpose. You will need to show that the loan was used for business, not a vacation in the Bahamas.

Likewise the business portion of credit card interest is deductible. You must be able to substantiate that the card was used for business for the portion of business interest that you are deducting. Unless you enjoy number puzzles, this will be a burdensome chore. You'll need to decide whether the amount of work calculating the business expense is worth the small tax benefit. I suggest using one credit card for all **big** business purchases.

Home equity or line-of-credit finance charges are deductible as **INTEREST** expense, but again, you must be able to show that the loan was used for business purposes.

The mortgage finance charge on a business building is of course a business deduction. Mortgage interest on the part of your personal residence used for business will show up on the Studio or Office in the Home Worksheet. And the finance charge for the business portion of your vehicle used for business will be deducted on the Auto Worksheet.

While writing this book I had to check a number of points with the IRS, which I did by calling its Small Business/Self-employed Unit at (800) 829–4933. You may find this number useful if you need answers, and I expect you'll find the people friendly and personable. Various people specialize in varied areas depending on the topic and the complexity or unusual nature of the question. Often the person you ask won't be able to answer your question but will have someone else get an answer back to you. Sometimes the answers aren't a straightforward yes or no. Here's an example:

Until a few years ago, student loan interest was not a deductible personal expense. Now it is deductible as an **adjustment to income.** So my logic works this way. If an **EDUCATION** expense meets the criteria for a deductible business expense, then any student loan interest acquainted with that specific **EDUCATION** expense is a deductible business **INTEREST** expense. I ran my idea by the "tax law specialist" at the IRS Small Business department. This was his conclusion: "I see your logic, but I don't know if it's deductible." I asked him how to find out. His response: "Through an audit." I said that if my client borrowed money from his brother to take a business course, and he paid back his brother with interest, the interest was a business **INTEREST** expense. Right? "Right," he said. So then I'm going to tell my clients and readers that the student loan interest is a deductible business **INTEREST** expense. He suggested I do that. So I have been taking that deduction for my clients. So far there hasn't been an audit of a return that includes this deduction, so I can't tell you if the IRS agrees with me.

Legal and Professional Services

LEGAL & PROFESSIONAL SERVICES for attorneys and accountants that directly relate to the operation of your business are deductible as business expenses.

Whether the fees come out of a zoning case, a lawsuit with a client, or a dispute with the government about business taxes owed, all are business deductions. Fees for services in a business-related lawsuit—win, lose, or draw—are deductible. Professional fees incurred in negotiating a business contract or in registering a copyright are deductible business expenses. Here's a reliable test of whether professional fees are deductible: Will the outcome affect the bottom line of your business? If the answer is yes or maybe, you can take the deduction. With that in mind, what about the fee you paid a lawyer for your will? Clearly, it's not a business deduction but a personal expense. (By the way, it's not a personal tax deduction either.)

Perhaps the most obvious deductions are bookkeeping and tax preparation fees. You cannot deduct the cost of the preparation of your entire tax return. Your preparer will allocate a portion to the business part of your return.

Your tax preparer will scrutinize any legal fees you pay to acquire or set up your business, or to acquire a business asset, to determine how they must be treated on your return. The biggest misconception: Indies assume that if

they paid many thousands of dollars to an attorney to help set up a business, the entire amount can be deducted in the first year. No way. Check out Chapter Seven to get a grasp of how these fees are deducted.

Repairs and Maintenance

This one seems like a straightforward deduction. Your computer crashes and you take it to be fixed; the expense is a **REPAIR** deduction. You purchase a one-year service contract on your new giclée printer; it's a **REPAIR** expense. You hire a rug shampoo service to get your office looking spic and span; that's a **MAINTENANCE** expense.

Any upkeep that keeps your business premises, property, or equipment in a normal efficient operating condition is a deductible **REPAIRS & MAINTENANCE** expense. However, if such care adds to the value or usefulness of the property or equipment, the expense will have to be written off over a number of years. This is a judgment call for your tax preparer to make.

Taxes as an Expense

In Part V you will read about the taxes you must pay as a sole proprietor. Here we'll look at the kinds of **TAXES** that are deductible business expenses.

Various kinds of taxes incurred in operating your business are generally deductible. How and when to deduct taxes in your business depends on the type of tax.

Any sales tax you pay on things used in your business is treated the same as the item purchased. For instance, sales tax or gross receipts tax on office supplies is deducted as part of **SUPPLIES** expense. The same goes for a tax on a computer purchase; it becomes part of the **EQUIPMENT** expense.

If you collect sales or gross receipts tax on services or products that you sell, you have a choice of how to handle that inflow of money. IRS publications tell you not to include it as income and not to deduct it as an expense. But for many indies it is much easier to include it as income and then tally up their checks to the local government to determine their sales tax expense. How you handle this is up to you as long as you are consistent. If you do not claim the sales tax as income, be sure that you do not deduct the amount you forward, or pay, to the state or city as an expense.

Here are some other taxes that may be deducted as business expense:

- Excise taxes
- Local occupational taxes
- Personal property tax on property used in your business
- Payroll taxes paid for your employees
- Real estate tax on business-use property

You cannot deduct federal or state *income* taxes as business expenses. However, city or state *business taxes,* such as the New York City Unincorporated Business Tax, is a deductible business expense. If your local government requires a commercial rent tax, that too is deductible.

In Part V you will see that you get to deduct one-half of the self-employment (SE) tax that you pay; however, it is not a business expense. It is deducted as an **adjustment to income** and helps lower your taxable income.

Other Expenses

The preceding expense categories are all specifically named on your Schedule C. Now for some of the items that go on the Other Expenses lines of your Schedule C:

Business Bad Debts

The concept of **BAD DEBTS** is confusing. If I get stiffed by a client or customer, most sole proprietors think, I can write the bill off as a business expense. Unfortunately that's not how it works.

You can only deduct an unpaid fee as an expense if you've already claimed it as income. And in the **cash method** for recording income, which most sole proprietors use, an unpaid fee from a client was never recorded as income in the first place—in which case there's no deduction when you give up on the "friendly reminders," call off your collection attorney, and throw in the towel.

You may, of course, deduct any expenses incurred for that in-the-red client, such as telephone and travel, but you cannot deduct the value of your time and your services as a business expense.

Woody Awlwood put a lot of time and materials into a new railing for Shifty Scofflaw's beach house. He billed

Cash vs. accrual recordkeeping

As a self-employed in business, you get to choose when to report your income and expenses. Don't get too excited—it's not as liberal a choice as it sounds.

You may opt for a **cash basis** method of bookkeeping. This is one that claims income when it is received and deducts an expense when it is paid.

Or you may choose an **accrual basis.** This bookkeeping method claims income when the client is billed, regardless of when the client pays you. You deduct an expense when you become liable for it, which is usually when you get the bill. You must use the same method for both income and expenses. The cash method is simpler and is used by most self-employeds.

Shifty $5,000, sent a half-dozen "friendly reminders," and tried a collection attorney, but Shifty hasn't responded and Awlwood knows he'll never get a dime. Since he uses the cash basis, Awlwood never claimed the $5,000 as income and can't deduct it.

Reality Frank Boyd White runs his architectural business using the accrual method. He billed Diners Delight $7,500 for preliminary design drawings two years ago. That's also when he claimed the $7,500 as income. Construction on the highway fronting the diner caused so much traffic congestion that business for the entire strip mall plummeted.

Diners Delight went out of business. Mr. White can write off the $7,500 as a business **BAD DEBT**.

Business Bank Account Fees and Credit Card Fees

Yes, these fees are deductible business expenses if—but only if—they are for your business. If you have only one checking account for both business and personal use, you will have to prorate the fees. A bounced check fee charged for a client's bad check is of course a business expense.

The same holds for a safe deposit box fee. If the box contains only business papers and CD backup of your business creations, then deduct the whole thing. If your Mom's turquoise necklace is stashed in there, too, prorate you must.

Be careful about credit card "fees." Often a credit card company will call a finance charge a "fee." It's trying to trick you into thinking that you're paying less interest that you actually are. Interest charges belong in the **INTEREST** expense category, not in Other Expenses.

Work Clothes and Uniforms and Their Care; Hair and Makeup

UNIFORMS are deductible. But what about the only three-piece suit that you own, which you wear only to meetings with important clients? No, it is not a business **WORK CLOTHES** deduction: Although you may feel like you're in uniform, the IRS considers it street clothing. Buying a whole new wardrobe to replace your jeans and T-shirts so that you can look the part of a prosperous business owner won't get you a deduction either. Streetwear-type business clothing must have your business name on it—and not held on by a safety pin or Velcro—in order to be deductible.

Nonstreet clothing such as a tuxedo or an evening dress purchased for a presentation are business expenses, as long as you don't wear them to your weekly block parties with friends and neighbors.

If you are a performer, the same rules apply. If you can wear the clothing as ordinary streetwear, it is not a business expense. So toe shoes are deductible. But tights? You see them every day on the street. The amount of income you make as a performer and what kind of backup you have proving your professionalism will influence which and how much performance wear you can deduct. Do you have posters showing you arabesquing in pink tights? Is there a photo of you in your oversize business suit and orange wig doing clown tricks for the school assembly? This is something you will need to discuss with your tax preparer.

Required **PROTECTIVE CLOTHING**—such as hard hats, safety shoes, work gloves, and rubber boots—is deductible.

If any clothing does fall into the narrow groove of special business attire, then the care and upkeep of that clothing is also a business expense.

There is an exception. You may deduct the cost of dry cleaning and laundry of all your clothes while on a business trip. You may deduct the first cleaning bill after your return for clothing used while traveling. But don't get too creative and save all your winter's dirty clothes for cleaning the day after you return from a three-day business trip.

Hair styling and **HAIR-CARE** costs and **MAKEUP** purchased solely for use on specific business occasions—not for everyday business wear—are deductible business expenses. A brunette who had her hair dyed black so that she could play Lady Macbeth would get a deduction, but fifty-five-year-old Raina Realtor, who gets a weekly facial because she believes it keeps her looking younger and so gives her more confidence, cannot deduct the weekly expense.

Dues, Memberships, Admissions, and Fees

Before reading here about which **DUES** are deductible as a business expense, be sure to read about **DUES** in **MEALS & ENTERTAINMENT** and the **LOBBYING** sections of Chapter Eight.

If it's a social club, country club, or athletic club, forget about it. You cannot deduct the cost of membership even if you belong only to further your business. The IRS states flatly: "No deduction [is] allowed for business clubs operated to provide meals under circumstances generally considered to be conducive to business discussions." If you take a business associate to lunch at the club, you can deduct the cost of the meal, but not the club dues.

So what **DUES** and **MEMBERSHIPS** can you deduct? Well, first, the group must not be organized for fun or entertainment purposes. And of course it must be related to and useful to your profession. So an artist could deduct membership in a museum, a nonfiction writer could deduct dues to the historical society. In general the following kinds of organizations (with a typical example) are looked upon favorably by the IRS:

- Trade boards and associations: Greater Washington Board of Trade
- Business leagues: United Agribusiness League
- Chambers of commerce: San Diego Regional Chamber of Commerce
- Civic or public service organizations: Rotary Club of Portsmouth, New Hampshire
- Professional organizations: New York Bar Association
- Real estate boards: Honolulu Board of Realtors
- Professional unions and guilds: Authors Guild

Publications

Depending upon your business, some or all reading material may or may not be considered a business expense. In IRS parlance, these materials are **Brilliant Deduction** PUBLICATIONS.

A writer can pretty much write off everything he reads—books, newspapers, magazines. If he's not reading it for content, then he's reading it for style.

An indie who is a public relations consultant must keep abreast of politics, social and arts information and trends, and technological advances that affect her business. Without a well-grounded awareness and knowledge of the world, how could she run a successful business? Developing a PR campaign for a teen product, for example, would require her to keep up with the music, fashion, and other interests of teen life.

A tour director must also be conversant in many fields. Her clientele is young, old, business executives or retired, couples and singles. She will be planning their trips and conversing with them on history, geography, art, social trends. She must have a wide knowledge base. I'd be hard pressed to say what publications she could **not** deduct.

On the other hand, the only reading material that the security alarm system installer can legitimately write off are his professional journals, and maybe the local newspaper since his knowledge of crime news may help him promote his business.

Taboo Expenses

The following expenses are not allowable deductions.

Penalties and Fines and Bribes and Kickbacks

Most indies think that if they have to pay a parking fine because their client meeting ran late, the cost should be deductible. And that they should be able to deduct a penalty paid to the local tax authority because they misread the confusing sales tax form they had to fill out. I agree—but the IRS doesn't.

The IRS says you cannot deduct penalties or fines you pay to any government agency or instrumentality for any kind of violation. These include:

- Civil actions
- Criminal actions
- Housing code violations
- Late payments for taxes
- Traffic violations
- Trucker violations of state maximum highway weight laws and air quality laws

Anything you pay trying to beat a fine or penalty is a deductible business expense if the offense relates to business. You can deduct legal fees and related expenses to defend yourself. These costs would be **LEGAL & PROFESSIONAL SERVICES** expense.

And there's an exception to the nondeductibility of penalties: the **nonconformance penalty.** You can deduct a nonconformance penalty assessed by the Environmental Protection Agency for failing to meet certain emission standards. That means if you couldn't move the repairman fast enough to get the emissions filter installed on your chimney and you are fined, you can deduct the cost of the fine on your tax return. I want to let you know that it's one of many IRS regs with which I disagree. Many of the big guys would rather pay the fine than fix the chimney! Hey, it's deductible.

When I visited Mexico a while back, I met an American running an American business there. He told us many interesting stories of business dealings in Mexico, including how his company dealt with the notoriously corrupt Mexican police. He said that he always made sure that his truck drivers had five hundred dollars in cash hidden in the truck ready to pay off La Policia when his trucks were stopped on trumped-up charges. The payoffs were actually in his company budget. I never did get an answer to my question: "Under what budget category?"

Bribes and kickbacks are not deductible expenses. (However, if you're on the receiving end, they are taxable income.) There are a few exceptions, and if yours is a profession that engages in such practices, then you need to consult with your tax preparer. Find out whether the illegal payment you are making violates a law that is "not generally enforced." That's in quotes because the IRS says that if the law is not generally enforced by a state government, then you get to deduct the payoff.

Charitable Contributions

A sole proprietor cannot deduct charitable contributions as a business expense.

If country doctor Emma Emdee pays for an ad in the Girls, Inc. newsletter announcing the new hours of her family clinic, even though the

Brilliant Deduction

organization is a charitable organization, Emma may deduct the cost of the ad as an **ADVERTISING** expense. However, were Emma to write out a check to the organization as a charitable contribution in hope of promoting more women in medicine, she could not deduct the contribution as a business expense. She could deduct it only as a personal charitable donation on her federal Schedule A: Itemized Deductions. Emma's medical practice is an LLC run as a sole proprietorship and so it is a pass-through entity; therefore, only she personally, not her business, may deduct any business-related charitable contributions.

CHAPTER FIFTEEN

A List of Deductible Business Expenses

In the following list of deductible business expenses, you will find more than one hundred typical and not-so-typical business deductions. Some have been addressed previously and some have not. All expenses are listed so as to help you readily determine into which IRS business expense category they would likely fit. More will be explained in Part IV: Record-keeping, on categorizing expenses.

IRS categories are of little concern at this point. The main thing is to have a grasp of legitimate business deductions. Keep in mind what I said in Chapter Six, Thinking Like an Indie Business: **Anything** you do that relates to your work, that stimulates or enhances your business, nurtures your professional creativity, improves your skills, wins you recognition, or increases your chances of making a sale is a likely business expense and therefore deductible. If you maintain your indie way of thinking, you needn't worry about missing any potential business deductions.

If you **know** that an expense is deductible, don't concern yourself with which expense category it fits into. Simply stick it into the closest match you can find or give the expense its own category and deduct it. The IRS will not disallow the deduction for being in the wrong category as long as it is a legitimate expense.

1. Advertising/promotion
- Business cards
- CDs/DVDs about you or your business
- Christmas/holiday cards
- Mailing lists
- Newspaper ads
- Photos, film, and processing
- Posters
- Professional registries: e.g., Players' Guide
- Résumés
- Web site development and hosting

2. Auto/truck/motorcycle:
See the Auto Worksheet

3. Commissions and fees to agents
- Franchise fees

4. Subcontractor fees
- Business coach
- Models
- Proofreader
- Supervisor for psychologists
- Virtual assistant

5. Equipment—costs more than $200 and lasts more than one year
- Alarm system
- Camera and accessories
- Computer and accessories
- File cabinets
- Furniture
- Lamps

- Music system
- Rugs
- Stand-alone shelves
- TV/DVD recorder or player

6. **Business insurance**
   - Business interruption
   - Disability—for non-spousal employees only
   - Fire and theft
   - Liability
   - Malpractice
   - Overhead expenses paid during period of illness
   - Workers' compensation for employees

7. **Business loan interest**
   - Mortgage on business property
   - Business portion of credit card finance charges

8. **Legal and professional services— must be for business services**
   - Accountant fees
   - Attorney fees
   - Bookkeeper fees
   - Lobbying expenses (with restrictions)
   - Pension administrator fees

9. **Supplies—general supplies used in your office or workplace**
   - Office materials: e.g., paper, toner, light-bulbs
   - Cleaning supplies and paper products: e.g., tissues, towels
   - Coffee, bottled water, hard candy for clients
   - Fire extinguisher

- Flowers or plants for the office
- Plant hangers
- Software

10. **Postage**
    - FedEx, UPS
    - Freight
    - Messenger service
    - Post office box (business percent if used for personal as well)

11. **Equipment rental or lease**
    - Chairs
    - Copier
    - Workshop tools

12. **Rent on business property**
    - Office
    - Studio
    - Rehearsal space
    - Warehouse

13. **Repairs/maintenance**
    - Equipment: e.g., piano tuning, service contract
    - Office: e.g., cleaning service, repair of a window
    - Laundering of linens used in office
    - Landscaping/lawn care for business property

14. **Supplies**—incidental supplies used in your specific business, not office supplies and not supplies used in the production of your product
    - Animal treats for a dog sitter
    - Linens for a massage therapist
    - Music scores for a music teacher
    - Props and scripts for a performing artist

15. Business taxes

- Employer's share of payroll taxes
- Federal highway use tax
- Franchise tax
- Gross receipts or sales tax
- New York Unincorporated Business Tax
- Personal property tax on business assets
- Real estate tax on business property
- Zoning permit

16. Licenses and fees

- Yearly business license
- Franchise fees
- Regulatory fees to state and local governments

17. Travel:

See the Travel Worksheet

18. Meals and entertainment

- With business associates: e.g., clients, potential clients, colleagues, employees
- At your office
- At a sporting or entertainment event
- Parties for business associates
- For the general public: e.g., for a grand opening, gallery show

19. Telephone and other communication utilities

- Monthly service plus accessories for business line
- Business percent of personal line—exclude basic line charge
- Cell phone
- Answering service
- Personal digital assistant (PDA)

- Internet service provider (ISP)

20. Office or studio utilities

- Electricity/heat/water
- Exterminator service
- Security company monthly fee
- Trash pickup

21. Wages to employees

22. Bank services charges—if account is both personal and business, then must allocate

- Business bank account fees
- Check printing fees
- Client returned check fee
- Safe deposit box

23. Copyright fees/royalties/patents

24. Costumes/cleaning/makeup

- Tuxedo/evening dress
- Hair done for award presentation
- Makeup for a performer
- Uniforms—clothing with the business name on it

25. Dues/entrance fees

- Civic and public service organizations: e.g., chambers of commerce
- Competition fees
- Museums
- Professional societies: e.g., bar or medical associations, real estate boards

26. Business gifts—maximum $25 per person per year

- To clients
- To potential clients
- To business associates

- Thank-you to mom for fixing your computer
- Tips: e.g., for travel assistants, backstage help

 27. Studio/office in the home:
See Office in the Home Worksheet

28. Photocopies/printing

29. Publications—anything you read
- Books
- Magazines
- Newspapers
- Newsletter subscriptions

30. Recording costs

31. Study/education/seminars/research
- Cable TV or computer—may need to allocate
- Classes
- Concerts
- Conventions
- Document gathering
- DVDs (purchase or rental)
- Galleries
- Lessons
- Library fee
- Movies
- Museums
- Performances
- Tuition and fees
- Workshops

32. Public transportation
- Bus
- Subway
- Taxi
- Train

33. Supplies used in the production of your product

Income

Chapter One: W-2 or 1099, introduced the concept of income. If you haven't already read that chapter, you need to do so before continuing. As I explained there:

Earned income is payment for services performed. It is money or goods that you receive in the form of salary, wages, professional fees, commissions, royalties, stipends, tips, etc., for work that you do. Earned income is not money or things you receive for reasons other than work. For instance, earned income is not a gift from Grandma, nor unemployment compensation, nor dividend income, nor insurance proceeds.

There are only two types of earned income:

- W-2 earnings
  and
- Self-employed income

Part III explains the latter: income earned by a self-employed.

CHAPTER SIXTEEN

Camels or Cash: What Is Self-employed Income?

Self-employed income is compensation for a service you have performed or a product you have provided. Does the source matter? No; it could be paid by your sister or the government of Egypt. Does the form of payment matter? No; it could be cash or check, or you could be paid in camels.

THE IRS SAYS ABOUT

Self-employed Income . . .

If there is a connection between any payment you receive and your self-employed trade or business, the payment is self-employed income. A connection exists if it is clear that the payment would not have been made but for your conduct of the trade or business.

Let's look at a few indies and their sources of self-employed income:

Carpenter: Woody Awlwood

- Building a porch
- Selling a desk he made
- Designing a layout for kitchen cabinets

Writer: Nadine Novella

- Book advance
- Royalties (These royalties differ from the kind of royalties received from a copper mine in one's investment portfolio.)
- Kill fee for a magazine piece
- Speaking honorarium
- Gold bookmark received as a writing contest prize (Its fair market value is determined and reported as income.)

Real estate broker: Raina Realtor

- Commission on a sale
- Referral fee from a fellow broker
- Fee for a real estate appraisal in a divorce case

Software developer/computer consultant: Syd System

- Hourly fee for repairs
- Payment received for cost plus markup for hardware parts
- Two massages in exchange for setting up massage therapist's computer. (The fee generally charged by the masseur is the amount reported as income by the computer consultant.)
- Corporate payment for analysis of current system
- "What to Look for in Buying a Computer" lecture fee at local men's club

Each of these transactions results in income for a self-employed person—even the bartering that took place between the computer consultant and the massage therapist. I'll explain bartering later in the chapter. Don't be fooled into

thinking that because the payment you receive is out of the normal course of your business or is not in good ol' American currency that it is nonincome. However unorthodox, it is still self-employed income. Remember: The IRS says, "If there is a connection between your self-employed trade or business and the payment, then the payment is self-employed income."

Understanding Income Lingo

There are many terms used in connection with self-employed income. It is your responsibility to claim all your income and it is the responsibility of your tax pro to put the right income on the correct line of your tax return. Recall the example of Rick Reporter from Chapter One. The two income terms you must know are *gross* and *net.*

Rick received $1,000 self-employed income for a magazine piece he wrote. That was his *gross* self-employed income. He had a $20 expense, which left him with $980 in *net* self-employed income. The $1,000 is also called his **gross receipts** or **gross sales,** and the $980 can also be called his *profit* or **net profit** or **net income** or his bottom line.

His income situation was simple. Most self-employed income scenarios are more complex than Rick's and may call for additional income terminology. But don't worry—if you understand Rick's self-employed situation, you understand the basics: *Gross self-employed income minus expenses leaves you with a net self-employed income.*

While we're on the subject of gross versus net income, let's take a look at two entrepreneurs, Whoopi Happenin and her sister Groovi Happenin. Each is a special events planner. Last year each had a *net* income of $40,000. If you looked only at the bottom line, you'd think they were equally savvy businesspeople.

However, Whoopi's *gross* self-employed income was $60,000. Her staff costs and expenses totaled $20,000. Apply a little arithmetic and you see that her costs were 33 percent of her *gross* (20,000 / 60,000). Her income formula looks like this:

$$\$60,000 - \$20,000 = \$40,000.$$

Groovi's *gross* self-employed income was $100,000. Her expenses were $60,000. That's 60 percent of her gross—almost double the rate of her sister. She probably had to work a lot harder and longer to bring in $100,000 than her sister did to bring in $60,000, and yet they both ended up with the same $40,000 net profit. Her income formula looks like this:

$$\$100,000 - \$60,000 = \$40,000.$$

Now which one do you think is the more savvy businessperson? Don't be fooled by the numbers. A very large gross income doesn't signify anything until it's compared to the bottom line.

Paying Tax on Income

A self-employed pays self-employment (SE) tax—and that's different from income tax—on his *net profit.*

On a self-employed's tax return, the amount of *net profit* is added to other kinds of income—interest, dividends, capital gains, alimony—to come up with **total income.** After various adjustments and personal deductions,

the result is **taxable income.** Income tax is calculated on *taxable income.*

A self-employed may have a *net profit* but have no *taxable income.* In that case he would pay self-employment tax but no income tax.

 Reality "It must be overwork!" That was the only explanation Woody Awlwood could come up with for the nonsensical thing his tax preparer told him. "Woody, good news," said his preparer. "With all your deductions, your income tax is zero. You need to send the Feds only another $1,239." "No income tax but I have to pay more than a thousand to the Feds! That's absurd. I already paid them $3,000. How could this be?" shouted Woody.

Here's how: Woody's net profit for the year was $30,000. He had no other income but he had a loss in the stock market, high mortgage interest, property taxes, and donations of used clothing to a local charity. He also supported his two children. This is how he got to zero taxable income.

Net profit from business	$30,000
Stock market loss	(3,000)
Mortgage Interest	(12,000)
Property tax	(4,000)
Contributions to Goodwill	(2,000)
Three exemptions (Woody plus two kids)	(9,000)
Taxable income	0

Net profit and *net income* are often interchangeable terms. Neither term means the same as *taxable income.*

In the example on the previous page, Woody's SE tax was just under 15 percent of his $30,000 net business profit and his income tax was zero. I'll explain more about taxes in Part V.

You're the Boss: Pay Yourself Whatever You Want

Many self-employed people have a misguided idea about their own business profits. They think that the weekly, monthly, or occasional checks they write to themselves—often called "draw"—is their income or their profit. They are wrong.

The checks a self-employed makes out to herself have no bearing whatsoever on her income, expenses, profit, or taxes. Whether you write yourself a $100 or $1,000 check every week, you are doing nothing other than altering cash flow by moving money from one place to another. It's called draw because you are drawing money away from someplace.

Let's examine this concept by means of the example of Raina Realtor.

 Reality Raina thought she managed her business finances well last year. She brought in $130,000, and after subtracting $20,000 in expenses and the $60,000 she paid herself in $5,000 monthly checks, she had $50,000 left in the bank. At the end of the year she "knew" she'd have to pay taxes on the $60,000 "income" she'd paid herself.

Here's what Raina thought:

Gross income	$130,000
Minus expenses	(20,000)
Minus money left in the bank	(50,000)
Raina paid herself and thought she had to pay tax on	$60,000

Here's how Raina's numbers really add up, or subtract out:

Gross income	$130,000
Minus expenses	(20,000)
Net profit	$110,000

You can see that Raina's profit on which she had to pay tax was much higher than the amount she had "paid" herself.

To Sum Up Self-employed Income

- If the payment is related to your self-employed venture, then it's self-employed income no matter how you're paid.
- Don't let the fine distinctions in the various terms for income confuse you. Keep in mind Rick Reporter, and be aware of the difference between **gross** self-employed income (everything you bring in) versus **net** income (what you're left with after business expenses).
- Self-employment tax and income tax are paid on two different income amounts.

CHAPTER SEVENTEEN

What Daddy's Accountant Forgot to Tell You about Income

Sammy Segar, CPA, may be a whiz at retirement planning and may know just when your daddy should cash in his stock options, but Sammy lacks the know-how to advise an independent professional, whose business life—in every respect—is more complicated than that of the guy who receives a company paycheck. Here are some aspects of self-employed income that are often overlooked.

Situations Too Tricky for Sammy

Take It—Don't Fake It: Constructive Receipt

If you can get at the money, you are considered to have received it. As a result, as soon as money or property is available to you, or is credited to your account, it becomes income to you. If you received a check in November, it was income to you in the year that you received it, even if you didn't deposit it until January.

If Nadine Novella's literary agent receives her royalty check, that's income to Nadine on that day even if her agent doesn't forward the money to her for a month. This approach to when payment becomes income is called **constructive receipt.**

Income after the Doors Close

P. R. Bernays closes up his solo shop as a public relations consultant to work as an employee in the PR department of Masdrogas Pharmaceuticals, Inc. Months later he receives a late payment check from a client for whom he had developed a PR package. Is it self-employed income? It sure is.

Trading Products and Services

If your work is paid for with a product or a service instead of with money, that's called **bartering.** And guess what! It's income just the same. The fair market value of the item or service you receive is part of your gross receipts.

The massage therapist earlier in this chapter, whose computer was fixed by Syd System in exchange for two massages, claimed $200 ($100 per massage) as part of his gross income and subtracted $200 in computer repairs for a net income of zero. If there is no net income there is no SE tax nor income tax liability. You

WHATTA**CONCEPT**!

Income that is not self-employed income

As you read the following pages about what is and what is not self-employed income, keep in mind that if it is not self-employed income, then no SE tax is due. Remember from Chapter Four that SE tax is the self-employed's Social Security and Medicare tax.

Although payment received may not be self-employment income, it may still be taxable income subject to income tax.

may still need to show the transaction, however, because some states require that sales tax, gross receipts tax, or a general excise tax be paid on **gross** income. New Mexico, for example, would have required approximately $12 in gross receipts tax on the $200 bartering income. Hawaii would have required about $8.

Syd, on the other hand, had $200 of income for the work he did, but because the massages were not ordinary or necessary business expenses, he could not deduct them. He must show the transaction.

A lot of bartering goes on that the IRS isn't aware of—but now you know the rule.

Grants, Awards, and Prizes

When you receive money under a research grant or an award, *if you perform a service or produce a product for the use of the grantor,* the money you receive is self-employed income. If you get a grant to go on retreat, think alone in a cabin, or converse with other thinkers, but do not have to present your thoughts to the grantor *for his use,* the grant money (although taxable) is not self-employed income.

Reimbursement for Expenses

A client reimbursement for expenses is **not** income. There are two different bookkeeping methods for handling client reimbursements, and they will be explained in Chapter Twenty-one.

Worldwide Income

No matter where your self-employed income comes from, it is part of your gross income. If Miles Mingus sells 100 CDs while on his European tour, the sales are included in his US income. Same thing with the jewelry Trixy Trinkets sells internationally on the Internet.

Special rules apply if you live outside the United States. If you spend all but the holidays virtually communicating with your clients from a beach in southern France, you'd better get advice from a tax professional who has experience with freelancers living out of the country.

Borrowing Cash

Short on cash? It's OK to borrow from yourself or someone else. As a self-employed, if you borrow against an asset that you own, the loan proceeds are not income.

 Anton Antique had a vast collection of first editions that his brother admired and envied. Big Brother loaned Anton $5,000 using the books as collateral. The $5,000 was not taxable to Anton. He 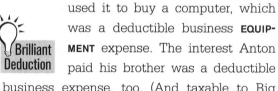 used it to buy a computer, which was a deductible business **EQUIPMENT** expense. The interest Anton paid his brother was a deductible business expense, too. (And taxable to Big Brother.)

The same treatment would apply had Anton borrowed the money from a bank or taken a cash advance on his credit card.

Interest on Bank Accounts

If your business checking account earns interest, that income is **not** self-employed income. It is personal interest income. But if you charge interest to clients on balances owed to you—

often called a late fee or finance charge—then that interest is self-employed income.

Sale of Business Property

A gain or loss from the sale of equipment, property, or other assets used in your business that is not held primarily for sale to customers is **not** self-employed income.

Rental Income

Rental income that you receive from tenants, although taxable income, is not self-employed income unless your profession or business is that of a real estate dealer, or you provide services such as cleaning, linens, meals, etc., for your tenants.

You are a real estate dealer if your business is buying and selling real estate with the purpose of making a profit. You are not a dealer if you buy and hold real estate for investment or speculation.

 Mike Mobile had a sizable piece of land near the lake. He let visitors park their campers there for a fee. He provided no services. The fees he received were rental income, not self-employed income subject to SE tax. Within a few years the spot had become so popular that he added some amenities and raised the rent. He provided things like a laundry facility, fax and phone line hookups in the main office, fresh water, etc. Now he's receiving income as a self-employed.

 Billy Bridesnapper rents out a part of his photo studio space to Victor Visual. The easier way for him to treat the money from Victor is to include it as income and then deduct the entire amount that he pays for rent. (Be careful of state gross receipts tax regulations with this method, though.) The alternative method is to not include the rental income in his gross income, but then he must also reduce his rental expense by the amount received from Victor.

If Billy owns the building from which he runs his wedding photography business, then the rental income from Victor is taxable rental income and does not get included with his self-employed income.

Hobbies

Any money you make on your hobby is not self-employed income. (To refresh your thinking about what is a hobby, see Chapter Three.)

 Shane Scriptwrite earns his self-employed income as a scriptwriter, and his hobby is collecting comic books. His sales of comic books are not part of his self-employed income.

In the same vein, a one-shot deal does not a business make:

 Dennis Dubya-two retired at age sixty-five from his job at Toys 'n' Things. He spent his summers playing golf and winters skiing. His golf skills were so impressive that he was asked to give lessons to teens at the local youth club. Dennis was paid to give lessons to the young people over the course of the summer. The youth club sent him a Form 1099 at the end of the year.

This was not self-employed income for Dennis because he was not in business as a golf instructor—that is, it was not a continuous or regular activity.

The IRS made a ruling on a case like this in 1992 regarding a nonbusiness activity for a man named Batok. If you should have a similar situation, be sure your tax pro is familiar with this case. She'll need to write "As per the Batok Case, TC Memo, 1992-727" next to the "Other Income" line in the personal section of your tax return. In this way you may avoid correspondence from the IRS as to why you haven't paid SE tax on the income. If you are wondering how this might apply to you, since you are a self-employed in business, here's a typical example:

 Charlotte Salesrep runs a profitable solo enterprise representing several children's toy makers. Every once in a while she is paid to babysit for the neighbor's kids. Her babysitting earnings are not self-employed income.

Charlotte's tax professional should know that her babysitting earnings are not subject to self-employed tax. Charlotte can help her tax pro make that distinction by keeping a complete record of all money received.

I hope the tax situations illustrated in this section have convinced you that you need a tax professional knowledgeable and experienced in advising independents. As for keeping a complete record of money received, I'll explain how to do that, in detail, in Chapter Twenty-one.

CHAPTER EIGHTEEN

Getting Paid in the Parking Lot: Cheating by Hiding Income

Under the table. In the parking lot. Off the books. Of course it's income. And yes, you must report it on your tax return.

 Miles Mingus plays a regular gig at Jazzy Jack's Pub. Jazzy Jack has a cash business; all his barflies pay for their drinks with hard currency—no plastic or checks, thank you. And Jack pays Miles the same way—in cash, which he takes from an envelope in his desk in the back office. Nobody's claiming a lot of the income and nobody's paying a lot of the taxes—until Jack gets audited.

The IRS says that a review of Jack's sizable purchases for liquor just don't match up with the tiny income he reports from bar sales. Whoops! Now the IRS checks out the waiters, the staff, and the tax returns of the musicians.

The IRS is not a morality agency, it is a monetary agency. It doesn't care what you do for a living as long as you pay taxes on the income you make doing it. If you make your living as a hit man or a lady of the night or a drug dealer, be sure to pay the IRS its fair share. Remember the Chicago mobster Al Capone? He wasn't sent to prison for murder, bootlegging, or racketeering; he was convicted of tax evasion for not reporting the money he earned in his self-employed endeavors.

When the IRS calls for an audit, its only purpose is to collect more tax money with some interest and penalty to boot. Criminal activity is not suspected. But if you are caught in outright cheating—particularly in deliberately failing to report a significant amount of income—the IRS will not hesitate to prosecute you.

Getting Paid "Off the Books"

I've always understood "off the books" to mean that the worker doesn't claim the income and the person paying doesn't claim the expense of the worker, nor pay benefits, keep records, or send W-2s or 1099s to the government.

An attendee at one of my seminars told me that he thought it meant he was "not an employee on the employer's books." That is, he was an independent contractor—a self-employed. To me it was obvious from the nature of the job that he was an employee. Apparently the employer was trying to bamboozle the worker.

There is no legitimate "off the books" category of employment. If someone wants to pay you that way, find out what he really means and don't agree to anything crooked. It's not worth it!

Getting Paid in Cash

Clients and customers may request that if they pay you in cash, could you lower the price? Their reason: "Oh, you know, cash means less

paperwork." Yeah, right. Cash means it's off the books. They're offering you a chance to hide income. If you did it, you would be committing a crime. If you feel you really want to get or keep this client but feel you can only do so by lowering your price, then tell him, "Cash is too troublesome for my recordkeeping, I much prefer a check. But I can give you a discount off my regular fee." Then give the client a "new customer" discount or your "February discount" or your "friend" discount. If the client insists on paying cash, then still give him a receipt.

On any receipt or invoice, always show the total fee and any discount you give.

Hiding income does not give a positive, professional image of your business. It raises questions, such as:

- Are you a legitimate business?
- Do you want your service or your product to be treated seriously?
- Do you want to be looked upon with respect in your business community?
- Do you want to get the best payment possible for your service or product?

We've all run across the trail of the underground economy, with its little hole-in-the-wall operations that seem to be running on cash and are probably not reporting their income. For the most part these operations are secretive and secluded little businesses that won't go anywhere and will never amount to anything. The people who use their services know that they can treat them and dismiss them in any way they wish. Illegal businesses are at a great disadvantage; they have no recourse because they can't come out of hiding. I've helped businesses go legit. They've come out of the closet and they've never regretted it. The owners sleep better, too.

And you need to know that there is no limit on how long the IRS can come after you if you have intentionally failed to report income. If you're claiming a Hyundai income, you'd better not be leading a Lexus life. The IRS might make you take the "economic reality" test: Can you do the things you're doing on the income you reported?

Clearly, simply, bluntly: **Don't hide income.** If you get caught, it's fraud. And if you're caught, you can be sure the IRS (and the state as well) will scrutinize much of your other financial dealings.

If you are ever audited, and the IRS refuses to accept some of your deductions, you will have to pay the additional tax on the lost deductions and interest on that additional tax amount. You also may have to pay a late payment penalty of up to 25 percent of the tax owed. You'll be out some money, but you've simply had a legitimate disagreement with the IRS about a deduction: You will not be hit with criminal charges or fraud penalties for hiding income. A fraud penalty can be as high as 75 percent of the tax owed. That is in addition to the tax owed plus interest.

There are ways to cut your taxes that are not criminal. One way to get your taxes as low as possible is to consult a tax pro with experience in guiding self-employeds. Make sure you talk with her as soon as you consider going into business for yourself. There are ways to time income and treat deductions that can work most advantageously for you if discussed early and planned ahead of the transaction.

To Sum Up Cheating

The best way to pay the least tax is knowledge! Start by understanding the basic tax and financial concepts regarding your self-employed venture. Know what you can deduct as a business expense and how to keep the best records. Part IV will continue to guide you in your quest for that know-how.

Recordkeeping

"Keep good records." That's what you read in all the self-employed how-to books, that's what you hear from financial advisors, insurance agents, and your father. As if everybody was born with recordkeeping skills but just needs some occasional prodding to stay up to date. Well, as you have probably learned, recordkeeping is a skill that doesn't come with the first slap on the bottom the moment you're born. It is a skill that, like cooking, can be done a myriad of ways, either in-house or sent out, using different flavors and different styles to please a lot of different palates, but all satisfying a universal need: Everybody's got to eat.

It is important to remember that recordkeeping systems are as unique and different as the people using them. There is no "ideal system" that will work for everyone, but as we all know: Everybody's got to keep records.

The Most Simple System is going to show you the basics of how to keep records for tax purposes in the easiest and quickest way possible. You can adapt the method to fit your style; keep it simple or expand it to fit the unique needs of your solo venture. Once you've mastered the basics, you'll be ready for a more advanced beyond-the-basics approach should you choose to move on to a computer bookkeeping program.

Now, before we get into the how-to of recordkeeping, I want to go over a few reasons other than taxes and Uncle Sam why good records benefit *you.* I will also answer that pressing question in space-strapped households: How long should I keep which tax records?

CHAPTER NINETEEN

Records as Resource: Why Keep Records?

As a self-employed it is important that you keep business records not only because of your dealings with the government—its requirements and your wish to pay as little tax as possible—but also because of other likely events and circumstances in your life.

Independent professionals grumble about the detailed records that a meddling Uncle Sam requires them to keep. Yet many self-employeds, once they start keeping records, realize that they have a resource in their hands that helps them monitor their businesses. Records can tell an indie not only how her business is doing but can also help predict how it may do next year. Perhaps Astrid Astrologer doesn't need records to look into the future, but the rest of us do.

There are nontax reasons why a self-employed might need business information at her fingertips. The examples that follow, by no means an exhaustive list, should get you thinking about the ways that business records may benefit your financial situation—whether professional or personal.

Getting a Loan

Whether you apply for a business loan, a personal loan, a mortgage for a new home, or you refinance your present home, the lender will want to see your business records. If you don't want to show business records, you may be able to get a "no-doc" loan (no income verification documents required), but it's going to saddle you with a higher interest rate.

Although mortgage companies are adopting new criteria that give the self-employed a more level playing field, it's still standard practice that, all things being equal, Emma Employee has a better shot at any kind of loan than does Indira Independent. Even all things not being equal, even if Emma makes less money, the lending institutions tend to think of her salary as more dependable. (Maybe they haven't heard of downsizing.) And in the nature of things, Emma's pay is more predictable. Lenders tend to get nervous thinking that Indira is more likely to run into hard times when the cash flows out instead of in, and then she might fall behind in the repayment schedule.

In most instances in which Emma Employee would have to show a W-2, Indira Independent would have to confirm her income via a federal Schedule C, Profit or Loss from Business (a part of her tax return). If the loan were applied for in midyear, Emma would have to show a pay stub with year-to-date earnings, and Indira would have to show a year-to-date profit-and-loss statement, often required on an accountant's letterhead.

College Financial Aid

When applying for student aid for yourself or your child, you will be required to complete financial aid forms. You must have records that will provide you with the correct information in order to fill out these forms accurately. You cannot guess. If you estimate because your records are incomplete, then you may be asked to submit a revised application when your records are complete. Often you will be required to submit documents to substantiate the information you provided. False or misleading information on a federal request for college aid can subject you to a $10,000 fine or prison or both.

Grants

When applying for a grant for any kind of project, you may need to show your project expenses to date as well as expected research and other costs necessary to completing the work.

Court Cases

Records are the very lifeblood of litigation.

In a divorce, proof of income—or lack of it—is often required whether debating a division of assets, amount of alimony, or child support. Just as an ex-spouse-in-waiting must prove the $70,000 assistant manager salary via a W-2, an independent professional must show by means of accurate records that even though the project sold for $70,000, the net income was only $10,000.

If you are a plaintiff in a negligence case in which you were injured, and your suit includes reimbursement for lost income, your business records are essential. You'll need them to show your income over past years and that you expected to earn even more this year had you not been laid up in traction for many months.

Insurance

Without sufficient records there is no way to substantiate a loss for insurance purposes. A home that went up in flames, a burglarized storage unit: Without proof of the cost or value of a computer or a camera, how are you going to get your insurance company to reimburse you for those items? You'll have trouble enough even with the records.

When you do record your possessions—whether via camcorder or still camera—keep a copy of your records in a safe place off premises, such as a friend's house or a safe deposit box.

Later in this chapter we'll discuss the time periods that various *tax* records need to be kept, but here's a note on insurance policies: If you have umbrella coverage or liability insurance for your business or home, keep the old policy records for past years in case someone files against you claiming injury in a past year.

The records ought to be kept for as long as your state's statute of limitations is in effect. The same goes for the auto insurance.

Warranties

Most warranty agreements are inflexible about expiration dates. Whether it's the laser printer or the washing machine that dies a week before the warranty runs out, it helps mightily to be able to prove the purchase date to the seller or manufacturer.

Equipment, Investments, and Other Assets

Not only for your own tax preparation do you need to know the basis of assets, stocks, and other investments sold, but also if you gift an asset to someone, you need to provide basis information to the recipient of the gift.

Other Important Stuff

In Chapter Twenty-two, The Most Simple System at Work, you'll learn an easy method of business recordkeeping, but here's a note on some personal records: Don't throw away your birth certificate, marriage certificate (even if the marriage is long gone), will, divorce decree, Social Security card, passport, various licenses, title to your automobile, insurance policies. Although it's best if all these records are organized in a filing system of your own devising, if you lack any sense of organization, at least keep them all in one place—a file box labeled "Important Stuff"—not divided among a kitchen drawer, summer home, attic, bedroom closet, car, and office desk. The latter is called the "sloppy spouse system" and is hazardous to your mental health.

Recordkeeping is a lot like exercising at the gym. It's really hard to get started. You have to want to get better at it. You have to make an effort. And you have to do it consistently. If you take time off, it takes three times as long to catch up. The Most Simple System will get you to the treadmill with the right attitude and the right gear. There's no telling how high or fast you can go after that.

CHAPTER TWENTY

What to Cast and When: How Long to Keep Which Records

A Sad Tale

Since she first started in business, Lisa Locksmith had her taxes prepared by Cousin Careless. But Careless retired and Lisa had to find a new preparer. She asked other independent professionals for suggestions, and that's how she came to use Fanny Flawless.

To the initial consultation Fanny asked Lisa to bring copies of all tax returns since the start of her business. Lisa searched her garage, and behind the winter tires, in a box marked "Keep," she found returns for 2002, 2003, 2004, 2005, and 2006.

"Why, Lisa," says Fanny after reviewing the five previous years' tax returns, "you've never deducted any costs for use of your car. Don't you use your car in your business?"

"Of course I do," says Lisa. "I put about 10,000 miles a year on my car just going to lockouts from my home office."

"Well, there are no auto deductions on any of these returns," says Fanny. "And 10,000 miles could save you about $1,000 a year in taxes."

"Good grief!" says Lisa. "Can't I go back and fix those returns or something and get my money back?"

"That's called amending your return, and you can amend for only three years after you filed your return. Let's see. Today is March 10, 2008, so you lost out on amending 2002 and 2003. But we can refile for 2004, 2005, and 2006. Can you review your records and get an accurate tally of your auto miles for those three years?" asks Fanny.

"Are you kidding?! Careless told me I didn't need to keep anything but a copy of my tax return. I threw all that stuff out ages ago."

The End

Yes, it is a sad tale, with a cost to Lisa of about $3,000. When most folks think or ask about record retention, they are concerned about an audit and how far back the IRS can go in requiring substantiation for deductions. They rarely consider that *they* might need old records to claim a tax refund or credit. The rules are clear-cut when looked at from the taxpayer's side of the fence. You have three years from the due date of your return to change—that is, amend—your tax return and claim a credit or refund. If you were an energetic early bird and filed before the due date, you still have three years from the due date.

To Cast or to Keep

Contrary to popular opinion, people don't usually get into trouble for not saving records but for saving the wrong ones or outdated ones, or not knowing where the right ones are. The huge stack of papers in the attic is often a monument to inertia complicated by not knowing which records need to be kept and which can be tossed.

Record Retention Simply Stated

- Keep tax returns (not records, but actual returns) forever. Label a box "My Tax Returns" and put them in there.

- Keep every year-end summary of your pension forever. Label a box "Pensions" and make a folder for each plan you have. Put that plan's year-end statement in the folder and close the box.

- Keep everything else for seven years from the last time it had any impact on your financial life. Label a box "2008 Tax Records: OK to throw out 12/31/2015."

You'll also find a quick reference table near the end of the chapter.

This section on the basics of record retention is your starting point. You will take a big step forward in your organization proficiency once you know which tax records to keep and for how long.

1. Your Tax Returns

Your tax returns are historical information—save them forever. They can be a source of horror or amusement. I was working with a graphic designer who had been a client for some time and whose income had made giant leaps in the last few years. But he was struggling to make ends meet. He had trouble managing his money and he didn't know where to start. I pulled out his tax return of five years earlier and showed him that his income at that time was the same amount as his current yearly credit card finance charges. That got his attention!

Tax records can be valuable in unexpected ways.

 Reality Really old returns proved useful in a divorce case. The father told the judge he expected his daughters to work part-time while in college and contribute toward the expense of school. The ex-wife thought that this would be too much to expect from the children. To show that his expectations were reasonable, the father found his tax returns from his college days showing his income earned while attending college. He graduated with honors. The judge decided for the father.

Another client, let's call her Dr. Endie Naturopath, was stopped at a light not far from her alma mater when her car was struck from behind. Serious neck injury prevented her from working for the next year and severely limited her future practice. It was the fault of the sweet young thing driving the VW Beetle—thank goodness it wasn't an SUV. In preparing for the court case, Endie's lawyer told her to present proof of her income since the start of her practice to show how her income had been reduced by not being able to work after the accident. Unlike the traditional medical professions, there is scarce statistical information on typical income and growth of income for naturopathic doctors. Endie's tax returns were crucial to a fair settlement of the case.

More routine but also very useful is using the previous year's tax return as reference when gathering material for the current year's return.

You can obtain back-year tax returns from the IRS, but this entails unnecessary time and expense. So be sure to save all your returns.

2. Records Substantiating Your Tax Return

The main reason to save tax records is to substantiate the items of income and deduction on your tax return in case of an audit. You should keep those records at least through the time when the IRS can question your return's accuracy. This time is called the **statute of limitations.**

In general, the statute of limitations is either three years after the due date of your return, or three years after the date you filed—whichever is later.

For example, if you filed your 2007 tax return on March 20, 2008, it could be called for an audit through April 15, 2011. If you filed your 2007 return on October 15, 2008 (the extension deadline), it could be questioned through October 15, 2011.

This is the easiest way to think about it: The IRS can come after you for questions about a transaction up to four years after the transaction. That is, 2007's records are vulnerable through 2011.

There are exceptions to the rule:

If you paid late. If you filed your tax return but couldn't pay your tax right away, you are open for an audit until two years after you paid the tax, regardless of when you filed your return.

If you forgot some income. If you filed a return in which you understated your income by 25 percent or more, the IRS can come after you for *six* years, not just three. Six years after filing is usually seven years after the transaction. That's why the rule of thumb is to keep your records for seven years.

Suppose that, in all innocence, Prudence Pas de Deux, in the year her net profit was $10,000, didn't claim as income the $5,000 grant she received to choreograph the winter pageant for the School for the Deaf. That's more than 25 percent of her income that she didn't claim, and the IRS has six years to come and get the tax and interest and penalty from her.

Prudence's ignorance of tax regs shows us how susceptible we all are to oversights—our own and those of our financial advisors. Because the IRS can go back to overlooked income six years after you've filed, I urge you to keep records for seven years. For example, for events that took place in 2007, keep records through 2014. You will keep 2008 records through 2015.

If you committed serious tax misconduct. No limit! There is no statute of limitations if you intentionally fail to report income. The IRS can come after you anytime if you file a fraudulent return or fail to file a return. That's why you should permanently keep records for any year that you didn't need to file a return. Your records will provide evidence in case the IRS ever questions why you didn't file for that year.

If you voluntarily extended the deadline. A taxpayer can agree to extend the statute of limitations if the IRS asks. This happens if some item on the return needs more time to be resolved. Check with your tax pro before signing on to this.

If you live or work in a state with a different statute of limitations. Be careful: Some states may have a longer statute of limitations than the Feds. For example, in California the statue of limitations is four years, not three.

3. Records for Multiyear Deductions

Even if you filed everything on time and on the up-and-up, there are situations in which records must be retained for a longer period.

If you have a business expense that you do not entirely deduct in the year you incur the expense, but instead spread the cost over a period of years, then you must retain the records at least long enough to meet the statute of limitations for the *last* return on which you deducted the final portion of that item.

This kind of expense deduction is called depreciation or amortization. It applies to expenses like business EQUIPMENT, VEHICLES, and BUILDINGS, as well as OFFICE IN THE HOME and START-UP COSTS.

 Clarissa Clothier purchased office furniture in 2008. It will be deducted on her tax returns through 2015. Were the IRS to suspect hidden income, her 2015 return could be questioned through 2022. So the records for the 2008 purchase of furniture are open to question by the IRS fourteen years from the date of purchase. (This is seven years from the last year it appeared on her tax return.)

Records for business equipment and property that must be written off over a period of years should be kept for as long as you own the property and then for seven additional years after you've disposed of it. Equipment and property are things like:

- Office equipment
- Furniture
- A warehouse building
- Vehicles

Reality

Clarissa finished deducting the 1999 business truck on her tax return years ago, but the truck still runs like a charm. If she sells it in 2009 and her 2009 tax return is audited in 2011, she may need to show records for the purchase of the truck and deductions for its use over the years, as well as records for its sale in 2009.

Segregating Multiyear Records

Chapter Twenty-two will give you additional instructions on recordkeeping how-to, but at this point it would be good to think about a file folder or box labeled "Equipment and other Long-Term Things." This can be the place where you put receipts, bills of sale, and instruction manuals for equipment, autos,

office furniture, etc.; and active warranties and service contracts on equipment.

What about records relating to your residence? The new, larger tax exemption for gains on the sale of personal residence has prompted some homeowners to question whether they need to bother saving any of their home-related tax records. Well, you may be a homeowner today and a self-employed with an office in the home tomorrow. And tomorrow you'll need all your home purchase and capital improvements records.

When you deduct expenses for an **OFFICE IN THE HOME,** the same record-retention rules apply as for any other multiyear deduction. Keep records for seven years after you sell your residence.

HOW LONG TO KEEP TAX RECORDS

THE RECORD	THE SITUATION	KEEP RECORDS FOR HOW LONG
Tax returns	Any	Forever
Records substantiating tax return	Filed on time, including extensions	7 years from the year of the transactions
	Filed late	6 years from filing date
	Paid late	6 years from last payment
	Filed a fraudulent return	Forever
	Never filed a return	Forever
Receipts for a multiyear deduction	Any	Seven years after the year you disposed of the item

Although most audits take place within two years from the time you file your return, the IRS can wait as long as three years—and in some circumstances even longer. For instance, when Prudence Pas de Deux neglects to include at least 25 percent of her income on her tax return, the statute of limitations extends for six years: That's seven years from the time of the transaction. (The time periods in the table on the previous page take such circumstances into consideration.)

Casting with Assurance

As I said in the beginning of this section, people don't usually get into trouble by not saving records but by saving the wrong ones. Don't confuse keeping records with never throwing out a piece of paper. The table on the previous page—How Long to Keep Tax Records—will guide you in pitching to the round file with assurance, but keep in mind that there are non-tax records not included in this table. Keep the records listed below, each in its own file folder, clearly labeled, in a safe place.

- Birth and death certificates
- Marriage and divorce papers
- Adoption papers
- Military service records (You'll need them when you file for Social Security.)
- Wills (Do not keep these in your safe deposit box.)
- Asset lists (so your estate can be properly administered)
- Medical records (one for each family member)
- Loan and lease agreements
- Personal and business insurance policies (See note in previous chapter.)
- Employment agreements
- Pension documents and pension tax returns (This is Form 5500 or 5500-EZ.)
- A complete record of pension contributions and withdrawals (found on the year-end statement)

CHAPTER TWENTY-ONE

It Ebbs, It Swells: Why and How to Record Income

Cash flow! I'm sure many of you have heard the term. There's all the goofy comments that cash does anything but flow. Very often it just stops. For the lucky ones it's a tidal wave; for the unlucky ones it backs up. For most of us it doesn't flow evenly but surges once in a while and ebbs when we need it most. It may help you to understand the term **cash flow** if you think of money coming in to you as **inflow** rather than *income.* Interest from your savings account is income; a birthday check for $500 from your great-uncle is not income; on a sale of stock, some of what you get may be income, but some of it is a return of your own money; health insurance reimbursements are generally not income. Some inflow is income while some is not. Inflow is any money you receive. Sometimes it is called cash receipts.

And think of any money you spend as **outflow** rather than as an *expense.* A utility bill is an expense; it might also be a business expense. Buying a vacation home is money out but not an expense, because you are exchanging one asset (money in the bank) for another asset (real estate). A birthday check to your house sitter is money out, but is it an expense? Outflow is money spent or disbursed, and so it is often called cash disbursements.

Earlier in Part IV we looked at the benefits of general recordkeeping. Let's examine the importance of an accurate record of all money coming in to you—*inflow.*

THE IRS SAYS ABOUT
Recordkeeping . . .

Except in a few cases, the law does not require any special kind of records. You may choose any recordkeeping system suited to your business that clearly and accurately shows your income.

Income versus Inflow

To show your income you need to be able to distinguish income from all other inflow. Therefore, you need a record of the *source* of each and every deposit made to each and every one of your financial accounts—checking, savings, investment, retirement. Only by being able to identify every cash receipt can you isolate that which is income, that which is not, and those that are transfers from other accounts.

In a simple audit of a self-employed, the IRS will want to see monthly bank statements for that year from all accounts. The IRS will add up every deposit. You must be able to explain any difference between the total deposits and the amount of income shown on your tax return. A written record of inflow may save you time and stress as well as untold amounts in taxes, penalty, and interest charges.

 If Syd System's tax return shows gross self-employed income of $30,000 and Syd's bank statements show $35,000 in deposits, then Syd had better have a good explanation for the extra $5,000. A note from Mom saying she loaned it to him will not do.

If Syd's bank statements show $25,000 in deposits but his tax return showed $30,000 gross self-employed income, the likely assumption is that he had $25,000 income in checks and $5,000 cash income. If that is the case, it means he is not depositing all of his income into his checking account. This may lead the IRS to question how much more than the claimed $5,000 cash income he's not putting into his checking account. Many indies think that as long as they claim "some" cash income the IRS will be happy and not look to see how much other cash income is not claimed. The IRS knows this ploy.

Both situations—bank statements showing less in deposits than claimed as income and statements totaling more than was claimed as income—lead to more thorough scrutiny by the IRS.

And what if Mom did loan Syd $5,000? His written income log should show just that to the IRS. In a situation where money comes from a family member, a copy of the check from Mom would be an invaluable addition to the inflow log.

Income Records and Estimated Tax Payments

The amount and timing of your estimated tax payments ("estimateds") may be based upon how much income you receive and when you receive it. Part V provides a complete discussion of taxes, but here I'd like to give you a perspective on income records and paying tax on income. There is no need to pay tax on income not yet received. For instance, if Luisa Lifecoach received a $40,000 project payment from her corporate sponsor in January, she would be required to make her first estimated payment on the following April 15. If, however, she did not receive the payment until early September, then her first estimated payment would not be due until September 15. An income log, with backup, would enable her or her financial advisor to calculate estimated tax payments.

If Luisa didn't consult with anyone about estimated tax payments but just paid them when she had the money, as an after-the-fact remedy, her income records could help her tax preparer show the IRS why a payment made in September instead of April was acceptable, thereby saving Luisa some interest and late payment penalties.

Don't Rely on the Sleepy Bookkeeper

Perhaps the best reason to keep a record of your income is because someone else's error can make your life miserable.

Depending upon your business, you may receive a Form 1099 from every client you worked for during the year, or some may send a year-end payment summary, or each of your clients may have a bookkeeper you can call to get a tally. However, you do not want to rely on their recordkeeping!

People to whom you sell your service or product make mistakes. Their bookkeeper had a bad day, there was a glitch in the new computer program, someone was too lazy to double-check an entry.

Many first-time clients have come to me having no idea of their income. Their plan was to add up all the 1099s they received from clients and use that as their income amount. How foolish to rely on the accuracy and honesty of others for such an important part of your financial well-being! One typo can plunge you into a tax inferno!

 Raina Realtor kept an accurate record of her commissions for the year. When the realty firm sent her a Form 1099 erroneously stating $5,000 more in income than she had received, she could prove the correct amount. A copy of the incorrect Form 1099 went to the IRS, so Raina must get the realty company to send a corrected form to her *and* to the IRS.

In a case such as Raina's, I would include a copy of the corrected 1099 with the tax return along with an explanation, just in case the

What to do about an incorrect Form 1099-MISC

The company or individual who pays you $600 or more in one year is required to send you a Form 1099-MISC stating your income. A copy goes to the federal government and in some cases to the state as well. Compare your record of income to all Forms 1099-MISC that you receive.

You must claim the income you received whether correctly stated on a 1099 or not.

If a 1099 understates income, as long as you are satisfied with the explanation given you by the payer, there is no need to insist on a corrected Form 1099.

If a 1099 overstates the amount paid to you, contact the payer for an explanation and correction. For instance, if all your 1099s total $60,000 but you received only $50,000 in gross income, then you need to get the discrepancy corrected. Contact the issuing party quickly. The rule is that 1099s must be sent to the recipient (that's you) by January 31 and to the governments by the end of February, so you have only one month—the month of February—to get the original 1099 changed before it is sent to the Feds. But if the original erroneous 1099 has already been sent to the government, more effort is required: The issuing party must file a *corrected Form 1099.*

If you receive an overstated 1099 and you have income from many sources, it may not be necessary to have the 1099 corrected. You'll need to discuss this with your tax pro.

Keep copies of any correspondence regarding incorrect 1099s.

realty firm didn't get around to sending the corrected form to the IRS.

Errors happen whether your income is from many sources or from only one. And it doesn't matter whether the source is some mom-and-pop shop or some by-the-book corporation. A client of mine who is a freelance headhunter for the big and powerful accounting firms marvels at the inaccuracy of the income statements she receives from these firms every year. To our amusement, we compare her accurate amounts to their faulty 1099s and come up with thousands of dollars' difference. And financial recordkeeping is their business!

Writers across the country know that small—and not so small—publishing companies are notorious for their faulty recordkeeping. It is often a hassle and sometimes impossible to get accurate royalty statements from many of them. The least that should be done when receiving royalties is to record the income received and note the period of time that the royalties cover. Save the royalty statements for the life of the book.

If trying to collect from a delinquent client, accurate records are indispensable in arguing your point. For instance, if you've not received final payment because the company that owes you the money changed bookkeepers and your invoice has been put in the "paid-in-full" bin, you should be able to show any partial payments received, when, and for how much.

 Reality When Attila Atelier sold three of Clement Creator's paintings for a total of $20,000, Clement knew his 60

percent share should be $12,000. When he received three checks totaling only $10,900, he used his income record to show Attila's bookkeeper where the mistake had been made and that he was still owed $1,100.

Real estate salespersons paid by commission from one realty company, authors paid solely through a literary agent, musicians paid by numerous clubs and bandleaders, personal trainers paid by multimillion-dollar corporations—all these people have run into serious problems when they have relied upon someone else's records. Be smart: Rely on yourself.

How to Record Inflow

Astrid Astrologer gets paid mostly in cash; Wally Windowasher mostly by check; Bulky Benjamin's customers pay for their watch repairs in cash or by check or credit card. What should each indie do with the income when it's received? Well, as I said before, most important: Don't hide it.

Next: Keep it simple. If you receive payment by check, deposit the *entire* check into your checking account. **Do not split the check.** That is, if you receive $500 and you need $100 cash, deposit $500 and then write out a check to yourself for $100.

You probably think that it would be simpler to deposit only $400 and keep the $100 cash. No way. Here's why.

The IRS is not interested in deductions alone. In an audit of a self-employed, its expectation is that not all income is being claimed. Make it simple on yourself and the auditor by

keeping a clear record of the flow of money. In financial circles that's called an **audit trail,** and you want to keep the trail neat and tidy. To do that you must deposit **all** money initially into the *same* account. Whether it's payment from a client, your spouse's paycheck, or a birthday present from Mom, deposit the entire amount into your primary account. Then, if you want to move some money into savings or an investment account, write out a check or have money electronically transferred from your primary account to another account. This way your audit trail will directly lead from one stepping-stone to the next rather than zigzagging sideways and backward. (Yes, I did say into the *same* account. I called it a *primary* checking account. You will read more about personal and business checking accounts in the next chapter.)

An example of a zigzag: You receive a $1,000 payment by check. You *split* the check and put $500 into checking and $300 into a savings account, and keep $200 cash. Then two days later, when your balance is running low in your checking account, you transfer $300 from savings back to your checking account. When you look at your bank statements a year later, will you be able to recall which deposits were income and which were transfers?

By depositing everything initially into your primary account, it is easy to see that anything that went into a savings or investment account was not income but a *transfer* from your primary account and that only the deposits into the primary account are to be looked at as possible income. You can easily show a transfer *out of* the primary account matching a transfer *into* another account by the matching dates and amounts and "transfer" written on the deposit slip. Should you need to prove your income to the IRS, you can take them down a straight path rather than scrambling through a financial maze.

For example:

$1,000	income deposited into checking
(300)	transfer from checking matches a $300 deposit to savings
(200)	check for cash
$ 500	remains in checking account

Consider Keeping an Inflow Log

Some call an inflow log a "receipts journal," "cash receipts ledger," or a "spreadsheet." How simple it is will depend upon the type of freelance endeavor you have, what else is happening in your financial life, and how much information *you* want readily available. You may choose to create an inflow log; however, in the Most Simple System, an inflow log is not mandatory. Let's look at a few.

Clarissa Clothier, dressmaker, will accept only cash or checks as payment, and there's no sales tax in her state. Her income log is on lined paper on which she writes down the date and the amount of money received:

Date	Dress Money	Invoice #	Other	Other Description
7/15/08	175.00	208		
8/1/08			990.45	Med reimbursement
8/27/08			1000.00	Transfer from savings
9/16/08	320.00	212		

Rusty Rustic, horticulturist, gets paid in cash and by check and does some bartering. He also wants to know who paid him and how. His log has more columns and looks like this:

Date	Amount	From Whom	Check	Cash	Barter	PRSL	Description
7/15/08	175.00	F. Frolic	✓				
7/22/08	200.00	Ron Renew			✓		fixed mower for gardening
8/8/08	150.00					✓	Ron loan payback

Miles Mingus, musician, laid his out this way (note his subtraction for a student's bounced check):

Date	Gigs check	Gigs $	Teaching	Personal	Amount of deposit	Description
2/1/08			85.00			Grillo
2/1/08		500.00			585.00	Jazzy Jack's
2/8/08				100.00	100.00	Mom B'day
2/10/08			- 85.00			Grillo—bad check

P. I. Snoop, private detective, has his own variation. Note his page 1 total:

Date Received	Total Received	Amount From Client	Amount From Other	Date Deposited	Notes
2/1/08	500.00	500.00		2/9/08	L. Legal
2/8/08	100.00		100.00	2/9/08	Mom
2/10/08	623.14		623.14	2/11/08	wife's payck
P1 Total	1223.14	500.00	723.14		

Luisa Lifecoach accepts payment in any form:

Date	Client	Other	Amount Received	Checks	Checks Deposit	Credit Card	Credit Card Deposit
11/5/08	CC		500.00	500.00			
11/5/08	RR		300.00	300.00			
11/5/08	PRB		400.00			400.00	
11/10/08		sister	24.00	24.00			
11/10/08	BB		600.00			600.00	
11/15/08			1824.00		824.00		1000.00

Customize your inflow. Your inflow log must suit you. It must also give clear information, whether it is prepared on loose-leaf paper, graph paper, or ledger sheets or on your computer using a spreadsheet program such as Works or Excel. (A spreadsheet program is not a bookkeeping program. Using a computer spreadsheet program is simply mechanizing some manual work. It's like using a calculator instead of manually adding up a column of numbers.) If you do use a computer spreadsheet program, it should be easily convertible into hard copy.

Use as many columns as you need in your inflow log. Use one page per month or per quarter, or simply tally the columns when you come to the end of a page. Always start a new year on a new page. Instead of a date-deposited column, you can just check off that you did deposit the money. You can note gifts from Mom in red pen, color code clients, highlight all cash. There are lots of variations on how to record income. Whatever format you use, however sophisticated or folksy, **write the source of the money—the inflow—on the bank deposit slip.** The source of the inflow is usually a client's name or a shorthand phrase like "Mom gift." Some indies write down the client's check number as the source instead of the client's name. That's not useful to you. Be sure your deposit slips have a duplicate that you can keep for your records, because the original goes to your bank.

If you choose not to keep an inflow log because payments to you are straightforward or seldom, then be even more careful in denoting every deposit on the deposit slip. For instance, if three clients pay you in cash, then list each client on the deposit slip and the amount paid by each. Save every deposit slip and tally them for your year-end inflow/income record.

If photocopying every check that comes in makes your recordkeeping easier for you, then by all means, copy away. Attach the check copies to your copy of the deposit slip.

Anything that works for you is fine as long as there is a **tangible, clear record of what you received, when you received it, and from whom.** The less elaborate the better, because you will stick with something simple.

How and where do you file your deposit slip? The most simple thing to do is label one folder "Deposit Slips" and label another "Bank Statements." As you make deposits, put the deposit slips and any attachments verifying deposits into the Deposit Slips file. When your bank statement arrives, compare your deposit slips to the bank statement. If everything checks out—that is, if everything reconciles—attach the deposit slips to the back of the bank statement in the order that they appear on the statement, and put the statement in the folder labeled Bank Statements.

Log Reimbursements from Clients

P. R. Bernays bills his clients for expenses and wants a clear inflow record.

When you receive reimbursement from your client for expenses (such as telephone, travel, or supplies), log the reimbursement as inflow and classify it as a reimbursement in a way similar to P. R. Bernays, on the next page.

Date	Total Received	Fee Received	Expense Reimbursement	Other	Date Deposited	Notes
4/5/08	5800.00	5000.00	800.00 invoice #261		4/10/08	ABC CO
4/8/08	3700.00	3100.00	600.00 invoice #255		4/9/08	XYZ CO
7/10/08	128.69			128.69	7/14/08	Jack owed me
P1 total	9628.69	8100.00	1400.00	128.69		

There are two different bookkeeping methods for handling client reimbursements. If it suits your business, this is the one I find easier: Let's say you bill a client $5,000 for services and $800 as reimbursement for telephone expenses. When you get the check for $5,800, note on the deposit slip and in your inflow log, if you keep one, that there's $5,000 fee income and $800 reimbursement income. Claim the entire $5,800 as gross income. At the end of the year, if your business phone bills total let's say $12,000, you may deduct the entire $12,000 because you have claimed the $800 reimbursement as income. This way, your deposits match your income and your checks to the phone companies match your expenses. A variation on this method may be necessary in states where tax is levied on gross income. Since reimbursement is not income, you will want to differentiate the fee from the reimbursement for state tax purposes.

The alternative recordkeeping method requires you to claim only the $5,000 as income. Then, at year-end, instead of simply totaling your $12,000 in **TELEPHONE** expenses, you'll have to remember to deduct the $800 reimbursement to come up with a phone expense total of $11,200 ($12,000 phone expense minus the $800 you were reimbursed).

It's easier to include the expense reimbursement payment in income and then deduct all expenses—reimbursed and not. The above examples were for one client with one category of expense. With many more clients, and a variety of expenses, keeping track of which expenses have been reimbursed and which have not can be very confusing, and your bookkeeping will suffer for it. Whichever way you keep your books, it nets out to the same income in the end.

See below for an example of a self-employed with $40,000 gross income and $27,000 in expenses, $11,000 of which were reimbursed by clients:

Gross fees (reimbursements not included)	$40,000
Minus nonreimbursed expenses	(16,000)
Net profit	$24,000

or

Gross fees	$40,000
Other income: client reimbursements	11,000
Gross income	$51,000
Minus all expenses including those reimbursed	(27,000)
Net profit	$24,000

Incidentally, if your client sends you a Form 1099 stating the annual income paid to you, will expenses be included on the 1099? Who knows? Some clients will not include expense reimbursements; others will. Since the IRS compares the gross income on your tax return with the income information they receive via Form 1099, including reimbursements in income may avoid a later explanation to the IRS.

ALERT! Be aware that there are some clever businesspeople who will write out a check for you dated December 31. For them it is deductible in the year they wrote the check. For you, a cash-basis business, it is income when you receive it. (Cash basis versus accrual method was explained in Chapter Fourteen, Write-off Wrap-up.) If that check doesn't reach you until January 31 of the next year, well then, that's when you claim it as income. The exception to that rule is when the client paying you includes that December 31 payment in the Form 1099 sent you for that year. In cases like that you should complain to the payer and discuss it with your tax professional. You may have to claim the income as reported to you on the 1099. If you must, then be careful not to claim it again in the following year.

The concept of constructive receipt, which deals with income received around the new year, is discussed in Chapter Seventeen.

Record State Sales Tax or Gross Receipts Tax

Many states have a sales or gross receipts tax that you as the seller of a service or product must charge your clients. Your income log needs to clearly show your collection of that tax. And depending upon your state, its regulations, and the amount of sales tax that you collect, you may have to tally your income on a frequent basis, such as monthly or semiannually.

If you do collect sales tax, be sure your income log includes the following three columns:

Total Received	Amount for Product or Service	Amount Sales Tax
106.00	100.00	6.00

How Often Should You Tally Your Income?

For tax preparation purposes you need tally your income at year-end only. Whether you do so on a weekly, monthly, quarterly, or an irregular basis will depend upon **your** need for information. For instance, if you are planning a major purchase, you may want an idea of your income to date, or if you must forward sales or gross receipts tax to the state, you'll need a tally of how much you have collected. In Chapter Twenty-six, you will see that if you want to fine-tune your estimated tax payments, you will need to tally income more often than only at year-end.

When you gather your material at year-end for your tax preparer, remember to keep separate totals for your self-employed earned income and for any other money that came in to you. It is important for your tax pro to be made aware of a gift from Uncle Thatcher of $10,000 or a loan from Aunt Ada of $5,000. Although that money isn't taxable to you, it is part of your cash flow and can explain how you managed to spend $5,000 more than you earned.

 After you have a yearly total for your self-employed income, write that amount on the top line of the Self-employed Summary C Worksheet. You will write your expense totals on this same worksheet. All worksheets are found in Chapter Twenty-three.

To Sum Up Income Records

- Not all inflow is income.
- Don't rely on others for a record of your income.
- Clearly identify all inflow on deposit slips.
- Review Forms 1099 as soon as you receive them.

An inflow log is easy. Although it must be accurate, it can suit your business and your recordkeeping style. The log must be configured in such a way that for all money received, it will be evident how much you received, when you received the money, from whom, and for what.

CHAPTER TWENTY-TWO

The Most Simple System at Work: Quick and Simple Manual Recordkeeping

Let's see: You now know if you're self-employed, you know whether or not you're running a business, you know how to record inflow and how to recognize income, you can spot a business deduction hidden under a rug, and you know all the benefits of good records.

Are you ready for the next step—keeping a record of your spending in a quick and simple way without a computer?

 Syd System helped Hildy Housewife install the genealogy software that she'd just purchased. Hildy paid Syd the $300 fee by check. It was late on Friday; Syd ran to the bank, deposited $100 of the check, and kept $200 cash. Then he made a quick trip to OfficeArsenal to buy a $20 printer cable, for which he paid cash; next he picked up a bottle of wine for his neighbor; then he met his friend Stella Sellit for dinner—his treat because she was advising him on his new advertising brochures. He paid cash for the wine and the dinners. Saturday morning Syd left on a ski trip.

Do you think that when Syd returned from his winter weekend, he remembered any of the hasty financial transactions he'd made on Friday? Or do you expect, as I do, that the memory of it all is buried deep in the snow and when tax time comes around, in spite of the spring thaw, nothing will be revealed?

Syd's hectic pace is characteristic of the business life of many independent professionals. That's why my Most Simple System works so well for solos. It is a quick, easy, accurate recordkeeping method that, used along with my worksheets, will ensure no missed deductions and will provide complete backup should substantiation be needed in the event of an audit. This is a basic, manual, noncomputerized method. Were we looking at a beyond-the-basics approach, you'd see how easy it is to incorporate what you learn here into a full-fledged manual system or a computer bookkeeping program. But for now you won't need any technology.

In Chapter Six, Thinking Like an Indie Business, I urged that you adopt a new mind-set based on the concept that you are an indie business. And that whenever you reach into your pocket for money, you may be engaging in a business transaction. If you've forgotten the basics in that chapter, reread it. It's a short chapter and imperative to understanding what comes next. The Most Simple System puts the "indie business" mind-set into action.

Although it does call for a different way of thinking, this is not theory: It is a method that you will incorporate into every day of your life. You are about to put into practice what you've learned about expenses for the self-employed.

Whether your freelance venture or sole proprietorship has been up and running for several years or you're planning to open for business the week after Labor Day, this part of the Most Simple System starts now!

In the last chapter I talked about inflow. Now you're going to learn about outflow—what to do before, during, and after you spend money.

There are four simple steps that will lead you out of the tax maze: Get, sort, tally, write.

Step 1: Get backup for every dollar spent.

Step 2: Sort and stack all backup.

Step 3: Tally all backup.

Step 4: Write it to the worksheets.

Let's look at each step in detail.

Step 1: Get Backup for Every Dollar You Spend

This is the cardinal rule, the keystone, the get-go, the core of the Most Simple System. There is nothing philosophical about it, and it doesn't involve debits, credits, trial balances, or ledgers. It's just something you do.

> From this day forward, pay for absolutely everything by check or credit card, or if you must pay by cash, then get a receipt. For everything and anything—personal expenditures or business expenses—follow this rule.

Do not take money out of your pocket—literally dollars, or their virtual equivalent, a check or credit card—without getting something back for the other pocket: a canceled check, a credit card slip, or a cash receipt. Let's call it backup.

I'll say it again: **Get backup for everything!** Groceries, a hat, a bottle of wine, a birthday card, a computer, diapers, office supplies, flowers, books, **everything!**

When paying by check your backup is your canceled check. When you pay by credit card, your backup is your credit card receipt slip—keep them all. If paying by check or credit card is impossible, pay with cash and get a receipt as your backup.

As long as you pay for **everything** by check or credit card, or get a receipt when you have to spend cash, there's little else you need to do all year. The trick is to get into the habit.

Furthermore, this rule applies not only to everything you spend but also to everything your spouse spends. Yes, even if your husband is not in business for himself and has nothing to do with your business. (The chair he purchased at the garage sale may have been intended for the kitchen, but when he brought it home you decided it was perfect for the sunny corner in your office.) And it applies to your children as well—whenever they pay for something for you, they must get a receipt.

Sometimes I have to talk reluctant indies into this new way of thinking. I remind you that this is the Most Simple System and this is the first step in the most simple way of keeping records. It's worked for my clients for more than twenty-five years.

Sure, it's a bother to ask for a receipt for everything you spend. After all, Sammy Segar, CPA, has advised you "just save business receipts"—and he handles a couple of big companies and was your father's accountant for years. Your brother never saves receipts and he got a huge refund. So I suppose you've got to be talked into it. Listen up: Here are some Reality Checks that will convince you.

 At the Total Foods checkout counter, Luisa Lifecoach decides against the hassle of writing out a check; besides, it's just groceries anyway. She puts four twenties on the counter, takes her change, and leaves the receipt on the counter. But that evening when the three women from the county senior center meet at her home to discuss the workshop she will present next month at the center, Luisa serves dessert and coffee that she bought that day at Total Foods. The expense of that food and drink is a deductible **MEALS & ENTERTAINMENT** business expense. Poor Luisa has no receipt. And some appetites those ladies had.

(If Luisa did have backup for the expense, she would deduct only the cost of the items she served to her business associates; she would not deduct the entire Total Foods amount if it included her groceries, for instance.)

 Nadine Novella must get her manuscript and Christmas cards mailed before leaving to visit her father in Vintage Village, Florida. Nadine follows the cardinal rule of the Most Simple System—she pays for **everything** by check. So in her haste, no need to think about the business deductibility of postage—of course she paid for the postage by check. Months later, when she goes though her canceled checks, she'll have her proof of the **POSTAGE** expense for mailing her manuscript and for the stamps used for that portion of Christmas cards sent to her business associates.

During that stop at the post office, resourceful Nadine also mailed a letter confirming her appointments with several board members and oldest residents of Vintage Village. She is planning to write a piece about the disposition and mood change of old folks when the "kids" arrive for the holidays. She had written the co-op board several months ago explaining her idea for the article and requesting interviews. Of course she is paying all her **TRAVEL** expenses by check or credit card.

Why do you get backup for every dollar you spend? So that you don't have to make decisions on the spot. You have the option of deciding later whether the expense relates to your business and therefore whether it is deductible. When pushing to meet a deadline or hurrying from a cab to make your next appointment, taxes are the furthest thing from your mind. But if you never miss that first step—getting backup for every dollar you spend—then should you find after rereading Chapter Ten that your Florida trip is a business deduction, or a partial deduction, all your receipts are available. You won't have to reconstruct your expenses after the fact.

So be sure the flashing light goes off: When money, in any form, leaves your pocket, you must get something in return—a canceled check (eventually), a charge slip, or a receipt for cash.

Before moving on to Step 2, let's examine in detail each of these methods of payment and the pieces of paper that are your evidence of expenses.

Checking Accounts

To get back a canceled check, well, that naturally means you have a checking account that returns canceled checks or copies of canceled checks to you. If your account doesn't provide originals or copies, change banks.

If that's impossible, you'll have to adjust the system, but a key element of its simplicity will have been lost.

You need only one checking account. Do not open a separate checking account for your business. Yes, that's the exact opposite of what Sammy Segar, CPA, told you. And it's not just Sammy who tells you that. In one IRS publication you are urged to open a business checking account and "although a bank may charge you an extra fee for a business account, the new account will more than pay for itself in accounting efficiency." The very next example from the IRS in the publication is the mixed use (personal and business use) of your automobile. So, let's see how efficient two checking accounts would be in this situation. Hmm ... guess you are expected to pay for each gas purchase with two checks—one for the personal use amount of gas and a business check for the business use portion.

Most accountants disagree strongly with my position. They don't know you like I know you! My system will save you money and time; their advice will cost you money and time.

Reality Let's look again at Luisa Lifecoach shopping for groceries at Total Foods. If she had both a personal and a business checking account, which one should she have used to pay for her groceries, assuming she knew that three business associates were coming over that evening? Oh! says Sammy, CPA, she should have divided the groceries into two piles: one for family and one for business guests. And paid with two checks. And what if Luisa's three-year-old was tearing at the display case while she was at the checkout and she was late picking up her ten-year-old at soccer practice?

Sammy Segar always insists that a business checking account is a must. But Sammy, if Luisa is just starting out, where does she get the money to put into her business account? Sammy says, transfer it from her personal account. But I thought that you're supposed to keep these accounts separate? OK, says Sammy, after she has made a little money, transfer the funds back to her personal account. But whoa, wait a minute, Luisa transferred too much out of the business account; now she'll have to move some back to the business account again. It's beginning to get messy already, and how will she keep a record of those transfers? Well, she won't get any help from

Sammy: He hates working with those eccentric indies.

As long as your records are accurate, one checking account is perfectly acceptable to the IRS. I think one big factor in the insistence on a business checking account is that it's supposed to cover up financial shenanigans. Many people like to believe that because something is paid by a business check that makes it a business deduction. Of course, that is not so! The attaché case for your daughter's twentieth birthday, even though purchased with your business check, is not a business expense. But the flowers, paid from your personal account, given to your mother as thanks for typing your business plan, are a business expense.

As I've said before, in the lives of self-employeds the line between personal and business is not clearly drawn; it wiggles around a lot. By the nature of the types of businesses that self-employeds are in and by the structure of a sole proprietorship, personal and business often intertwine—almost always so in the creative fields. You do not want to struggle with business versus personal decisions every time you spend money.

Use one checking account! One that returns canceled checks or copies to you along with your bank statement.

Besides, a business checking account costs money, while your own checking or savings account is usually free of charge. Who needs the extra expense? Well, sometimes it's unavoidable. It may be necessary to have a separate account if you do not use your own name as your business name.

Reality✓ Graphic designer Victor Visual decided to call his business the Double V Studio, and most folks pay him with checks made out to his business name. Because his bank does not allow both names—Victor Visual and Double V—on his account, he'll have to have an account in the name of his business in order to deposit his checks. The simple (and money-saving) alternative is for Victor to open a savings account in his business name, deposit the checks into it, and then have the bank do an automatic sweep of the funds from his savings to his checking account whenever the funds reach a certain amount specified by Victor.

Paying Bills by Check

Whenever you pay a bill by check, write the check number and the date paid on the invoice. For example, if you paid your phone bill on March 14 with check number 607, it might look like this:

TOUCHTONE TELEPHONE TITAN

One month service $987.65   *Check #607*
3/14/08

File the receipts consecutively, by check number, in a folder labeled "2008 Check Backup." You may do something with them later.

Reconciling a Bank Statement

Yup, that's what they call making sure you or your bank didn't make a mistake. Think of it as reconciling your differences. Once a month your bank sends you a statement along with your canceled checks. You need to reconcile the bank statement balance with the balance you've tallied in your check register. Register—that's the little lined pad that comes with your checkbook where you list deposits you've made and the checks you've written.

If you think that there's no need to look over your bank statement, here's an incentive: The sleepy-looking, surly bank teller—the one with the C-minus grade average who didn't say good morning when you made your deposit—is entering **your** numbers in the bank's computer system.

You saw in the previous chapter that after comparing your record of deposits to those on the bank statement, you were to take the deposit slips from the Deposit Slips folder and attach them to the back of the bank statement, which then went into the Bank Statements file.

Compare the originals or copies of the canceled checks to the amounts on the bank statement. When you are satisfied that you and the bank have no differences of opinion, put the canceled checks in a folder or envelope labeled "2008 Canceled Checks." You are going to do something with them later.

Credit Cards

Using one credit (or debit) card simplifies your financial life. If your finances can handle it, open two credit cards, but use only one. Hide the other for emergencies, such as when the first one is lost, stolen, or fraudulently used.

An exception to this dictum is credit card purchases on the Web, where fraud is rampant. I've had a $100 Christmas gift certificate fraudulently charged to my account. The crooks assumed, or hoped, that in the high volume of transactions during the holiday season, a mere hundred dollars wouldn't be noticed. Hah! They didn't know whom they were dealing with! On another occasion I had cheaters bill thousands of dollars in computer equipment to my card. You can reduce such risks by using a separate card for Internet purchases only and by requesting a low credit limit on it. Banks offer special cards or account numbers just for online purchases. Check it out. Stay vigilant anyway.

Save every credit card slip. Place a container convenient to your point of entry—a basket on your desk, a big envelope on the hall table. A creative but harried client uses a wooden breadbox with a rolltop door as her catchall on the kitchen table. Closed up, no one would ever know. Drop your credit card slips into the container at the end of the day.

Print out some sort of record for every purchase made online. Label a folder "Online Purchases" and put it near your computer.

By the way, whatever your backup—credit card, canceled check, or cash receipt—if what you purchased is not evident from the receipt—for instance, $125 spent at Deepak's Department Store—at the time of purchase, write a notation on the receipt such as "reference book," "scarf," or "desk chair."

Once a month, whether you give it your full attention or do it while on the phone with your marathon-talker sister, match your credit card slips and online purchases to your credit card statement. Don't pay your credit card until you've compared your receipts to the statement.

If you've lost the slip but know the charge is accurate, handwrite a receipt noting the needed information. For example:

10/28/08—Visa statement

10/16/08 $88.48 D.C. shuttle ticket

Attach all that month's receipts, including any handmade ones, to the statement in the order they appear on the statement. File the statement in a folder labeled "2008 Visa Statements." If you have more than one credit card, make a folder for each card. Label each folder with the name of the card, or perhaps label it using the last four digits of your card number—for example, MC 3210 for your MasterCard account number 1234-5654-3210.

In one year you will have twelve monthly credit card statements, each with its slips attached. You are going to do something with them later.

Review your credit card statement regularly. Remember the sleepy-looking bank teller? He quit the bank and is now working for Bigbank Visa. One step beyond incompetence takes us to the cheats. You'd notice a $1,000 watch that you did not purchase charged to your account, but what about the small stuff? A client charged $19 at Barnes and Noble during Christmas week. When her statement arrived it showed the B&N charge as $49. The credit card company sent her a copy of the receipt she had signed. It showed $49. Apparently the store clerk had made a 4 out of the 1 and took $30 cash out of the register so that the store's receipts still balanced at day's end. A nice holiday bonus for him if he did that several times a day.

Another client was erroneously charged for a $100 key deposit secured by a signed charge slip that was wrongly entered even though the key had been returned. A couple on vacation for three months had some bills paid automatically via their credit card. Careful scrutiny caught a heavy hand on the zero key that changed a $25.00 expense into $250.00.

You might not notice a discrepancy in your statement if you charge large amounts, or use your credit card for many transactions, or have a high balance and pay only the minimum, or if anxiety induces you to close your eyes and blindly pay the bill when the monthly statement arrives. As I noted earlier, Internet credit card cheats are getting subtler and shrewder. They don't steal your card number and charge like a bull, running up thousands of dollars in purchases. Instead, they steal a lot of credit card numbers and sneak one or two items onto a lot of cards. They get away with it because so few people check their statements.

I can't say it too often: Review your statement.

Handling Straddle Statements

In your recordkeeping, do not combine or straddle years. Start on January 1 and end on December 31. Stop using your check register on December 31 and put it with that year's records. Start a new register on January 1.

Most bank and credit card monthly statements do not start on the first day of the month nor end on the last. They straddle months, and

therefore they straddle years—for instance, December 14, 2008, through January 13, 2009. When you have a monthly statement that straddles a year, make a copy of the statement. Put the original and any deposit slips, canceled checks, or credit card receipts dated December 31 or before with the earlier year's records (2008); put the copy and all paper transaction records taking place January 1 or later with the later year's records (2009).

Some banks and financial institutions are willing to change your cycle so that it ends on the last day of the month.

For cash-basis taxpayers (you'd know if you weren't), an invoice paid by check on or before December 31, 2008, regardless of when it clears your account, is considered paid by you in 2008. If it's a business expense, it should be deducted on your 2008 tax return and put away with your 2008 records.

The same holds true for purchases made with a bank—not a store—charge card. Purchases on or before December 31 are deducted as expenses in that year, regardless of when you pay the credit card bill.

Paying Cash and Getting Receipts

Right next to the box you have for dropping off your credit card slips, put another container—a wicker basket or a shoe box (one of my clients uses a plaster skull with the cranium sawed off)—into which you drop your cash receipts. Receipts for anything that you did not purchase by check or credit card—from shelf brackets at the hardware store to newspapers and aspirins at the drugstore—all go into the cash container.

Write a $ (a dollar sign) at the top of the receipt. This way in case you throw a receipt into the wrong container, it'll be clear at sorting time that this is a receipt for a cash expense.

Without exception all cash receipts go into the container. This is also the time to note on the receipt a description of the item if it is not self-evident. But there is no need to make a spot decision as to whether or not the item is a business expense.

Oops! No receipt? If you forgot to get a receipt, make one. Get a scrap of paper and write down the important information: date, description, amount.

 You and a friend, Celia Ceramist, do lunch at Diners Delight. While waiting for your food, you express dissatisfaction with the work of your print shop. Celia tells you about the new Pronto Press that just opened in her neighborhood, which is offering first-time customers big discounts. Your response: "Thanks, Celia. I'll be able to get the postcards out on time. You've saved me a bundle. Lunch is on me." You both talked so long that you hurried out, paid cash, and forgot to get a receipt. When you get back to your home office later that afternoon, don't concern yourself whether the lunch is a business deduction or not (it is), but remember that in the Most Simple System you must have backup for **all** your expenses. So take one of those scraps of paper that you have in small piles ready for just such occasions and on it write today's date, the name of your business associate, the amount of lunch including tip, and the reason for the lunch.

6/14/08 with Celia Ceramist

lunch — $33.00 w/tip

printer re: Pecos Postcards

Throw that handwritten receipt into your cash receipts skull. For now you're finished with it.

 Celia Ceramist returned to her studio equally late, with just enough time to get the tiles ready for the kiln. She had taken the bus across town to buy supplies before meeting you for lunch. Now, while cleaning up in the studio, she remembered having no bus fare receipts, so on a scrap of paper she wrote the date, the destination, and the fare. She threw the note in the big urn that she keeps conveniently on the floor near the door to the studio. (She probably would not have written down this expense if first she had to clean her gummy hands and then get a ledger book from her desk located on the studio's second floor.)

6/14/08

errands & Victor Visual printer info

Bus $6.00

The IRS will accept these handwritten notations on scraps of paper as expense records. However, it is not a good practice to have **most** of your expenses backed up by handmade receipts. If you have $2,000 in business **SUPPLIES,** of which $1,900 is noted on scraps of paper, don't expect that to fare well in an audit.

Be creative. I remember explaining to a graphic artist that because for him all magazines he purchased were a visual resource of one sort or another, he could deduct all of them. When I told him he'd need to get receipts for his magazine purchases, he said, "Do you want me to get myself beat up trying to get a receipt for a magazine at a busy newsstand in New York City?" Back then, most magazines had the price on the front cover. The next year when he came to see me, with an air of accomplishment, he opened an envelope and poured out all these tiny triangles of paper. He'd cut the corner price off each magazine. The total was more than $1,100, a surprise to both of us.

The moral: Because of your unique business situation, to take full advantage of the tax laws, you must be creative.

Ready for the Next Step

In the Most Simple System, you do not do any recordkeeping in the sense that most people think of it—those intimidating ledger sheets that look like plaid paper, or business expense diaries that must have been designed for somebody else's business but not yours, or calendars that are never where they're needed when they're needed. All you need to do is pay for **everything** by either check or charge card or get a cash receipt. There is no need to be meticulous about keeping an expense ledger; you've tried that before and you were perfect at it—for a week. Using the Most Simple System,

just about everything you need at tax time will be on hand in your canceled checks folder, credit card statement files, or receipt box.

OK, it took some time to explain how to collect canceled checks, charge slips, and receipts. Now what do you do with them? Well, first, rejoice in your own good sense: You've got backup.

At our initial meeting, one of my new clients had no reason to celebrate. As we reviewed tax return material for him and his wife—both freelance writers—I asked if he had any records to substantiate their expenses. He told me that on the previous night, as he was getting ready for our meeting, he sorted all his papers and got so much into the swing of it that he cleaned his desk and threw away all the papers he thought I wouldn't need. He threw out all those wrinkled receipts and coffee-stained charge slips—even the canceled checks. Oops.

But you have all your records! You're following the Most Simple System. It's April 1 and you're preparing to go to your tax preparer to get your return done—starting early this year just as you promised yourself you would last year on April 15.

Step 2: Sort and Stack All Backup

You are about to take your backup records and put them into a format useful in the preparation of your tax return. You have a choice as to when you put together the information you've collected on money spent. You can do it once a year just before tax time, or you can do it incrementally, as the spirit moves you.

A year is twelve consecutive months

My bass player client's tax year, and yours, begins on January 1 and ends December 31. It's called a **calendar year** because it exactly follows our calendar.

A **fiscal year** (and don't laugh at people who think it's a physical year, because they may play bass better than you ever could) may conform to the calendar year but then again it may not. "Fiscal" means having to do with finances, and a fiscal year covers a span of twelve months, but they can be any twelve consecutive months. The federal government's fiscal year begins on October 1 and ends on September 30 of the following year, and Congress adopts a budget based on that time period.

You can file your returns and pay taxes on a fiscal-year rather than a calendar-year basis, but you must contact the IRS and receive permission to do so in advance. In some businesses it might make sense to follow a fiscal year. Say, for example, that you are making a great success of a ski shop, but most of your business comes between October and February—straddling the calendar year. Not only is it artificial in terms of your business to stop counting on December 31 and start counting anew on January 1, but in order to see how your business is faring, you probably want to compare not one calendar year to another but one winter season to another. It might make more sense to have a fiscal year that's in sync with your business, like from June 1 through May 31.

Let me warn you, though: Changing to a fiscal year isn't easy, involves unforeseen consequences, and complicates your financial life. Be sure that you want it and that despite the effort it will work better for you in the end.

Unless your self-employed endeavor is seasonal, use the calendar year as your tax year. As a calendar-year taxpayer your year ends on December 31, and even if your first year of business started in the middle of the summer, it still ends on December 31. Remember that. There are lots of forms that ask when your tax year ends. And you won't have to call your accountant to find out.

Every month is fine; every three months—that's called quarterly—is also OK; New Year's Eve if the snowstorm kept you from getting to the party or you are determined to fulfill last year's resolution; two days before your appointment with your accountant in April, if you're slow to muster; or early October with just enough time to make the extension deadline of October 15, if you're the procrastinator of the group.

The point is: The exact time frame doesn't matter; it is entirely up to you. Gather your backup whenever it suits you.

The deadline is: in time to get your paperwork to your tax preparer so that she can complete your tax return before the last extension deadline.

The wrong way to categorize: The proof is not in the writing

In this chapter I explain the right way to categorize your business expenses. But before that, let's look at the *wrong* way:

Get a piece of paper and label columns at the top with expense categories; get the check register; write amounts from the register on the piece of paper in the different columns; add each column to come up with a total for each expense category.

What's wrong with this cumbersome procedure? First, it's a lot of work. Second, it's a method prone to mistakes ($183 in the check register, for instance, gets transcribed as $138). And the third reason—and the most important—is that in an audit it's worthless. A handwritten list of expenses totaling $986 for SUPPLIES does not prove that even one dollar was spent for anything. The proof lies in canceled checks and receipts, and a column of numbers is just that—a list of numbers. To show the IRS that you did in fact spend $986 on SUPPLIES, you would have to retrieve your backup totaling $986. And that would be just for SUPPLIES; you would have to do the same for every other expense category.

The goal is: an accurate and complete total of your business expenses for the year.

What's a year? One of my clients collected all his records from April 16 through the follow-

ing April 15 because he knew that's when tax returns are due. He's a bass player and my only client who ever made that mistake. Actually, he's a very talented bass player.

OK, if you've adhered to the core component of the Most Simple System by getting backup for every dollar spent, then you are ready to go. You have:

- Twelve monthly bank statements in a folder labeled 2008 Bank Statements.
- Receipts or invoices for checks written for the year labeled 2008 Check Backup.
- A year's worth of canceled checks in the envelope labeled 2008 Canceled Checks.
- Twelve credit card statements with their receipts attached in a folder labeled 2008 Visa Statements.
- A box with the year's cash and home-made cash receipts.

The IRS does not look at your expenses chronologically; your tax return is done categorically. It's not how much you spent in the month of September but how much you spent for **SUPPLIES** that interests the IRS. So we are about to sort expenses by category.

The Whatta Concept! at left shows you what *not* to do. Now here's how to sort your backup the easy way. When done, you will know the amount spent in each business category for the entire year, you'll miss not one business expense, and you'll have the proof of all your expenses ready in the event of an audit.

It's a bit like playing solitaire. Clear a space—your kitchen or conference table, drafting board, desk, or the floor.

Get the List of Deductible Business Expenses from Chapter Fifteen, copy it, or if you're feeling aggressive, rip it out of the book. It will be your guide when sorting all your spending into appropriate business categories. You may also use the worksheets in Chapter Twenty-three as a guide. Here goes:

Sort and Stack Canceled Checks

Most folks hate to mix up their canceled checks. They prefer to keep them in numerical order in the envelope with the bank statement. (That's a neat way to keep them, although it's of little use.) But you know better. You have collected yours in an envelope, labeled "2008 Canceled Checks," for later sorting.

If your canceled checks come to you photocopied as part of your bank statement, then cut them up. Not comfortable with that? Then copy and cut. You need individual checks for this method.

Sort the checks into piles, each pile a different business expense—for example: **ADVERTISING, BUSINESS GIFTS, POSTAGE, REPAIRS.**

It is here, at the sorting stage, where you will finally make those decisions as to what is

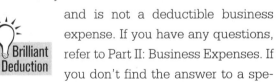

and is not a deductible business expense. If you have any questions, refer to Part II: Business Expenses. If you don't find the answer to a specific question, then put those uncertain expenses into an **ASK TAX PREPARER** category.

Make the Most of your Expenses

When you're sorting your expenses into stacks, have your calendar in front of you. Look for business activity around the dates of

those checks and receipts that don't spark anything in your mind. As you come to the check made out to Len's Liquor on March 20, look to your calendar. When you see that on March 21 you went to visit fellow freelance horticulturist Rusty Rustic to talk about organic fertilizing methods, you may remember that you brought over two bottles of wine for that occasion. That check goes into the business **MEALS & ENTERTAINMENT** pile. (Be sure to review Chapter Eight to note the special kind of annotation needed for a **MEALS & ENTERTAINMENT** expense.)

When you're sorting, if the check itself is not evidence of the expense or if it is not clear what the check paid for, go to your 2008 Check Backup folder; look up the check backup by number of the check, and staple the backup to that check. Then put the check with its attached backup in the appropriate pile.

 No specialist he, Warren Wordsmith prides himself on being a "generalist writer." He'll write about anything if a magazine will pay him for it. Therefore every check he sends to Publishers Clearance Quarters

 is a deductible **PUBLICATIONS** expense. But a check made out to the Country Store will need backup to show that it was for three magazines.

In addition to your piles for each business expense category, you may have separate piles for personal tax deductible expenses such as **MEDICAL** and **CHARITABLE CONTRIBUTIONS.**

There should be a pile for "Personal: Not

Too much work?

Some people think the government makes you jump through hoops for a few measly deductions. Is this method too much effort for you? Let's look at the numbers.

A $120 MEALS & ENTERTAINMENT expense means a $60 deduction. If you're in a zero tax bracket, it will save you approximately 15% in self-employment tax. That's $9.

If you're in a 28% tax bracket and you live in a high-tax state, it could save you 15% SE tax plus 28% federal income tax plus 7% state income tax. That totals 50%, which is a direct tax savings of $30 on a $120 business meal expense.

It's taken some effort, and it's made a difference of possibly $30 to you. Too much work for a piddling thirty bucks? Or do you hold to the view that thirty bucks here and thirty bucks there eventually adds up to real money? The decision is up to you: your time and effort measured against how much of your money you will send to government entities. It's up to you to value your time spent versus taxes saved.

Needed for Taxes" items and one pile for "Ask Tax Preparer" items.

What If You Had Multiple Expenses on One Check?

If you purchased personal items and office supplies at Megamall-Mart with one check, then get your check backup, circle the business items and their amounts, tally them, note the business amount on the receipt, and put the check—with the receipt attached—on your SUPPLIES pile.

During your sorting, when you come to the Total Foods check made out on the day the business associates came to your home for an evening meeting, get your Total Foods receipt from the 2008 Check Backup. If you didn't note on the receipt at the time of the purchase which items were snacks for the business meeting, then do so now. If you can no longer remember which items and amounts were for your business associates, then do some sensible estimating. If you know that you spend approximately $175 per week for groceries and this check is for $295, you can assume a $120 business expense. Write down the reasoning behind your calculation, the amount, who was there and why, and attach the note to the check. Put the check with attached note in the MEALS & ENTERTAINMENT pile.

Sort and Stack Credit Card Receipts

After you've finished sorting checks into appropriate piles, get your twelve monthly charge card statements. Double that amount if you have two credit cards, thirty-six if you have three credit cards, and so on.

Just as you copied your bank statement(s) that straddled December and January, do the same with your December–January credit card statement(s). File the original with the earlier year, the copy with the new year's records.

Remember the December 31 Rule

When sorting credit card receipts, keep in mind, as I pointed out earlier in this chapter, that every item charged on or before December 31 is an expense for that year, even if it isn't paid for until the following year. If you carry a large balance on your credit card and don't pay it off for several years, the business expense is still deductible in the year it was charged.

The exception to the December 31 rule is for store credit cards. Here's why: If you purchase a computer from OfficeArsenal on December 31, 2008, and charge it to your Bigbank Visa, Bigbank pays OfficeArsenal. You do not owe OfficeArsenal, you owe Bigbank. You've paid for your computer; it's the bank you haven't paid. Same as if you'd borrowed the money from Momma to buy the computer and plan to pay her back as soon as your client pays you.

However, if you charged that computer to your OfficeArsenal credit card, you could deduct only the amount of money that you had actually paid OfficeArsenal. You did not yet pay for your computer because OfficeArsenal had not yet received its money. If you failed to pay the balance owed, then OfficeArsenal could repossess your computer.

Now you're ready to work with credit card receipts. Over the course of the year, you have been attaching receipts to the credit card statements. The hour has come to go to the 2008 Visa Statements folder. Starting with January, detach the receipts; place each one in a category pile that you have already set up for the canceled checks. For instance, a credit card receipt for **MEALS & ENTERTAINMENT** goes on top of the pile of checks for **MEALS & ENTERTAINMENT,** and so on.

Perhaps as you do this you'll find the need for a new pile when an additional category

 Brilliant Deduction (such as **BUSINESS INSURANCE** or **EQUIPMENT**) appears among the receipts.

As you complete each month's statement, reattach the nonbusiness Personal: Not Needed for Taxes receipts to the monthly statement. Then put the credit card statement back in the 2008 Visa Statements file.

What If You Have a Receipt with More Than One Category of Deductible Business Expense on It?

Make a copy of the receipt. Note the amount for each expense, then distribute the original and copy or copies to the appropriate pile. If you don't have access to a copier, handwrite a receipt.

For instance, your receipt from the Heartbreak Hotel includes both your lodging, which you will put in the **TRAVEL** pile, and your restaurant and bar tab. You know from reading Chapter Eight that the restaurant and bar tab expenses must be separated from your other **TRAVEL** expenses.

Since you don't have a copier available, your handwritten receipt for the second expense looks like this:

> *see original in TRAVEL expenses*
> *VISA 8/15/08*
> *Heartbreak Hotel   Meals & Ent $226.89*

Sort and Stack Receipts for Cash Expenses

Next, get your skull, basket, or urn that is filled with cash receipts and handwritten scraps of paper detailing expenses for which you forgot to get a receipt. All the expenses you had that were not paid by check or credit card now get placed on top of the existing piles.

Here's the Sunday newspaper, that goes to **PUBLICATIONS.** Breakfast with Maxine, that's **MEALS & ENTERTAINMENT.** Oh yes, the book on sailing, that goes with the Sunday newspaper receipt to **PUBLICATIONS.** The desk and chairs purchased at a garage sale go to the **EQUIPMENT** pile. **TOLLS & PARKING** have their own stack. Gas and car repairs go to **AUTO.** The taxi receipt goes to **TRANSPORTATION.**

You'll know when you're done because no more pieces of paper or canceled checks will be uncategorized. All will be in one pile or another.

Step 3: Tally 'Em

Finally, you get to use something technological: a calculator with a paper tape. The tape is a must. The cost of the calculator—approximately $35—is deductible.

Add up each pile. Save yourself a lot of time and reduce your errors by not doing pennies. If it's 50 cents or more, round off to the next dollar; if it's 49 cents or less, drop the cents. Believe me, and those who know the law of averages can back me up, it always evens out within a couple of dollars.

$16.40	=	$16
$ 1.50	=	$ 2
$17.90	=	$18

After you've tallied each stack, tear the tape from the calculator, leaving about an inch of extra blank tape on the bottom. Write down the category of business expense (for instance, **DUES**) on the very bottom of the tape, with some space for writing between the total and the category name. You may use that space later. Staple or securely fasten the tape to its pile of checks, charge slips, and receipts.

A psychologist asked why the calculator must have a tape. One reason, which she professionally understood: "It's your security blanket. You can see just how the sum of $4,321 for **PHOTOCOPIES & PRINTING** was arrived at." There are other reasons. The tape is a convenient reference—you can check off each category total after you've transferred that total amount onto my worksheet. If you are audited and the IRS guy wants to see your **PHOTOCOPIES & PRINTING** expenses, you just pull out your stack of receipts with the tape attached. If he chooses to check your addition and comes up with a total of $3,321 instead of your $4,321, it will be easy enough to compare tapes and see who made the wrong tally. The tape is also convenient if you want to tack on a handwritten estimated additional amount for expenses that you know were missed because your honey forgot to get receipts. It will be easy to distinguish later between expenses for which you have backup and expenses for which you don't; the latter will be written in the extra space left on the bottom of the tape.

The Cohan Rule

Speaking of estimates, I noted earlier in the book that some expenses can be estimated if it can be shown that expenses were incurred. For instance, if you can show that you do a one-hundred-customer mailing three times a year but have no **POSTAGE** receipts, you may calculate what your mailing costs would have been and use that amount as a business deduction.

Estimated expense is a concession that was wrung out of the IRS many years ago, and it's called the Cohan rule. It's named after a man well known on Broadway and with a niche in tax history as well: George M. Cohan, the famous songwriter-playwright and all-around Yankee Doodle Dandy.

In the 1920s Cohan appealed an IRS ruling disallowing his travel and entertainment expenses because he couldn't document any of them. The appeals court decided in his favor, stating that absolute certainty of expense figures was not necessary. In 1963 a court case ruled that **BUSINESS GIFTS** and **MEALS & ENTERTAINMENT** expenses must be backed up (as I noted in Chapter Eight), but the Cohan rule still applies in other categories.

How Often Should You Tally?

Well, if anxiety nags at you when there's too much loose paper around and you feel the need to tally your expenses on a monthly basis, do it exactly as outlined above. Then put each monthly tally into an envelope or folder labeled by category: **ADVERTISING, EQUIPMENT, REPAIRS/MAINTENANCE,** etc. Tally your monthly totals at year-end.

Step 4: Write 'Em Up

Once you've tallied the business expense piles, you have done nearly all the necessary record-keeping for the business deductions portion of your tax return and your records are ready for IRS scrutiny in the event of an audit. If the IRS does question your return at some time in the future, you will have only to look over your finished tallies, and since they are in such good shape, the review should not take long. You don't panic (well, some of you probably will panic anyway but it's needless) because you know you have perfect, provable backup for your expenses. Once your tax return is filed, you never again have to concern yourself about that year or its records.

What Do You Do with These Tallied Piles of Expenses?

This is where my Most Simple System worksheets come in. You will learn all about them in the next chapter.

You will write your expense totals on the worksheets. When the worksheets are completed, they will provide your tax preparer with all the information she will need to prepare the sole-proprietor portion of your tax return.

You will also have ample information based upon your personal tax deduction tallies—**CHARITABLE CONTRIBUTIONS, MEDICAL, INVESTMENT FEES PAID,** etc.—to provide your tax preparer with much of the information needed to prepare the parts of your tax return not related to self-employment.

Other than any checks, credit card slips, and cash receipts that are in your **ASK TAX**

PREPARER pile, you do not have to bring the actual backup for your expenses to your tax preparer. You need only bring the worksheets.

If thinking as an indie business has become habitual, and if you follow these steps (as well as the instructions that accompany the worksheets in the next section), you will have, with a minimum output of your time, taken advantage of every deduction available, prepared the material for your tax return, and readied yourself for any inquiry from the government. You will also have cut a good chunk from your accountant's time and thereby reduced tax preparation cost.

CHAPTER TWENTY-THREE

The Worksheets: Put It Together with the Most Simple System

I've mentioned the Most Simple System worksheets throughout the book. You may have used some of these as reference when sorting and

tallying your expense backup. The worksheets are your means of presenting your self-employed tax information to your preparer. They are:

- Self-employed Summary C
- Travel Expense Other Than Auto
- Business Use of Auto, Truck, or Other Vehicle
- Auto, Truck, or Other Vehicle Purchase
- Studio or Office in the Home
- Residence or Real Estate Purchase
- Residence or Real Estate Sale
- Capital Improvements to Residence or Other Real Estate
- Equipment and Inventory

Accompanying each worksheet, if necessary, is a description or instructions. Some of the worksheets follow the format of an actual IRS form but modify it to make the entries more understandable and useful to you and your tax preparer.

You will put your tallied expense totals on the appropriate lines of the worksheets. On some worksheets additional information—such as total business miles—is required.

Don't cheat yourself by relying on only the worksheets. You need to have read much of **Self-employed Tax Solutions** to take full advantage of every Most Simple System tax maneuver and deduction.

Doing the worksheets is a simple and easy-to-follow procedure. Get yourself a cup of coffee

or a glass of wine. Now, let's start with the most important, the Self-employed Summary C Worksheet. Summary C mimics the federal Schedule C: Profit or Loss from Business. You'll find them side by side so you can make a comparison.

Under "Expenses" (Part II on the federal form), both the worksheet and federal Schedule C start at **ADVERTISING** and go through to **WAGES.** Then where

Schedule C asks for "Other expenses," Summary C continues with **BUSINESS BANK ACCOUNT FEES** and goes on.

The lightly shaded lines tell you that something must be done other than write an amount on a line. You are asked to list **EQUIPMENT** purchases on the reverse. Your tax preparer will decide how to deduct **EQUIPMENT.** Whatever her decision, you will see the result—your deduction—on the "Depreciation" line of the federal Schedule C. If, because of things like business auto use or working out of your home, you need to complete other worksheets, you will write nothing on that shaded line but go directly to the specified worksheet.

There are five columns on Summary C, and you can use them any way that suits your circumstances. Some suggestions:

- One column can be for backed-up expenses, the next column for estimated, and the third for the total expenses.
- A column can be used for notes.
- If you tally expenses quarterly, you can use one column per quarter and the fifth column for the year total.
- If you're an employee and self-employed, you can use one column for employee business expenses and another for your self-employed expenses.
- Husband and wife, each self-employed, may use the same worksheet. One column for him, one for her, and an either/or

column if they don't know how to split the expense or if the expense is to be proportioned to each based upon income or some other formula.

- Two businesses can use the same worksheet.

In Chapter Twenty-one you learned how to keep track of income. Now write your gross income amount on the top line, "Self-employed income." Here too you can take advantage of the columns if you've sorted your income into groups such as fees, reimbursements, and sales tax collected. The fifth column can be your total income

In Chapter Twenty-two you learned how to tally your expenses. Write your totals on the appropriate lines. If you use column 1 for actual expenses and also want to include expenses for which you forgot to get receipts, you may decide to do something like this:

	1	2	3
	BACKUP	ESTIMATED	TOTAL
Postage-shipping-freight	284	12 mos x $15/mo = 180	464

In the above example, you have receipts for **POSTAGE** in the amount of $284. You also know that you send out three packages a month at $5 per package to Clyde Client, but your brother runs them to the post office for you and he **always** forgets to get a receipt.

Turn the page to begin the worksheet.

SELF-EMPLOYED SUMMARY C WORKSHEET

	1	2	3	4	5
SELF-EMPLOYED INCOME					
Expenses					
Advertising					
Auto: see Auto Worksheet					
Commissions					
Assistants and other contract labor					
Equipment bought this year: Describe and list date of purchase on reverse					
Business insurance					
Interest expense					
Legal and accounting services					
Office supplies					
Postage-shipping-freight					
Rent: equipment					
Rent: office space					
Repairs and maintenance					
Supplies: also see cost of supplies below					
Business taxes: explain on reverse					
Travel, not meals: see Travel Worksheet					
Travel meals and entertainment: see Travel Worksheet					
Other meals and entertainment					
Telephone-cell phone-answering service					
Internet service					
Wages paid					
Business bank account fees					
Copyright and permission fees					
Dues-entrance fees					
Gifts (max $25 per associate)					
Photocopies and printing					
Publications					
Research-study-seminars					
Supervision-coaching					
Transportation					
Work clothes, costumes, cleaning, makeup					
Total expenses					
Office/studio: see Office Worksheet					
Cost of supplies used for production of your product					
Inventory: cost of supplies remaining at 12/31					

SCHEDULE C (Form 1040) Department of the Treasury Internal Revenue Service (99)	**Profit or Loss From Business** (Sole Proprietorship) ▶ **Partnerships, joint ventures, etc., must file Form 1065 or 1065-B.** ▶ **Attach to Form 1040, 1040NR, or 1041.** ▶ **See Instructions for Schedule C (Form 1040).**	OMB No. 1545-0074 2007 Attachment Sequence No. **09**

Name of proprietor	Social security number (SSN)

A Principal business or profession, including product or service (see page C-2 of the instructions)

B Enter code from pages C-8, 9, & 10   ▶

C Business name. If no separate business name, leave blank.

D Employer ID number (EIN), if any

E Business address (including suite or room no.) ▶ ....
City, town or post office, state, and ZIP code

F Accounting method: **(1)** ☐ Cash   **(2)** ☐ Accrual   **(3)** ☐ Other (specify) ▶ ....

G Did you "materially participate" in the operation of this business during 2007? If "No," see page C-3 for limit on losses   ☐ Yes   ☐ No

H If you started or acquired this business during 2007, check here . . . . ▶ ☐

Part I   Income

1	Gross receipts or sales. **Caution.** If this income was reported to you on Form W-2 and the "Statutory employee" box on that form was checked, see page C-3 and check here . . . . . ▶ ☐	**1**	
2	Returns and allowances	**2**	
3	Subtract line 2 from line 1	**3**	
4	Cost of goods sold (from line 42 on page 2)	**4**	
5	**Gross profit.** Subtract line 4 from line 3	**5**	
6	Other income, including federal and state gasoline or fuel tax credit or refund (see page C-3)	**6**	
7	**Gross income.** Add lines 5 and 6 . . . . ▶	**7**	

Part II   Expenses. Enter expenses for business use of your home **only** on line 30.

8	Advertising	**8**		18	Office expense	**18**
9	Car and truck expenses (see page C-4)	**9**		19	Pension and profit-sharing plans	**19**
10	Commissions and fees . .	**10**		20	Rent or lease (see page C-5):	
11	Contract labor (see page C-4)	**11**			**a** Vehicles, machinery, and equipment	**20a**
12	Depletion	**12**			**b** Other business property . .	**20b**
13	Depreciation and section 179 expense deduction (not included in Part III) (see page C-4)	**13**		21	Repairs and maintenance . .	**21**
				22	Supplies (not included in Part III)	**22**
				23	Taxes and licenses	**23**
				24	Travel, meals, and entertainment:	
					a Travel	**24a**
14	Employee benefit programs (other than on line 19) . .	**14**			**b** Deductible meals and entertainment (see page C-6)	**24b**
15	Insurance (other than health) .	**15**		25	Utilities	**25**
16	Interest:			26	Wages (less employment credits) .	**26**
	a Mortgage (paid to banks, etc.) .	**16a**		27	Other expenses (from line 48 on page 2)	**27**
	b Other	**16b**				
17	Legal and professional services	**17**				

28	**Total expenses** before expenses for business use of home. Add lines 8 through 27 in columns . ▶	**28**	
29	Tentative profit (loss). Subtract line 28 from line 7	**29**	
30	Expenses for business use of your home. Attach **Form 8829**	**30**	
31	**Net profit or (loss).** Subtract line 30 from line 29. • If a profit, enter on both **Form 1040, line 12,** and **Schedule SE, line 2,** or on **Form 1040NR, line 13** (statutory employees, see page C-7). Estates and trusts, enter on Form 1041, line 3. • If a loss, you **must** go to line 32.	**31**	
32	If you have a loss, check the box that describes your investment in this activity (see page C-7). • If you checked 32a, enter the loss on both **Form 1040, line 12,** and **Schedule SE, line 2,** or on **Form 1040NR, line 13** (statutory employees, see page C-7). Estates and trusts, enter on Form 1041, line 3. • If you checked 32b, you **must** attach **Form 6198.** Your loss may be limited.	**32a** ☐ All investment is at risk. **32b** ☐ Some investment is not at risk.	

The next worksheets to look at are Travel Expense Other Than Auto, then Business Use of Auto, Truck, or Other Vehicle, then Auto, Truck, or Other Vehicle Purchase. Be sure to read Chapter Ten before you complete these worksheets.

For a quick summary:

- **TRAVEL** is overnight. **TRANSPORTATION** takes place in the same day.
- If your stay is overnight, then the expenses go on the Travel Expense Worksheet.
- If not overnight then the expense is listed on the Transportation line of Summary C.

- Your means of getting from one place to another, whether for **TRAVEL** or **TRANSPORTATION,** may be the same.
- If you use your own vehicle, whether for **TRAVEL** or **TRANSPORTATION,** all information goes on the Auto Worksheet.

Sometimes it is easier to prepare one Travel Expense Worksheet for each trip rather than compiling all **TRAVEL** expenses together. If you need to, make many copies of the worksheet.

The Vehicle Purchase Worksheet, although repeating some of the items on the Auto Worksheet, is helpful as a reminder of what you need to do now that you own a new vehicle and what you need to get ready for your tax preparer.

TRAVEL EXPENSE / Other Than Auto

To differentiate between TRAVEL and TRANSPORTATION—
when you are away on business **overnight, it is travel.**

The following expenses must have been incurred **while traveling.**

This page: *Total travel* or
per trip total

(if per trip designate which trip this page: _____)

	HAVE BACKUP	ESTIMATED	TOTAL
Plane and rail fares			
Tips and baggage			
Taxis and public transportation			
Auto rentals			
Lodging			
Telephone			
Laundry and cleaning			
Other travel expenses			
Total travel expenses			
** Travel meals			
** Travel entertainment			
Total meals & entertainment while traveling			

** **Estimated amounts are not allowed for meals or entertainment.**
   Per diem amounts are accepted for meals.

Number of nights away from home on business: _____

Note on the reverse the city you were in and the dates you were overnight in that city.

BUSINESS USE OF AUTO, TRUCK, OR OTHER VEHICLE

	VEHICLE #1 OR SELF	VEHICLE #2 OR SPOUSE	VEHICLE #3	VEHICLE #4
Description of vehicle and date purchased				
Cost, or if first year of business use, then value on first day of business use				
Mileage @ January 1				
Mileage @ December 31				
Total miles for the year				
Business miles for the year				
_____ cents per mile =				
Business percent				
Actual expenses				
Loan interest				
Gas				
Repairs and maintenance				
Insurance (include AAA)				
Registration and license				
Car wash				
Garage rental				
Auto-only credit card				
Subtotal actual expenses				
Rental or lease costs				
Total expenses				
Business percent				
Business expenses				
Business tolls and parking				

(Please read and complete page 2 of the Auto Worksheet)

Auto expense is calculated as either a percentage of actual expense OR as cents per mile, NOT both.

If you purchased your vehicle this year, provide for your tax preparer:

- The bill of sale
- The loan agreement
- Any other papers relating to its purchase

and

- What is the weight of your vehicle? _____
  (This information is on a sticker on the door frame.)

If you made lease payments for more than 30 days, what was the fair market value

of that vehicle on the first day of the lease term? $_____

(Fair market value is what the vehicle would have cost to purchase.)

THE FOLLOWING INFORMATION IS **REQUIRED BY THE IRS.**
IT APPEARS ON YOUR TAX RETURN.
PLEASE RESPOND TO ALL QUESTIONS.

The IRS asks:

1. Do you have evidence to support your auto expenses? ☐ YES ☐ NO *(Well, you better.)*

2. Is the evidence written? ☐ YES ☐ NO *(But of course it is.)*

Note:

Commuting from your home to work is NOT business mileage. It is personal mileage.

3. What is your average daily round-trip commuting distance?

   Vehicle #1_____ Vehicle #2_____ Vehicle #3_____ Vehicle #4_____

4. What is your total yearly commuting mileage?

   Vehicle #1_____ Vehicle #2_____ Vehicle #3_____ Vehicle #4_____

5. Do you (or your spouse) have another vehicle available for personal use? ☐ YES ☐ NO

AUTO, TRUCK, OR OTHER VEHICLE PURCHASE

If you purchase a **car, truck, or other motor vehicle** that you use or will use for business, provide:

- The bill of sale

- The loan agreement

- Any other papers relating to its purchase

- The weight of your vehicle _____
  (This information is on a sticker on the door frame.)

Be sure to:

- Keep accurate records of the total mileage for the year

- Note the mileage reading when you purchase the car.

- Note the mileage reading on 12/31 . . . **New Year's Eve.**

- Keep accurate records of business mileage and use by noting:

  - Date of the business trip

  - Reason for the trip

  - Total mileage of the trip (recording on a calendar is fine.)

Keep records for ALL auto expenses, not just those that are business related. *Yes, that's right. Save records for ALL your auto expenses.*

For everything you spend on your car, pay by either:

- Check
  or

- Credit card

  - Get a gas credit card. In that way you will need only add up 12 checks at year-end rather than dozens of gas, oil, and repair receipts.

  - Use a different credit card for each vehicle.
  or

- If by cash, then get a receipt

At tax preparation time complete the Business Use of Auto, Truck, or Other Vehicle Worksheet.

Also be sure to tell your tax pro if you purchased an alternative motor vehicle such as a hybrid. You may be eligible for an energy tax credit.

The next worksheets to look at are Studio or Office in the Home, Residence or Real Estate Purchase, Capital Improvements to Residence or Other Real Estate, and Residence or Real Estate Sale.

You know from reading Chapter Twelve whether you are eligible to claim a deduction for **OFFICE IN THE HOME.** You also know how to measure the area used for business. Now all you need do is write the totals of your tallied expenses on the appropriate lines on the worksheet. The Office in the Home Worksheet mimics the federal Form 8829: Expenses for Business Use of Your Home, which follows the Office in the Home Worksheet. On Part II of the federal form, column (a), "Direct expenses," corresponds to my column A: "Expenses for Business Area Only—Not Those Included in Entire," and the federal column (b), "Indirect expenses," corresponds to my column B: "Entire." Be careful here. Column A is for expenses related to your business area only. A repair to the office lock or painting the office, for instance, would each be listed in column A, "Business Area Only." Column B, Entire, is for any expense that is related to your entire residence—for instance, a roof repair. If the repair were $1,000, that would be the amount that you write on the Repairs and Maintenance line in column B. If you use 25 per-

cent of your home for business, it is after expenses are subtotaled that the business portion of deductible repairs (and all the other Entire expenses) will be calculated.

If you had a home office, studio, or workshop in more than one place during the year, then you will have more than one Studio or Office in the Home Worksheet. **Do not combine** amounts for more than one location.

If this is your first year deducting **OFFICE IN THE HOME** and you own your residence, then review the Residence or Real Estate Purchase Worksheet. Bring all the information listed on that worksheet to your tax preparer.

Use the Capital Improvements Worksheet to record all of your residence improvements each year.

Even if you are not currently working out of your home, collect the information requested on the Residence or Real Estate Purchase Worksheet and the Capital Improvements Worksheet; file all that information in your ongoing "House" file. Then, should you decide to work from home, bring the House file to your preparer.

If you sell your home and have deducted home office expenses, you will need to review the Residence or Real Estate Sale Worksheet to determine what you will need to bring to your preparer in the year of the sale.

STUDIO OR OFFICE IN THE HOME

- Area of your home or apartment used exclusively for business _____
- Total area of your home or apartment _____
- Equals percentage of home or apartment used for business _____

	A EXPENSES FOR BUSINESS AREA ONLY–**NOT** THOSE INCLUDED IN ENTIRE	**B** ENTIRE
Mortgage interest #1 Mortgage interest #2 Home equity interest		
Property/real estate taxes		
Insurance		
Rent		
Repairs and maintenance		
Utilities: Water Electricity Gas/heat		
Trash collection		
Housekeeper: Only if a service or you pay payroll taxes.		
Lawn maintenance: Only if used exclusively for business area.		
Maintenance fees: Include co-op or condo statement.		

Fix up the house this year?

List improvements on the Capital Improvements Worksheet.

If you purchased your home this year, or if this is the first year you are deducting office in the home, be sure to review the Residence or Real Estate Purchase Worksheet.

Form **8829**	**Expenses for Business Use of Your Home**	OMB No. 1545-0074

Form **8829**

Department of the Treasury
Internal Revenue Service (99)

Expenses for Business Use of Your Home

▶ File only with Schedule C (Form 1040). Use a separate Form 8829 for each home you used for business during the year.
▶ See separate instructions.

OMB No. 1545-0074

2007

Attachment Sequence No. **66**

Name(s) of proprietor(s)

Your social security number

Part I Part of Your Home Used for Business

1	Area used regularly and exclusively for business, regularly for daycare, or for storage of inventory or product samples (see instructions)	**1**	
2	Total area of home	**2**	
3	Divide line 1 by line 2. Enter the result as a percentage	**3**	%
	For daycare facilities not used exclusively for business, go to line 4. All others go to line 7.		
4	Multiply days used for daycare during year by hours used per day	**4**	hr.
5	Total hours available for use during the year (365 days × 24 hours) (see instructions)	**5**	8,760 hr.
6	Divide line 4 by line 5. Enter the result as a decimal amount	**6**	.
7	Business percentage. For daycare facilities not used exclusively for business, multiply line 6 by line 3 (enter the result as a percentage). All others, enter the amount from line 3. ▶	**7**	%

Part II Figure Your Allowable Deduction

8	Enter the amount from Schedule C, line 29, **plus** any net gain or (loss) derived from the business use of your home and shown on Schedule D or Form 4797. If more than one place of business, see instructions	**8**	

See instructions for columns (a) and (b) before completing lines 9–21.

		(a) Direct expenses	(b) Indirect expenses		
9	Casualty losses (see instructions)	9			
10	Deductible mortgage interest (see instructions)	10			
11	Real estate taxes (see instructions)	11			
12	Add lines 9, 10, and 11	12			
13	Multiply line 12, column (b) by line 7		13		
14	Add line 12, column (a) and line 13			**14**	
15	Subtract line 14 from line 8. If zero or less, enter -0-			**15**	
16	Excess mortgage interest (see instructions)	16			
17	Insurance	17			
18	Rent	18			
19	Repairs and maintenance	19			
20	Utilities	20			
21	Other expenses (see instructions)	21			
22	Add lines 16 through 21	22			
23	Multiply line 22, column (b) by line 7	23			
24	Carryover of operating expenses from 2006 Form 8829, line 42	24			
25	Add line 22 in column (a), line 23, and line 24			**25**	
26	Allowable operating expenses. Enter the **smaller** of line 15 or line 25			**26**	
27	Limit on excess casualty losses and depreciation. Subtract line 26 from line 15			**27**	
28	Excess casualty losses (see instructions)	28			
29	Depreciation of your home from Part III below	29			
30	Carryover of excess casualty losses and depreciation from 2006 Form 8829, line 43	30			
31	Add lines 28 through 30			**31**	
32	Allowable excess casualty losses and depreciation. Enter the **smaller** of line 27 or line 31			**32**	
33	Add lines 14, 26, and 32			**33**	
34	Casualty loss portion, if any, from lines 14 and 32. Carry amount to **Form 4684**, Section B			**34**	
35	Allowable expenses for business use of your home. Subtract line 34 from line 33. Enter here and on Schedule C, line 30. If your home was used for more than one business, see instructions ▶			**35**	

Part III Depreciation of Your Home

36	Enter the **smaller** of your home's adjusted basis or its fair market value (see instructions)	**36**	
37	Value of land included on line 36	**37**	
38	Basis of building. Subtract line 37 from line 36	**38**	
39	Business basis of building. Multiply line 38 by line 7	**39**	
40	Depreciation percentage (see instructions)	**40**	%
41	Depreciation allowable (see instructions). Multiply line 39 by line 40. Enter here and on line 29 above	**41**	

Part IV Carryover of Unallowed Expenses to 2008

42	Operating expenses. Subtract line 26 from line 25. If less than zero, enter -0-	**42**	
43	Excess casualty losses and depreciation. Subtract line 32 from line 31. If less than zero, enter -0-	**43**	

For Paperwork Reduction Act Notice, see page 4 of separate instructions. Cat. No. 13232M Form **8829** (2007)

RESIDENCE OR REAL ESTATE PURCHASE

If you purchased a **house, co-op, or condominium** this tax year, congratulations!

The following is needed to prepare your tax return:

1. **Purchase closing statement.**

2. **List description and amount of all purchase expenses that are not included on the closing statement.**
   For example: inspection or legal fees, postage, telephone.

3. **List all capital improvements made since the purchase.**
   See Capital Improvements Worksheet.

4. If you have a mortgage, then provide the **year-end bank statement of total mortgage interest paid.**
   Your mortgage lender sends this information on Form 1098. If you did not receive one, ask your lender to provide it.

5. **Year-end statement of total property/real estate taxes paid.**
   If you paid real estate taxes through your mortgage lender rather than directly to your town or county, then the amount is usually on the same Form 1098 as your mortgage interest.

6. **Tax bill or statement for the year of purchase.**
   This must show how much property tax is for the land and how much is for improvements (the building). You can get this information from your town or county tax assessor.

7. **Co-op or condo statement on the breakdown of maintenance fees if that is the form of your ownership.**
   The statement must state either the exact amounts or the percentages for fees, property taxes, and mortgage interest.

Even though the rules for capital gains on personal residences have been modified, if there is a chance that you will use your home for business or as rental property at some future time, then you should start a House file. It will be an *ongoing file.* All the papers that are listed above should be in your House file. Any time you make a CAPITAL IMPROVEMENT to your home, the receipt that is proof of that expense should also be placed in the House file. Group those receipts by year. Do not put REPAIR receipts in the House file. A *new* roof is a capital improvement; *replacing* a toilet is a capital improvement; *fixing* the kitchen plumbing is a repair.

RESIDENCE OR REAL ESTATE SALE

If you sold a **house, co-op, or condominium** this tax year, congratulations!

The following may be needed to prepare your tax return:

If 1 through 4 are already on file at your tax preparer's office, or she has kept an ongoing basis tally of your real estate, then skip to 5.

1. **Original purchase closing statement.**

2. **List description and amount of all purchase expenses that are not included on that closing statement.**
   For example: inspection or legal fees, postage, telephone.

3. **List capital improvements made since the purchase.**
   See Capital Improvements Worksheet.

4. **Tax bill or statement for any year.**
   This must show how much property tax is for the land and how much is for improvements—that is, the house or building. You can get this information from your town or county tax assessor.

5. **The sale closing statement.**

6. **List description and amount of all sale expenses that are not included on the sale closing statement.**
   For example: inspection or legal fees, postage, telephone.

If you have a mortgage, then provide:

7. **Year-end statement of total mortgage interest paid.**
   Your mortgage lender sends this information on Form 1098. If you did not receive one, ask your lender to provide it.

8. **Year-end statement of total property/real estate taxes paid.**
   If you paid these taxes through the lender rather than directly to your town or county, then the amount is usually on the same Form 1098 as your mortgage interest.

9. **Co-op or condo statement on the breakdown of maintenance fees, if that is the form of your ownership.**
   This must state either the exact amounts or percentages for your portion of fees, property taxes, and mortgage interest.

CAPITAL IMPROVEMENTS TO RESIDENCE OR OTHER REAL ESTATE

YEAR	DESCRIPTION	AMOUNT	HAVE RECORDS	ENTIRE	YARD/ LANDSCAPING	PERSONAL ONLY	OFFICE/ STUDIO ONLY
EXAMPLES							
8/7/2006	Roof	10,000	YES	10,000			
11/30/2007	Bedroom windows	2,000	YES			2,000	
8/8//2007	Driveway paved	5,000	NO		5,000		
12/30/2008	Built-in shelves	2,500	YES				2,500

Next is the Equipment and Inventory Worksheet.

In Chapter Thirteen you saw that Clarissa Clothier, after sewing for her kids and friends for ten years, decided that it was time to do it professionally. All the money she had spent over the years on equipment and supplies was not lost. She could still get a deduction for many of her expenses. She could deduct her sewing machine at its current value and also put the value of her remaining supplies in her inventory. The Equipment Worksheet facilitates that calculation.

Remember here: A few photos to document these items, especially those that had been purchased many years ago, will be a good safeguard.

EQUIPMENT AND INVENTORY

If this is your first year as a self-employed, then complete the following list for
all equipment and supplies purchased **before**
you became self-employed
that you will now use in your business.

Date you became self-employed: _____

DESCRIPTION	DATE PURCHASED	ORIGINAL PURCHASE PRICE	VALUE @ START OF BUSINESS	NOTES: e.g., VALUE FROM WHAT SOURCE

CHAPTER TWENTY-FOUR

Most Simple System: A Summary

Now that you've looked over the worksheets, let's review the recordkeeping routine, including how to store records.

"Keep good records." That's how Part IV started. Now you'll no longer feel helpless and hopeless when you hear that directive because you know the basics of good recordkeeping.

Here's a review of the steps in the Most Simple System. Follow them for the easiest and most tax-advantageous approach to indie recordkeeping.

The Most Simple System Recordkeeping in Brief

1. Use one checking account. A business account is not necessary.

2. Clearly identify every deposit on the deposit slips.

3. Log inflow.

4. Get some sort of backup in return for every dollar spent:
   - Canceled check
   - Credit card receipt
   - Receipt for cash expenditures
   - Handmade receipt

5. Set up the Most Simple System basic catchall bins and files:
   - Catchall bins hold:
     All cash receipts
     All not-yet-sorted credit card receipts

   - Files hold:
     Check backup
     Bank statements (one for each account)
     Canceled checks
     Credit card statements (one for each card)

6. Log certain expenses:
   - Mileage
   - Telephone

7. Annotate certain expenses at the time of the expenditure:
   - Business gifts
   - Meals and entertainment

8. Tally income and sort expenses at year-end (more often if it suits your recordkeeping style).

9. Transfer totals to the Most Simple System worksheets.

When adapting the Most Simple System to suit your style, always remember simplicity and consistency. Avoid setting up a procedure that is too complicated to remember or carry out easily.

This is *your* recordkeeping system. If you have the right mind-set—that of an indie in business—it is foolproof and completely legitimate. Be comfortable with it even if Sammy Segar, CPA, might frown upon it. It works.

Laying It to Rest: Storing Your Records

Your tax material was given to your preparer; your returns were completed, reviewed by you, mailed to the governments. You're done—almost. Not so fast, you need to put away your records. There are two steps to this.

First: Segregate Multiyear Records

In Chapter Twenty you learned that some disbursement records need to be kept longer than seven years from the purchase date. They were expenses for things lasting longer than one year, such as **EQUIPMENT** and **AUTOS.** Now is the time to pull the multiyear records. Label a folder "Long Term"—that's because you're going to keep the papers in it for a long time. In the folder place the backup for all your long-term deductions. If you own a residence, you will also have an ongoing House file in which you will put purchase, capital improvements, and sale documents, as well as dated photos of your home office or studio.

Second: Store Your Records

The easiest method is to label a cardboard file box with a single year, for instance "2008." Then put all files for 2008 in that box. Place your tax returns—both federal and state—and your Long Term file and your House file *in the front of the box* for ready reference. You'll want to refer to them next year when collecting your tax material. Also at that time—next year—you'll remove your Long Term file and your House file and place them in next year's box.

You'll have a separate box for each year. Six years after you've filed a return, remove the tax return, place it in a box or folder labeled "Old Tax Returns," and throw out everything else.

WHATTA**CONCEPT!**

Outsource

If you really, truly hate to deal with financial recordkeeping, hire someone else to do it for you. That's better than not getting it done at all, or doing it badly. You can pay someone to keep a record of inflow, sort your receipts, balance your checkbook, keep track of who owes you money—that's called your receivables—and check your credit card statement. The cost of outsourcing will depend upon where you live, the competence of the bookkeeper, the size of your business, and (very important) how organized or disorganized you are. An hourly or monthly clerical or bookkeeping fee in the range of $15 to $75 an hour will very likely save at least that much in taxes, preparer fees, and psychological distress.

The Most Simple System works. My clients—indies just like you—have saved oodles in taxes, set up and maintained audit-proof recordkeeping, and done it simply, painlessly, and with confidence. Even though your expertise may be in astrology, technology, or musicology, you can do this, too.

Taxes

Real estate tax, payroll tax, sales tax, excise tax, city tax, federal and state income tax, personal property tax, fuel tax, breathing tax, luxury tax—only kidding, there's no tax on breathing. It may be a slight comfort for you as a highly taxed citizen to know that self-employeds pay the same taxes as everyone else. And just as with W-2 people, a self-employed's tax liability varies due to amount of income and deductions, and local and state tax laws.

In Part V we are going to look at taxes from the perspective of the self-employed.

WHATTA**CONCEPT!**

Tax liability

Tax liability is the total tax assessed on a tax return for the year—not what is paid in, not what is owed, nor what is refunded. It's the important number: the sum of income tax plus self-employment tax that is paid or will be paid on the year's income. Other taxes such as payroll tax for a domestic employee (e.g., nanny or housekeeper) may add to overall tax liability.

CHAPTER TWENTY-FIVE
Your Fair Share

"How do I pay estimated taxes?" is usually the first question on the lips of a self-employed. And it's almost always asked before the indie has any idea of what estimated taxes are. So before I explain how to calculate the amount of an estimated tax payment and when and where to send it, I want to give you an orientation on the taxes that a self-employed pays. The idea is that you should know what you're paying before you pay it.

Estimated tax payments are payments you make to the government. The amount of the payment is based on the income you **expect** to make in the current year.

Estimated payments to the IRS cover two taxes: income tax and self-employment tax. You can be liable for one but not the other because—as you read in previous chapters—each tax is based on different criteria.

- Income tax is based upon **taxable income.**
- Self-employment tax (SE tax) is based upon **net self-employed earnings** and is the self-employed's combined Social Security tax and Medicare tax. It corresponds to an employee's FICA and Medicare withholdings.

Which brings us back to the confusion that Woody Awlwood exhibited in Chapter Sixteen, Camels or Cash. Remember? He didn't get it when his tax preparer informed him that his income tax was zero, but he still had to send $1,239 to the Feds.

Woody did not understand the difference between income tax and self-employment tax. He owed taxes because on his net self-employed income of $30,000, his SE tax was $4,239 and he had paid only $3,000 in estimated taxes.

In the next few pages I will explain the difference between income tax and self-employment tax and things like who must file, filing status, tax bracket, and marginal tax rate. Don't get hung up on the terms; this is intended solely as a basic, fundamental explanation that will be useful to your general understanding of a self-employed's taxes.

Understanding Income Tax

As you learned in Chapter Sixteen, there are various kinds of income. Stock sale gains are one kind, for example, and payment for jury duty another. Most kinds of income are taxable—that is, subject to income tax. Some income, however, is not taxable, such as municipal bond interest. And some income is sometimes or partially taxable, such as Social Security payments received.

Just because income is **subject to tax** doesn't necessarily mean you will end up paying tax on it. You pay income tax on **taxable income,** and many items can reduce taxable income.

 Reality Let's take a look at Aunt Ada, the quilter from Chapter Three whose hobby was supported by her investment income:

Investment income	30,000
Deductible medical expenses	(10,950)
Property tax	(6,000)
Charitable contributions	(10,000)
One exemption	(3,050)
Taxable income	-0-

Aunt Ada has zero taxable income, which results in no income tax liability.

Who Must File a Tax Return?

Since Aunt Ada had no taxable income, did she still have to file a tax return? Yes.

If your gross income—that's all income subject to income tax before taking any deductions—is more than a specified minimum, then you must file a return. However, just because you must file a tax return does not mean that you will have any tax liability. Like Ada, you may have enough deductions to completely wipe out taxable income.

Filing status (such as single or married filing jointly) and **gross income** determine whether you must file a tax return. For instance, in 2007 a single person under 65 and not self-employed must have filed a return if his **gross income** was at least $8,750. A husband and wife, neither self-employed, both under 65, are not required to file unless **gross income** reached $17,500. The threshold amount creeps a little higher each year.

Aunt Ada's gross income—subject to tax—was $30,000. Therefore, she had to file a return.

In the determination above on when you must file, notice that I excluded the self-employed. I'll explain why I did that in just a bit. I also want you to be aware that the gross income in the above explanation is not the gross self-employed income of an indie's business but rather all income of the taxpayer (and his spouse) that is subject to tax.

What's a Tax Bracket?

As taxable income increases, so does the federal income tax rate. The rate at which you end up is called your **tax bracket.** Another term for tax bracket is **marginal tax rate.** They both mean the percentage at which your next dollar of income is taxed. If you're in a 15 percent tax bracket, for instance, then on the *next* $100 of taxable income you will pay $15 in income tax. If in a 28 percent bracket, then $28 of the next $100 taxable income will go to the Feds.

Gross income determines if you must file. Then filing status and taxable income determine the rate at which tax is paid. For instance, in 2007, a single person would have been taxed at a 10 percent rate from $1 *taxable income* through $7,825. After $7,825, the rate increased to 15 percent.

Advancing to a higher tax bracket does not mean that **all** your taxable income is taxed at the higher rate. It means that any income from that point on is taxed at that rate. So if Siegfried Single has $51,850 in taxable income, this is how it works:

The first	$ 7,825	is taxed at 10%	=	$ 783
Then	$24,025	is taxed at 15%	=	$3,604
Then	$20,000	is taxed at 25%	=	$5,000
Total Income:	$51,850	Total tax:	=	$9,387

He is in a 25 percent tax bracket. That is his marginal tax rate.

ALERT! Complex tax rules can alter your marginal tax rate. If you are considering a financial move in which your tax bracket is an important factor, check with your tax pro before making any decision.

Here's another term for you: the **effective tax rate.** Think of it as the real tax rate. In the Siegfried Single example above, a total of $9,387 tax was paid on a taxable income of $51,850. If we divide the tax by the taxable income, we get:

$$\$9,387 \div \$51,850 = 18.10\%,$$
or a little more than 18%.

Although Siegfried was in the 25 percent tax bracket, his effective tax rate was about 18 percent of his taxable income. The effective tax rate is somewhere between the tax bracket you are at and the previous lower rate. It is the percentage of your taxable income that goes to the federal government for **income tax.**

There's more than one income tax! All but a few states, and some cities as well, impose an income tax. Some tax at a flat rate, some at a progressive rate similar to the way the Feds do it. If you have self-employed income, you may need to pay estimated taxes to your state to cover state income tax and sometimes city income tax. Check with your tax pro and your state.

Understanding Self-employment Tax

While income tax is paid on any kind of taxable income, self-employment tax is paid only by people who work for themselves. It is the Social Security and Medicare tax for self-employeds and is paid on a self-employed's *net earnings.*

I have already told you about net profit, but not about **net earnings.** And, as you have been warned before, the IRS is disposed to set up similar-sounding names for similar—but not identical—kinds of income. Net profit is what you have left after subtracting all business expenses from your gross receipts. **Net earnings** are a portion of net profit and are tabulated according to the following formula:

Net profit x 92.35% = net earnings.

The reason for that peculiar percentage is not important. What is important for you to know is that you must pay self-employment tax if **net earnings from self-employment** are $400 or more. The other way to look at it: You must pay SE tax if your *net **profit*** is $433 or more. Here's the arithmetic:

$433 net profit x .9235 = $400 net earnings.

Reality If Agua Fresh grossed $3,532 cleaning pools his first summer in business and he had $3,100 in expenses, then his net profit was $432. He does *not* have to pay SE tax. And with no SE tax and a gross income less than $8,750, he does not have to file a tax return.

You know that filing status and gross income determine who must file, but now we have another must-file criteria: Regardless of income, if you are subject to SE tax, then you must file a tax return.

Reality Fred Fixit, who lives with his parents and has no income, decides it's time to earn a living. He starts his repair business on December 28. He does one repair job for the family across the street. He's paid $450; he has no expenses. Yes, he has to pay SE tax, and so he must file a return even though he is single and his only income is from that one repair job.

WHATTACONCEPT!

Watch your decimal point

Just in case your memory about decimals has faded, here's a refresher.

One dollar is made up of 100 cents. A dime (10¢) is 10% of a dollar. We could also write it as .10 or ¹⁰⁄₁₀₀ or ¹⁄₁₀.

If you cut a penny in half and have ten and one-half pennies, you'd have 10½¢ or 10.5% of a dollar or .105 of a dollar.

When a percent sign (%) is used, the decimal point is moved two digits to the right: .9235 is the same as 92.35%.

An inventor who claims to have received a six-figure payout for his car-waxing machine may be running out to buy a Porsche or a Hyundai depending on the placement of the decimal point. Did he receive $900,000.00 or $9,000.00?

The Basics of Self-employment Tax

- SE tax kicks in if net profit from self-employed income is $433 or more. You must file a tax return if your net profit is $433 or more no matter how much or how little your other income; no matter how young or old you are; no matter if you're collecting Social Security or in grammar school; no matter if you're married or single.

  In case you missed it: Yes, you must pay SE tax even if you are an elder statesman collecting Social Security with some income from business consulting, or a kid burning CDs and selling them to fellow students.

- SE tax is paid on 92.35 percent of *all* net profit.

- The SE tax rate is 15.3 percent and is made up of two components: 12.4 percent Social Security tax plus 2.9 percent Medicare tax. Social Security benefits are available to self-employed persons just as they are to wage earners. Your payments of SE tax contribute to your coverage under the Social Security system, which

provides you with retirement, disability, and survivor benefits. Medicare coverage provides hospital insurance benefits.

Many self-employeds (usually the younger ones) confuse Social Security payments and unemployment compensation. Employees receive coverage for both benefits. If a W-2 person has worked for a certain amount of time and leaves work under certain conditions, she can receive payments while not working. This is called unemployment compensation. It is taxable income. Self-employeds never receive unemployment compensation.

- Payments toward the Social Security tax portion of SE tax stop when earned income reaches a specified amount. In 2007, for employer, employee, or a self-employed, the cutoff was $97,500. That means if any combination of Social Security wages, tip income, and/or net earnings from self-employment reached $97,500, no more Social Security tax had to be paid. The cut-off point rises a little every year.

  In 2008 the cutoff is $102,000. If as a salaried employee you earned $102,000 in 2008 and you had a sole proprietorship as well, you would not have to pay any of the Social Security tax portion of SE tax no matter how high your net earnings from self-employment.

  If your total net earnings from self-employment or salary or a combination of both were $102,000, you would pay the same amount of Social Security tax as your neighbor who earned five zillion dollars.

- All earned income is subject to the 2.9 percent Medicare tax. There is no limit. You and your high-earner neighbor will pay very different amounts of Medicare tax.

- An employee pays one half of his Social Security and Medicare tax and his employer pays the other half. As a self-employed you pay both the employer's half and the employee's half of Social Security and Medicare taxes.

   You pay both halves and you get to deduct one half. The deduction is taken as an adjustment to income on the front of your tax return, in the same section as self-employed health insurance premiums and your pension contribution. The deduction reduces only income tax. It is not a deduction against net earnings from self-employment.

   The deductibility of SE tax, like health insurance, is under discussion in the halls of Congress. Check with your tax pro for any changes.

- The amount of Social Security you receive in your golden years is based upon your earnings over a lifetime. The Social Security Administration gets its figures on earnings from your tax return. If you've shown little or no income over the years, you will receive little or no Social Security when you get old. That's what happens to all the under-the-table housekeepers and nannies: no Social Security when the arthritis sets in and they can't work anymore.

Income Tax Plus SE Tax Equals a Lot of Tax!

Here's an eye-opener on a solo's tax liabilities:

   A $10,000 net profit for a self-employed at a 15% tax bracket means that $1,500 must go for federal income tax and another approximately $1,500 for SE tax. Add them up: 15% plus 15% equals 30%. Depending upon state and city, the indie may owe another 5% to 10%, or $500 to $1,000, for state and city income taxes. That could bring the figure up to 40% of net profit going toward taxes, or approximately $4,000 of every $10,000 net income. And remember, 15% is one of the lower tax brackets. For some the government takes a bigger bite—how about at a 35% federal rate! That would change the above total income going for taxes to 60% (35% plus 15% plus 10%).

Reality Kristin Knockoff received a $12,000 fee for her design work. With expenses of $2,000, she came out with a profit of $10,000. Whoop-de-do! But Kristin shouldn't start partying just yet. Other income on her return brings her to the 28% federal tax bracket, and she lives in New York with a state income tax of 7%. Kristin also has a pension plan that allows her to put away 20% of her net profit. With all these considerations, let's see what she's left to party with:

Consultation fee (gross SE income)	$12,000
Business expenses	(2,000)
Net profit	$10,000
28% income tax	(2,800)
15% SE tax	(1,500)
7% NY state income tax	(700)
20% of net for pension contribution	(2,000)
Remainder for other spending	$ 3,000

Kristen gets to spend only $3,000 of her $10,000 net profit. That's just 30% left after 70% is allotted for taxes and pension contribution.

It is important for indies to understand the relationship of gross income to what they really have on hand for household expenses, vacations, new cars, and kids' shoes.

The Flip Side: Deductions Reduce High Taxes

High taxes emphasize the importance of deductions. As I just showed you, being in the 15 percent tax bracket can result in 30 percent of your profits going to the Feds for taxes. On the flip side, a $1,000 business expense decreases your taxes by $300; expenses of $10,000 drop your taxes by $3,000.

A deductible business expense of $10,000 that saves $3,000 in taxes means that a $10,000 purchase reduces your cash flow by only $7,000. Yes, $10,000 is going out for the expense, but $3,000 is *not* going out for taxes. A business trip that costs $5,000 will save $1,500 in taxes, bringing the real cost of the trip to $3,500 ($5,000 minus $1,500).

Reality A few days after Christmas, with New Year staring him in the face, what could Ivan Inventor do to save some tax money? Luisa Lifecoach told him to go out and buy that $1,000 scanner he needed. But Ivan had no money until the end of January, when he expected to receive the big royalty check for his latest Gizmo. Luisa told him to charge the scanner to his Bigbank VISA. He could write it off this year. He'd save three hundred tax dollars (30% times $1,000), and he needn't pay anything toward the $1,000 expense until the following year when the January credit card bill arrives.

ALERT! Even though a business expense can save you 30 to 65 percent in taxes—depending upon your tax bracket and state and city tax rates—*never* spend just to save taxes. It is not a dollar-for-dollar write-off.

Other Types of Taxes

Only federal, state, and some city income taxes and self-employment tax are paid via estimated tax payments (to be explained in a moment). But there are other taxes of special importance to the self-employed, such as sales tax and excise tax.

ALERT! If your city or state requires you to charge sales or gross receipts tax, you must collect the tax from your customers and forward it to the appropriate government agency. That collected tax was *never* your money. You collected it for the government. Therefore, if you don't send it in on time, you're in big trouble. The same holds for employment taxes that you have withheld from your employees. It's the government's money, not yours.

As I noted in Chapter Five, federal excise taxes are imposed on items such as guns; tobacco and alcohol or their ingredients; fishing rods and arrows of a certain length or their components; fuel; and certain vehicles. If in your self-employed business you sell or lease products, you need to check with your tax professional as to whether you need to pay excise taxes.

Every state, county, and municipality has its own tax requirements. Get to know the local requirements. Messing up can be costly. Ask questions. Then ask the same questions again in a different way. Compare the answers. Do they make sense? If not, get more information.

CHAPTER TWENTY-SIX
Estimated Tax Payments

Federal income tax, Social Security tax, and Medicare tax are pay-as-you-go taxes; that is, the tax must be paid as income is earned. Dennis Dubya-two, shipping clerk for Toys 'n' Things, receives a paycheck every week. Each week Toys 'n' Things withholds all applicable taxes from Dennis's pay and forwards them to various government agencies. At the end of the year, Dennis receives a W-2 that shows income earned and taxes paid.

Self-employeds must follow the same pay-as-you-go method as do wage earners like Dennis. As an entrepreneur brings in income, he withholds taxes from himself—that is, he puts money aside—and then sends his taxes to the government via estimated tax payments.

Not every self-employed has to make estimated tax payments. I know, you have a self-employed cousin who doesn't have to pay estimateds. It's the overall tax liability of a self-employed that determines whether estimated

tax payments are required, and there's a good chance that Cuz is not required to make any payments because of his other financial circumstances.

A self-employed's total tax liability is made up of SE tax on his net earnings and income tax on all his and his spouse's income as well as any other taxes due with his federal tax return. SE tax and income tax on net profit or loss are not necessarily the only factors in calculating estimated tax payments. If, for instance, you had a self-employed business income of $10,000 and also had investment dividends of $30,000, both these sources of income (totaling $40,000) would be elements in your estimated tax calculation. And if your wife earned $90,000 at her W-2 job, the taxes withheld from her income would also be a factor in those calculations.

Because someone is self-employed doesn't necessarily mean that he *must* make estimated tax payments. Consider the following situations:

- When all deductions are subtracted from income, there may be no tax liability.
- Enough tax may be withheld via a W-2 job to cover the entire tax liability. (In order to avoid making estimated tax payments, you may choose to increase tax withholdings at yours or your spouse's W-2 job. To do this, request that an additional sum be withheld every paycheck. You may have to complete a Form W-4 for the employer.)
- Enough taxes may be withheld from pension withdrawals to cover the entire tax liability.
- The previous year's tax refund may be carried forward in a sufficient amount to eliminate the need for estimated payments.

Who Must Make Estimated Tax Payments

Although there are exceptions, here's the safe and simple rule: *You must make estimated tax payments to the federal government if you had a tax liability for the previous year and you expect to owe tax of $1,000 or more when you file your tax return.*

You may want to read that again. It says "owe" $1,000 when you file your tax return; it does not say have a "tax liability" of $1,000. If you forgot what a tax liability is, check out the beginning of Chapter Twenty-five.

The IRS says it doesn't want anyone to pay more than her fair share. And you want to make sure that when you pay your fair share, you do so at the last possible moment, keeping your hands on your money for as long as possi-

ble while at the same time avoiding any interest or penalty fees.

There are three approaches to paying estimated taxes. At tax filing time, you can:

1. Break even.
2. Owe something to the government.
3. Get a refund from the government.

Breaking even is smart. Owing something to the government is even smarter, if it can be done without paying interest or penalties. The third approach, paying so that you get a refund, is dumb, dumb, dumb.

The Four Methods of Calculating Estimated Tax Payments

1. Prior Year Method

This method is simple: Pay this year what your tax liability was last year.

This is the easiest calculation and the safest if your income ***increases*** every year. Whatever your total tax was last year, divide that amount by four and make four payments to the United States Treasury.

For instance, if last year's tax was $8,000, then make sure you pay at least $8,000 this year. If neither you nor your spouse have federal income tax withheld from jobs or pension payments, you should make four payments of $2,000 each. If you had a part-time job and $1,000 federal income tax was withheld (do not include FICA or Medicare taxes withheld), and $500 of the previous year's refund was carried forward to this year, your calculation would be as follows:

Payment required for this year		$ 8,000
Less withheld		(1,000)
Balance to pay		$ 7,000
Divided by four	$ 1,750	per payment
Less carry forward subtracted from first payment		(500)
First payment		$ 1,250
Second, third, fourth payments	$ 1,750	each

If your federal tax for this year came in higher than $8,000, using the prior year method you do not owe any interest or penalty on the balance owed as long as it is paid by April 15!

High rollers beware! The above method applies to an adjusted gross income (AGI) of up to $150,000. If your AGI exceeds $150,000, instead of paying 100% of last year's tax, you must pay 110%. If you are married and filing separately, the 110% will apply if your AGI is over $75,000.

WHATTA**CONCEPT!**

Adjusted gross income—AGI

Adjusted gross income (AGI) is the amount of total income subject to tax, minus various deductions called adjustments to income–such as IRA or self-employed pension contributions, one-half of self-employment tax, and alimony payments. Your AGI is the amount on the last line of the first page of the tax return, Form 1040. It is from adjusted gross income that personal itemized deductions and exemption amounts are subtracted in order to arrive at taxable income.

The prior year method—called a "safe harbor" by the IRS—is easy and avoids interest and penalties for self-employeds with a rising annual income. The IRS frequently uses the term **safe harbor**—a place where harm cannot befall a vessel—to mean that although a taxpayer can choose several alternatives, no penalty will ensue if the safe harbor alternative is followed.

Once again, to be clear: If you use method 1, Prior Year Calculation, no matter how much tax you owe come April 15, you will not have to pay any penalty or interest.

2. Current Year Method

Pay 90 percent of this year's tax.

If you expect this year's income to be less than last year's, your tax will probably be less. (I say probably because factors other than income play into the calculation. Be careful.) In this method you pay the Feds 90 percent of this year's tax in four equal installments.

Typically, your tax preparer will set up estimated payments for you at the time she prepares your previous year's return. If your crystal ball tells you that your income will decrease this year, let her know so that she can calculate your payments.

The drawback of this method: Your income projections for the remainder of the year have to be accurate. For many solo operators that's a hard trick. If you send in less than 90 percent of your taxes and you owe $1,000 or more, you are liable for interest and penalty.

3. Annualization Method

This is the most complicated method and the most time consuming—for both you and your preparer. It requires several tax reviews over the course of the year.

In this method your taxable income is calculated to determine the amount of tax liability for each quarter of this year. It's like doing your tax return four times a year.

If you plan to use this method to calculate your estimated payments, discuss the procedure with your tax pro.

So why would you even consider method 3? Because in rare instances, if your income is very high or very irregular, it could work to your tax advantage. I'm talking about the computer games developer who had a really good previous year—net income of almost $300,000. Didn't know what this year would bring. Made no money right through the summer, then on Halloween sold his patent for a payment of $190,000. That was his only business income all year. Since he is not required to pay taxes on income before it's received, putting off the tax payment on this income was to his advantage.

4. Government as Savings Bank Method

The next time Friend Freddy tells you that Sammy Segar is a great accountant because every year he gets Freddy a big refund, ask him this: "Are you sure CPA Segar doesn't work for Uncle Sam part-time? Why else would he set you up so that you loan your money to the IRS for a whole year—interest free?"

How so? If you get a $1,000 refund from the government at the end of the year, that means that *your* money was sitting in the IRS bank earning interest for Uncle Sam. If it earned 5 percent, that's $50 in the Feds' pocket, not yours. And to rub salt in the wound, let's say you had a $1,000 balance on your credit card all year that you didn't pay off because the IRS had your $1,000. At 18 percent that cost you $180 in finance charges. The IRS made $50 on your money, while you lost $180. So much for Sammy Segar's big refund.

I know, lots of folks like getting a tax refund. They say it's the only way they can save money. I say, get it together and quit throwing money away. Whether through withholding or estimated taxes, if you are paying so much to the government that you get a sizable refund, then change your ways. If you or your spouse have a W-2 job, then reduce your withholding at work and have the difference *automatically* deposited into your own special savings account. Or cut back on your estimated tax payment and when writing out the estimated checks to the government, write one to your savings account.

All Methods

The smartest way to pay estimated taxes is to send the government as little as possible as late as possible, using one of the above methods.

No matter what the method, remember to look at total tax liability, not just self-employed income. And be sure to take into consideration any tax paid through withholding at a job or via other payments to you.

ALERT! If you must make estimated tax payments and you have a household employee, you must include any employment taxes for your domestic employee when figuring your estimated tax.

When to Pay Estimated Taxes

Under most circumstances you will make four estimated tax payments to the IRS and also possibly to your resident state. If you earn self-employed income elsewhere, you may need to make payments to a nonresident state as well. The methods used to calculate the IRS estimated payment amount usually apply in the same way to the states, but you ought to confirm this with your tax preparer or state tax office.

The following chart shows the dates for making estimated payments.

WHEN TO PAY: ESTIMATED TAX PAYMENT DUE DATES

For the period:	Due date:
January 1 through March 31	April 15
April 1 through May 31	June 15
June 1 through August 31	September 15
Sept. 1 through December 31	January 15 the following year

It is not a crisis if you're late on a payment due date. Depending on the amount of tax payment, an interest and/or penalty amount will be calculated at the time your tax return is prepared. The IRS rate is lower than most credit card finance rates.

How to Pay Estimated Taxes

There are several ways to pay estimated taxes.

Carry Forward a Previous Year Overpayment

When you file your tax return, if you have an overpayment of tax you can choose to have the refund returned to you or you can apply part or all of it to your estimated tax for the following year.

The amount you have carried forward as payment toward the following year should be taken into account when figuring your estimated payments. You can use all the carryforward amount toward your first payment, or you can spread it out in any way you choose among any or all of your payments. If you find the January 15 payment difficult because of holiday spending, then use your carryforward to ease your cash flow and have it applied to the fourth payment.

Pay by Check

Use Form 1040-ES, Payment Voucher, to pay federal estimated tax. There are four numbered vouchers. Include one with each payment by check.

Be sure the voucher is filled in accurately. If you are married, then put the names and Social Security numbers in the same order as they appear on your tax return.

Make the check or money order payable to the United States Treasury. On the check or money order, write your Social Security number, the year for which you are making payment, and "Form 1040-ES." Don't staple or clip the check to the voucher.

Most indies have their estimated tax payments set up for the next year when they have their tax returns prepared. If you made estimated tax payments in the previous year, you'll receive IRS payment vouchers in the mail for the current year. Or ask your preparer to supply them when she calculates your estimated payments. Or get vouchers and mailing address (it is not the same as that to which you mail your tax return) by calling the IRS at (800) 829–1040 or logging on to www.irs.gov.

ALERT! Never send a payment to the IRS (or any government agency) without the correct document, properly filled out, accompanying it.

Pay by Credit Card, Electronic Payment, or Withdrawal

ALERT! Be careful if you pay your estimated tax, or any other tax, by credit card. To pay by this method, you must use a service provider who charges a fee. And your credit card company will treat it as a cash advance. Wow! That'll be a huge finance charge. The options for credit card and electronic tax payments or funds withdrawal are changing rapidly. You can get the most current information at www.irs.gov.

CHAPTER TWENTY-SEVEN

What Daddy's Accountant Forgot to Tell You about Taxes

Let's look at why paying penalties on unpaid taxes should be avoided, but paying interest—well, that's not the end of the world. And if you need extra time to file your tax return, an extension is not only easy, it may be to your advantage.

Penalties and Interest

If you do something wrong, the IRS can't flog or pummel you, but it can hit you with penalties and interest, such as:

- Underpayment penalty: 9% per year.
- Late payment penalty: ½ of 1% per month.
- Interest on balance due: Rate changes every three months.

- Failure-to-file penalty: 5% per month of the tax not paid by the due date, for a maximum of 25% of the unpaid tax.
- Failure-to-pay penalty: ½ of 1% per month of unpaid tax.
- Penalty for a frivolous return: $500.
- Accuracy-related penalty: 20% of the underpayment.
- Fraud? We're not even going there. For starters you're looking at 75% of the unpaid tax added as penalty to the tax owed.
- And the list goes on . . .

In this section I'll cover only those few penalties and interest assessments that would most likely affect a solo entrepreneur.

With the seemingly never-ending list of penalty and interest that can be imposed upon you, deciding whether you should beg or borrow the money to pay the government rather than arrange to make installment payments depends on what kind of tax you owe to which government.

State or city sales or gross receipts tax that you collect—as I've said before—is not your money. It is the government's money that you are holding. The same is true if you have employees. Any payroll tax that you withhold from their pay is not your money. It belongs to the government. You are the government's collecting instrument and you must pass the collected tax on to the government on specific due dates. If you don't hand it over, you have in effect stolen the government's money. On these taxes, yes—you beg or borrow to get them paid. If you have employees, there is no out for not paying payroll taxes. You must pay them. If you haven't paid them, then hire a tax attorney. Pronto.

On the other hand, tax that is paid via estimated payments—income tax and SE tax—is *your* money that you owe to the government. If you can't make a timely payment, you will be charged some interest and some penalty. No need to go to pieces. You'll see below how the costs are calculated. But first, let's look at the most reliable and least stressful way to prepare for estimated payments.

You saw in the beginning of Part V that for a self-employed, a combination of federal income tax, SE tax, and state income tax can typically add up to about 40 percent of net income. That means when you get a check from a client, 40 percent of the after-expense amount is not yours to spend. It must be earmarked for taxes. A simple method is to ballpark an expense amount against that income, then sock away 40 percent of what's left. If you think it's hard to do when you get the check, that's nothing compared to how difficult it will be three months later when your estimated tax payment is due.

The 40 percent figure is of course an estimate. You may be in a higher tax bracket or have so many personal deductions that you have no income tax liability, or you may live in a state with no state income tax. However, 40 percent is a good starting point.

And just how do you sock away 40 percent? That depends on you. Some of us are so disciplined about money that just telling ourselves not to spend it is enough, while others must actually remove the money from sight. There is no good or bad way. There is only a way that works or a way that doesn't—for you. If you want to open a separate bank account and call it the "not-my-money" account or the "TAX" account, that's fine. When you get a check from a client, deposit the entire check into your checking account, then immediately write a check to yourself and deposit it into the TAX account. Or if you get lots of small payments from customers, deposit them all and then at the end of the week, or end of the month, make your TAX account deposit. Your TAX account could be a checking account, savings, money market—it doesn't matter. But don't put the money into an account in someone else's name. One client thought the safest course was putting his tax money into his domestic partner's account. Safe, maybe, but not good in the eyes of the IRS. No straight audit trail there.

As you read in Chapter Twenty-six, there are different ways to calculate estimated tax payments. The money you have put aside most likely will not match the amount of estimated tax payment due. If you find you are putting aside a lot less or a lot more than is required for your estimated payment, discuss the situation with your tax preparer. Keep in mind that if you're using method 1, prior year calculation, then your payments reflect last year's income, not the current year income. Even if you do not need to send as an estimated payment all the money you have put aside for taxes, don't spend it. It may be due come April 15.

And what if you just don't have the money to pay your taxes on time?

 Reality Stella Sellit received payment from *Glitzy Glamour* magazine in May, but because she had to pay for brochure printing for another client, Total Foods, she could not put money aside for her second estimated tax payment due June 15. She paid for the printing, and then when Total Foods paid her in July, she paid her second estimated payment one month late.

As I said at the beginning of this section, the when and why of IRS interest and penalty charges can be very complicated, so I'm going to give you only the basics.

Underpayment Penalty: 9% Per Year

The underpayment penalty, also called the estimated tax penalty, kicks in if your estimated payments are made late or they are not sufficient. The penalty is 9% per year.

If you have a $1,000 estimated payment due on June 15 and can't come up with the money until July 15, you will be charged 30 days interest at 9% per year. On the tardy $1,000 payment that would be about $7. This is calculated at the time your tax return is prepared and is added to your total tax liability.

The same would hold true if your required June 15 estimated payment were $1,000 short: for instance, if $5,000 were due and you paid $4,000 on June 15 and then paid the remaining $1,000 on July 15. (If you foresee that kind of situation, photocopy the voucher so that you have it for the later payment. Never send money to the IRS without some official form!)

Here's the arithmetic on the $7:

June 15 (estimated due date) to
July 15 (payment made) = 30 days.

$1,000 x 9% = $90 x 30/365 days = $7.40.

Late Payment Penalty: 1/2 of 1% Per Month

The late payment penalty kicks in if you have not met the safe harbor payments of 100% (or 110%) of the previous year's tax or paid at least 90% of your tax by April 15. The rate is ½ of 1% per month. That's 6% per year, but it is calculated monthly. The maximum penalty is 25% of the tax owed.

If you file your return by April 15 but can't pay the $1,000 tax owed until August 15, your late payment penalty would be $20.

The arithmetic:

April 15 (date all tax must be paid) to
August 15 (date paid) = 4 months.

$1,000 x ½% = $5 per month x 4 months = $20.

Interest on Balance Due: Rate Changes Every Three Months

If all taxes due are not paid by April 15, in addition to the 6% per year late payment penalty, there is interest charged on the tax owed *and* on the late payment penalty that is owed.

The interest rate changes every three months. Figure it to be pretty close to a typical home equity loan rate. If I use 7% in the example above, total interest would come to about $24.

The arithmetic:

April 15 (date all tax must be paid) to
August 15 (date paid) = 122 days.

$1,020 ($1,000 tax + $20 penalty) x 7%
x 122/365 days = $23.86.

What does all of this add up to?

- If you pay a $1,000 estimated payment one month late, it'll cost you $7.
- If you pay a $1,000 estimated payment five months late, it will cost you about $35 (five times $7).
- If you owe taxes of $1,000 after April 15 and don't pay it until August 15, it'll cost

you $44 ($20 late payment penalty and $24 interest).
- If you owe $5,000 come August 15, it'll cost you about $220 (five times $44).

You can see from the numbers above that being late or missing an estimated payment is not the end of the world. It costs you money. Depending upon how much you owe and how late you are, it could cost you a lot of money. Plan ahead so that you don't get bogged in a financial quagmire—paying last year's tax this year, and then this year's gets paid next year. However, if you need a month or two because of cash-flow problems, it doesn't mean the swamp monster is around the corner.

ALERT! Don't file your return late. If you do, in addition to any other penalties and interest, you could also be hit with a late filing penalty. (See below for how to file for an extension.)

Has there been death or destruction in your life? The IRS will waive penalties for failure to file tax returns and for failure to pay tax if the failure is due to reasonable cause and not willful neglect. Death, illness, divorce, fire, and theft are reasonable causes. Talk to your tax pro if any of these kinds of events prevented your paying or filing on time.

Tax Return Extensions

Tax returns are due April 15. There's an automatic extension that gives you until October 15 to file.

Automatic Extension

An extension of time to file your return is just that—more time to file your return, not more time to pay your taxes. Taxes are due by April 15. IRS Form 4868: Application for Automatic Extension of Time must be filed by April 15 and gives you until October 15 to file your return. You can download the form from the IRS site or file online or by phone.

On the extension form you need to write your total tax liability for the year, then subtract how much you've paid already. If there is a balance due, pay it if you can. If you can't, you are now aware of the penalties and interest that could be assessed.

Yes, I said write in your total tax liability. Well, what if the midnight hour of April 15 fast approaches and your tax preparer is not returning your calls? How do you figure out your total tax? Do this:

Use last year as your guide. If your income is higher than last year, your tax will most likely be higher. If expenses are less—didn't buy another $5,000 computer—then your income will be higher and so will your taxes. Be conservative in your calculations. Estimate your income higher than you think it is and your expenses lower. Come up with a net income.

Compare it to last year and use a simple proportion to figure your tax. An income 25 percent bigger means your tax will be at least 25 percent higher than last year.

Here comes a homemade safe harbor: Both your extension for last year and this year's first estimated payment are due on April 15. Instead of sending two separate payments to the government, combine the amounts and send one payment with your extension. The amount would include whatever you expect to owe for last year plus the amount of the first estimated payment due this year.

Just in case you miscalculated last year's tax, part of what you had allocated to this year's estimated may be used for last year's tax due. Your tax pro can make adjustments in your estimateds when she completes your tax return and you won't be hit with penalties for last year.

You may need to file a state extension.

Ignore the old husbands' tale that filing an extension sets you up for an audit. It just isn't so. If it gives you more time to collect your material, review your return, or make sure everything is as it should be, all the more reason to give yourself more time.

Conclusion: Beyond the Basics

My aim throughout this book has been to guide you through the tax and recordkeeping basics of an indie business. You will find that as a book of basics, *Self-employed Tax Solutions* cannot cover all circumstances; it does, however, provide a firm foundation for the more complex situations that will arise as your business grows and changes.

Had we the space here to go beyond the basics, a look at more advanced topics would include things like payroll and computerized records. You'd learn the guidelines for hiring subcontractors and employees—and how to handle them quickly and at a tax savings. You'd be introduced to the often-missed opportunity that could save you a bundle of tax money by putting your helpful and competent spouse on your payroll. Or how you could save some money by employing your child while teaching him or her the ropes of your indie business.

You'd learn how even medical expenses for you and your family could be completely deducted as a business expense.

You'd see how the Most Simple System, with a few addenda, works easily if you have more than one self-employed business—let's say a travel writer who also sells jewelry that he purchases in his travels.

Were we to go beyond manual recordkeeping, we could use your understanding of the Most Simple System to adapt any computer bookkeeping program—even though written for the world of employees—to fit into and work for your solo enterprise.

And, finally, the last **ALERTS!**

Remember to explore pension possibilities. I've warned you to watch out for Sammy Segar and others telling you to incorporate. Well, in the old days (Sammy's going to be 103 on his next birthday), a big reason for incorporating was that it provided the only way someone working for himself could sock away a lot of money into a pension. Sammy's still working with the old rules, but those old pension laws are gone. A wide choice of pensions with tax-saving opportunities are now available to the indie. If you find that you are bringing in more money than you currently need to live on, be sure to talk with a savvy tax pro who can explain all the pension possibilities to you—including giving your employee-spouse a generous retirement plan.

Never ignore a letter from the IRS. Some years ago a woman who cleaned house for me showed up at my door in tears. The IRS had put a lien on her checking account. When I asked her if the IRS had contacted her earlier, she cried harder and sobbed, "under the sofa." After some coffee she explained that all the unopened letters from the Feds were under her sofa. However daunting it may be, you must deal with the IRS if they contact you. The longer you wait the greater will be the impact on your life.

Pick your tax professional as carefully as you would any other pro in your life. How many solos does she have as clients? Do you understand what she says? Does she treat you with respect and have an understanding of your solo business? If not, is she interested in learning more about it?

Be careful of tax software. All through this book I've encouraged you to do the record-keeping and information gathering and let your tax professional prepare your return. But if you choose to prepare your own tax return using one of the available software tax programs, be careful! Just as the tax laws and computer bookkeeping programs are written for the W-2 world—for employees or for "small businesses" (which by the way are defined as those with assets of ten million dollars or less)—so are the tax preparation programs. I have seen them mess up OFFICE IN THE HOME,

auto use, SE tax, and a lot more. A new client, with fine-tuned solo business skills, came to me having prepared his own return using a tax preparation program. He did everything right. The program did not. After I corrected the errors made by the program, he saved an additional $3,973 in federal taxes on an income of $150,012.

Tax laws change; some of the specifics in this book may change—who knows, the $25 per person gift limit on deductions may soar to $30—but the general concept and your grasp of the indie way of thinking as presented in this book will not change. You can use **Self-employed Tax Solutions** as a reference book for as long as you work for yourself.

To all my readers, may you find simple solutions to all your tax and financial queries. I wish you success in whatever you choose to do.

Glossary

Accrual basis. A bookkeeping method that claims income when the client is billed regardless of when the client pays, and deducts an expense when it is incurred.

Adjusted gross income. Total income after the subtraction of adjustments to income. It is the amount on the last line of page one of Form 1040.

Adjustments to income. Adjustments are expenses that may be deducted from total income on the front of the Form 1040 and include things like alimony paid, self-employed health insurance premiums, and a self-employed's contributions to a pension.

Amortization. The deduction of the cost of assets in equal amounts over a period of time.

Audit trail. A clear record of the flow of money.

Backup. In the Most Simple System, documentation of an expense: canceled check, credit card slip, cash receipt, or handmade receipt.

Bartering. Trading for work done or products bought using products and services instead of money.

Basis. The amount paid for and the cost of improvements made to equipment or property.

C corporation. Known as a regular corporation. It is a business entity independent of its owners.

Calendar year. A tax year that begins January 1 and ends December 31.

Capital asset. Things of value that last longer than a year, such as equipment or vehicles used in your business.

Capital expense. An expenditure made for a capital asset. Such expenses are usually written off over a period of years.

Cash basis. A bookkeeping method that claims income when it is received and deducts an expense when it is paid.

Cash flow. How money moves in and out of a business. Positive cash flow means more comes in than goes out. Negative cash flow means that there's more going out than coming in.

Constructive receipt. A tax rule that says income is yours if it is available to you even if you haven't received it or have chosen not to receive it. This includes income for you received by your agent or a check you received that you did not deposit.

Earned income. Compensation for services performed.

Effective tax rate. The actual percentage of your income paid as income tax. It is always lower than your marginal tax rate.

Estimated tax. The amount of tax that a taxpayer expects to owe for the current year after subtracting withheld tax and tax credits. Estimated taxes are usually paid to the government quarterly.

Fiscal year. A tax year that covers a span of any twelve consecutive months.

Goodwill. The value of a trade or business based not on capital assets but on intangibles such as expected continued customer patronage due to its name, reputation, product innovation, service, etc.

Gross receipts. A self-employed's total earned income before any deductions.

Independent contractor. The IRS term for self-employed people.

Inflow. All money that comes in. This includes income and all other receipts such as loan proceeds and gifts.

Limited liability company (LLC). A legal business structure set up under the laws of a state that limits the liability of the owners. LLCs can be formed as a sole proprietorship, partnership, or corporation.

Limited liability partnership (LLP). A legal business structure for certain professionals that has the tax structure of a partnership.

Marginal tax rate. The tax bracket (rate) at which the next dollar of income will be taxed.

Most Simple System. This is both a record-keeping process and a way of thinking for an indie in business. It ensures no missed deductions, facilitates an accurate record of income, and provides complete backup documentation

in the event of an audit. It is quick and easily understood.

Necessary expense. An expense that the IRS defines as appropriate and helpful for your business.

Net earnings. A portion of net profit that is calculated by multiplying net profit by 92.35 percent and on which SE tax is calculated.

Net income. The result when business expenses are deducted from business income. The profit or loss of a business.

Net loss. The negative result when business expenses are greater than business income.

Net profit. The positive result when business expenses are less than business income.

Ordinary expense. An expense that the IRS defines as common and accepted in your field of business.

Outflow. All money that goes out. This includes deductible expenses as well as non-deductible expenses such as loan repayments.

Partnership. The most simple structure for a business with more than one owner.

Pass-through income. Income that passes from the business directly to the taxpayer on a dollar-for-dollar basis. Sole proprietorships and partnerships are typical pass-through business structures.

S corporation. A business structure that is treated as part partnership and part corporation for tax purposes.

Self-employed income. Compensation to a self-employed paid as commissions, fees, royalties, or stipends. Sometimes called freelance or 1099 income.

Self-employment (SE) tax. The Social Security and Medicare tax paid by a self-employed. It is calculated on net earnings.

Sole proprietorship. The most simple structure for a one-owner business.

Statute of limitations. The amount of time in which the IRS can audit a return and assess additional tax, interest, and penalties.

Tax bracket. The tax rate at which income at a specific level is taxed.

Tax credits. Incentives created by the government to influence the way taxpayers behave. For instance, a tax credit is given if money is spent to make a business more accessible to the disabled. A tax credit directly reduces tax liability dollar for dollar.

Tax deduction. A term that indicates a process rather than a specific. When business and personal expenses are subtracted from income, then tax liability is reduced.

Tax home. Your principal or regular place of business.

Tax liability. The total tax assessed on a tax return for the year.

Taxable income. Income subject to tax after all deductions and adjustments have been applied. Income tax is calculated on taxable income.

Total income. All income including net profit, interest, dividends, alimony, unemployment compensation, etc., before subtracting adjustments or personal deductions and exemptions.

W-2 income. Compensation paid to employees. Sometimes called salary, wages, paycheck, take-home pay.

Index